BIRNBAUM'S
Disneyland ®

STEPHEN BIRNBAUM
EDITOR

WENDY LEFKON
EXECUTIVE EDITOR

PAUL POSNICK
DESIGN DIRECTOR

TONI SACCOMAN
ART DIRECTOR

LESLIE WESTBROOK
ASSOCIATE EDITOR

TRACY SCARPINO
EDITORIAL ASSISTANT

AVON BOOKS & HEARST PROFESSIONAL MAGAZINES, INC.

CONTENTS

a perfect visit: When to Go; How to Get There; Answers to Tough Questions on Budgets and Packages; Hints on Traveling with Children; plus Hints for the Handicapped, for Singles, and for Older Visitors—plus lots more information that will prove invaluable.

AND ACCOMMODATIONS

on all the important transportation opportunities around Southern California, as well as our appraisal of the best available accommodations. Our listings cover Anaheim, plus prime stopping places in Buena Park, Newport Beach, Los Angeles, and San Diego.

THE MAGIC KINGDOM

its multitude of attractions and amusements, the entertainment and the shops, as well as hints on how to avoid the crowds and other special tips to make your visit most memorable.

GREAT TIMES

are nearly endless numbers of gastronomic experiences to enjoy. We've organized these eating opportunities—both inside' and outside Disneyland—into a meal-by-meal guide that allows prospective diners to know which restaurants are where and what specialties they offer.

golf ball sail onto the green, chances are you'll be able to fulfill your fondest athletic dream in this land of continuous sunshine. These activities make the perfect complement to the magic of the Magic Kingdom.

CONVENTIONS

any sort of get together. Here's all the pertinent information needed to start planning a perfect conference or seminar.

attractions, cultural diversions, and sports events (the California Angels and the Los Angeles Rams both have their home bases here); and then there's that irresistible phenomenon of Southern California—the monumental shopping mall.

even longer tour of the area. The available options are as diverse as the landscape—ranging from the urban sophistication of Los Angeles to desert trails and/or the spectacular Pacific coastline.

For Alex, who merely makes this all possible

ISBN: 0-380-71785-9

Printed in the United States of America

Other 1992 Birnbaum Travel Guides

Acapulco
Bahamas, Turks & Caicos
Barcelona
Bermuda
Boston
Canada
Cancun, Cozumel, and Isla Mujeres
Caribbean
Chicago
Eastern Europe
Europe
Europe for Business Travelers
Florence
France
Great Britain
Hawaii
Ireland
Italy

Ixtapa & Zihuatanejo
London
Los Angeles
Mexico
Miami & Fort Lauderdale
New York
Paris
Portugal
Rome
San Francisco
South America
Spain
United States
USA for Business Travelers
Venice
Walt Disney World
Western Europe

A WORD FROM THE EDITOR

To tell the truth, I came upon Disneyland a little bit backwards. For most people in this country, Disneyland was their first experience with Walt Disney's remarkable idea of what outdoor amusement could be like, and they were understandably dazzled by the scope and breadth of his original concept. Once having been so totally impressed, they later ventured off to Walt Disney World in Florida, where they were even further entranced by Disneyland's larger, younger sibling.

Not me. As an easterner, I had visited Walt Disney World many times before I ever made my first foray onto Disneyland's Anaheim premises, and I went with a fair amount of skepticism. After all, wasn't Disneyland created when Walt Disney himself had to risk every farthing of his financial resources, and didn't Walt Disney World really represent his ultimate concept? Furthermore, wasn't Disneyland just an identical copy—albeit the original one—of the Magic Kingdom at Walt Disney World?

ground associated with America's best-known attraction is one of the prime objectives of this guide.

Visitors to Disneyland break down into two very distinct categories: those who live within 100 miles or less of Disneyland's Anaheim site, and those who travel to Disneyland from often very distant points. For the former, our *Essential Guide to the Magic Kingdom* will be their prime focus. For the latter, the elements we've included that will aid in crafting a complete vacation experience should be of significant value.

I think it's fair to say that Disneyland is a unique entity. It's far larger and more complex than most first-time visitors imagine, and the depth of its diversity is scheduled to increase exponentially as several new attractions and amusements are added as part of what Disney President Michael Eisner calls the "Disney Decade."

It turned out that all my doubts were totally unfounded, for although certain of the basics of the two extraordinary establishments are undeniably the same, Disneyland is possessed of a unique charm, intimacy, and hospitality that can only be experienced at an attraction of such manageable size. The special personality of Disneyland is every bit its own, with singular attractions and special niches that are almost too numerous to catalogue. So there's almost no way that even a regular, frequent visitor could possibly hope to know all of the small nuances that help a visitor to enjoy all that Disneyland offers. Describing some of this back-

And that doesn't include all the goings-on planned for the new Port Disney complex down the road in Long Beach.

So the 1990s will only increase the opportunities to waste a surprising amount of valuable time waiting in line at attractions that are best left for another time of day, and thereby end up missing most of what's there to enjoy. Similarly, a focus only on rides and attractions misses much of the enjoyment that exists in the lovely shops, glittering shows, special events, and interesting restaurants. So knowing the full inventory of what's available—and the best time and order in which to enjoy it—is absolutely essential for maximum enjoyment.

At the same time, no region in the United States is more complex than Southern California, where sights, transportation, and basic unfamiliarity confound every new visitor. That's why we've tried to put Disneyland inside a fixed, comprehensible, geographic context, so that a visitor planning a trip to Disneyland is aware of all there is to see and do within a reasonable radius of the park's Anaheim premises.

In designing this book, we've also tried to keep you and your family from making the same mistakes that dogged my own early encounters with Disneyland. Even the most willing vacation planner needs adequate information in order to prepare an intelligent itinerary and daily plan, and what we hope we've done is to organize all the information necessary for a productive visit into as accessible and coherent a context as possible. Anyone who will take the time to read even the outlines of the chapters that follow will find an emerging pattern that fits his or her special tastes; for those unwilling to exert even that much effort, we've compiled specific, prospective, day-by-day itineraries for several lengths of visits in order to protect you from yourself.

Travel guides of any sort are ultimately reflections of personal taste, and putting one's name on a title page obviously places one's preference on the line. But I think I ought to clarify exactly what "personal" means with reference to this book. Literally dozens of very talented people have worked on preparing this guide, and what you will read on the pages that follow is the collective wisdom of myself and these others, amplified and expanded by comments from other knowledgeable editors, friends, and Disneyland staff members whose tastes most closely approximate our own. I've tried to avoid doggedly alliterative or oppressively onomatopoeic text in favor of simple, straightforward descriptions of what I think is good and bad.

So despite the considerable numbers of contributors, what follows is as close to the gospel according to Birnbaum as you're likely to find. It represents as many of my own tastes and preferences as possible, and it's likely, therefore, that if you like your steak medium rare, your ice cream served only in a sugar cone, and can't tolerate fish that's been frozen and then overcooked, we'll probably have a long and meaningful relationship. Readers with dissimilar tastes conceivably may be less enchanted.

This guidebook also owes an enormous debt to the ladies and gentlemen who created, manage, and run Disneyland. Despite the designation of *Official Guide*, I must hasten to add that *the Disneyland staff has exercised no veto power over the contents of this book*. Quite the contrary, they have opened their files and explained operations to us in the most generous way imaginable so that we could prepare the comprehensive appraisals, charts, and schedules that were necessary to help visitors understand the very complex workings of a very complex enterprise.

I daresay there were times when the Disneyland folks were less than delighted with some of our opinions or conclusions, yet these analyses all stayed in. Furthermore, we've been flattered again and again by Disneyland staff members who've commented about how much they've learned about some unfamiliar aspects of Disneyland from the material in this guide.

But the fact remains that this guide could never have proved as useful as it is without the extremely forthcoming cooperation of Disneyland personnel on every level. Both in the park and behind the scenes, they've been the source of the most critical factual data. I can only hope that I'm not omitting any name in thanking Stan Freese and Mickey Aronson (Entertainment); Gary Burson, Glen Hicks, and Steve DeWitte (Food Administration); Bob Risteen and Jerry Wright (Finance); Chuck Ousley (Merchandise); Bob MacKinnon (Business Relations); John Cora (Operations); Ray Sidejas (Custodial); Lee Lowman (Equal Opportunity); Karl Andrews and Rich Ruescher (Walt Disney Travel Company); Van France (Disney University); Dick Butler and Dale Burner (Maintenance); Ron Dominguez (Administration); and Ken Inouye (Landscaping).

In addition, John Hench, Marty Sklar, Tony Baxter, Raellen Lescault, Ken Anderson, Betsy Richman (WDI), and Elaine Martinez Cali of the Anaheim Area Visitor and Convention Bureau deserve a special tip of the editor's hat for the assistance they provided that was well beyond the call of duty. To Bob Roth, Bob Baldwin, Renie Bardeau, Lou Anne Cappiello, and Barbara Warren who did so much to make our job easier (and often possible), more thanks are due for their extraordinary help.

Most of all, we owe a debt of gratitude larger than we can say to those Disneyland executives (past and present) who believed in and nurtured this project, and who allowed us to do it—often against their basic instincts and better judgments.

Lastly, I also should point out that every worthwhile travel guide is a living enterprise; that is, this book may be our best effort at explaining how best to enjoy Disneyland at this moment, but its text is in no way cast in bronze. In this edition and subsequent annual revisions, we expect to refine and expand our material to serve our readers' needs even better. To this end, no contribution is of greater value to us than *your* personal reaction to what we have written, as well as information about *your* own experiences while you were trying our suggestions. We eagerly and enthusiastically solicit your comments about this guide, and your opinions and perceptions based on your own visit. In this way, we are able to provide the best and most current information—including the actual experiences of individual travelers—and make it more readily available to others. So please write me at 60 East 42nd Street; New York, New York 10165.

I sincerely hope to hear from you.

Steve Birnbaum

GETTING READY TO GO

Planning is the key element that most often insures a trouble-free vacation, and a holiday in Southern California is no exception. The geographical area is just too broad and filled with too many attractions to allow a visitor to see even the best of all that's available—even during a full week (or even two)—without careful preparation.

That doesn't mean that every detail must be decided before departure—just that the major options should be known before leaving home. This helps in choosing just which sights and attractions are simply too good to pass up.

The chapters that follow describe Anaheim's attractions and the other California musts (see *Anaheim* and *In All Directions*), and they will provide assistance, as will the pages that follow in this chapter, which is designed to supply all the data necessary to help you decide when to go and how to get there (for the amount of money you have available to spend). It also provides a variety of helpful hints on how to make your Disneyland holiday most enjoyable, relaxing, and free of unexpected problems. (Unless otherwise noted, all phone numbers are in area code 714.)

WHEN TO GO

When weighing the very best times to visit Disneyland, the most obvious possibilities seem to be Christmas, Easter, and summer vacation months—especially if there are children in the family. But there are some very good reasons to avoid these periods—the major one being that almost everybody else wants to go then, too. On the busiest of those days, you may encounter lengthy lines at one or more attractions, thus limiting the amount of time spent in pure enjoyment. In general, busy days tend to be the least satisfying.

Other times of the year are more pleasant. The week before Thanksgiving, for example, is notably uncrowded. The week after Christmas Day is frantically busy—but the week before stands out for its peaceful atmosphere, with the additional bonus that the fabulous Christmas decorations and special yuletide activities are all available to be enjoyed. Though most of the summer is very busy (the park's summer season runs from June 22 through September 8 this year), the period before July 1, the last week in August, and the first week of September are usually less crowded, so these weeks are good times to visit. They also allow a visitor to see the park at its twinkling nighttime best, complete with fireworks—but without the crowds of most of the rest of the summer. Spring months are lovely because of the abundance of seasonal flowers. So is February, when there are spectacular displays of tulips in the Central Plaza.

Saturday is usually the busiest day of the week year-round. (In summer, Mondays and Fridays are next busiest, Tuesdays, Wednesdays, and Thursdays slightly less crowded.) If it's necessary to visit the park on a weekend day, try to make it on a Sunday.

When not to go: If you hate crowds, avoid the week between Christmas and New Year's Day and the weeks from mid-June through the third week in August. The Fourth of July weekend is very busy.

DISNEYLAND WEATHER

If dry, sunny weather is your ideal, Anaheim may indeed seem like heaven. Rainy days are few and far between, and generally occur between the months of November and April, which is also the coolest time of the year. Santa Ana winds during this season occasionally produce short periods of dry, crisp, warm, desert weather and sparkling clear air that unveils the distant mountains that the smog hides most of the rest of the time.

In summer, Southern Californians are accustomed to thin, low morning clouds that make it wise to plan expeditions to the beach in the afternoon, when the haze burns off and the mercury rises; mornings and nights are generally cool.

| | Temperatures(ºF) | | Rainfall (in.) |
	Average high	Average low	Average
January	65	44	3.62
February	67	45	2.09
March	68	46	2.00
April	70	50	1.63
May	72	53	0.29
June	77	56	0.02
July	82	61	0.01
August	83	60	0.04
September	81	59	0.10
October	77	55	0.26
November	72	50	1.01
December	67	46	1.60

SPECIAL EVENTS

Disneyland itself sponsors nearly a dozen annual special events during the year, and nearby communities stage as many more, all adding considerable spice to the Southern California scene. Any of the following is worth considering when making plans to visit Disneyland. For information about other annual activities at Disneyland see *An Essential Guide to the Magic Kingdom*.

JANUARY

New Year's Eve, Disneyland: There are fireworks and well-known entertainers on hand for this big end-of-the-year bash, one of the prettiest times to visit the park. For more details about this and other Disneyland activities mentioned below, contact Disneyland Guest Relations; Box 3232; Anaheim, CA 92803; 999-4565.

FEBRUARY

Dana Point Harbor Festival of Whales: This event, held for three consecutive weeks in late February or March (depending on the whale migration itself), highlights the southward migration of California gray whales by holding a marine movie festival (featuring films by the likes of Jacques Cousteau), plus slide-illustrated talks by marine biology experts, musical performances by the sea, Navy and Coast Guard ship tours and rides (weather permitting), and displays of whale-related artifacts. A program for youngsters features children's art exhibits, musical performances, and other entertainment. Whale-watching cruises, offered in the area from January to March, are frosting on the cake. Dana Point is about 35 miles south of Disneyland. Details: Festival of Whales; Box 701; Dana Point, CA 92629; 496-2274.

MARCH

Winter Festival, Laguna Beach: At this three-day arts festival, held March 8, 9, and 10 this year, some 100 to 120 specially selected artists are on hand to exhibit pottery, jewelry, macrame, and the like on the grounds of the Festival of Arts (described below) at 650 Laguna Canyon Road. Music, poetry readings, mime, and an international food fair round out the festivities. Details: Laguna Beach Chamber of Commerce; Box 396; Laguna Beach, CA 92652; 494-1018.

Fiesta de las Golondrinas, San Juan Capistrano: The townspeople here have been welcoming the March 19 arrival of the celebrated square-tailed cliff swallows (from their wintering grounds in Goya, Argentina) ever since the founding of the community's mission in 1776. But during the last 2 decades, the birds' return has been celebrated with special fervor. Radio stations from all over the world broadcast coverage of the week-long event. There are Spanish and Mexican folk dances, programs for children, a "hairiest man" contest, and more. On one of the festival days, people not wearing proper Western attire are clapped into a portable 19th-century-style jail. A $1 bail fee secures their release. A parade (the largest non-motorized parade in the U.S.), featuring individuals in Mexican and Native American attire, is a highlight. As for the mission itself (see *In All Directions*), it is one of the ten most active archaeological sites in this country, and the chapel is the oldest building still in use in the state. A smaller celebration is held in October to bid farewell to the famous birds. Details: San Juan Capistrano Fiesta Association; Box 532; San Juan Capistrano, CA 92693; 493-1976, or call the Chamber of Commerce, 493-4700.

APRIL

Toyota Grand Prix of Long Beach: A CART (Championship Auto Racing Teams) race using Indy-type cars turns the streets of Long Beach into a racetrack each year during a weekend in late March or early April. Details: Grand Prix Association of Long Beach; 100 West Broadway, Suite 670; Long Beach, CA 90802; 213-437-0341.

MAY

Summer Preview Weekends: Beginning during the spring, the park stays open until midnight on Fridays, Saturdays, and Sundays. The Main Street Electrical Parade is presented all three nights, and a fireworks display is an extra bonus during May and June. Details: Disneyland Guest Relations; Box 3232; Anaheim, CA 92803; 999-4565.

Strawberry Festival, Garden Grove: Between 30,000 and 50,000 holidaymakers show up for each day of this Memorial Day weekend in Garden Grove, not far from Anaheim. The Strawberry Festival Parade of floats, bands, and equestrians is one of the highlights. Gourmands smile at the cutting of an enormous strawberry shortcake, big enough to cover a whole stage and substantial enough to provide most festivalgoers with at least one portion. Radio and TV celebrities are on hand for autographs, and there are plenty of contests—such as the one for redheads that's open to all ages, with prizes for the oldest and the youngest carrottops, and for the longest, shortest, and curliest tresses. Details: Strawberry Festival Association; Box 2287; Garden Grove, CA 92640; 638-0981.

Wooden Boat Festival: More than 60 classic and contemporary wooden boats are displayed, both in and out of the water. There are also demonstrations, seminars, a wooden boat sailing regatta, a boat parade, and a boat-building contest. Details: Newport Beach Area Chamber of Commerce; 1470 Jamboree Rd.; Newport Beach, CA 92660; 644-8211.

JULY

Orange County Fiesta, Fountain Valley: This six-day-long festival (held during the July 4th weekend) features a chili cook-off, bluegrass and country music, fireworks, and other entertainment in the Mile Square Park area in Fountain Valley. A carnival is held in conjunction with the festival. Along with a fireworks show on July 4th, the festival features contests, arts and crafts, food stands, and bands. The park is located on the corner of Brookhurst and Heil Streets, Fountain Valley. Details: Chamber of Commerce; 10101 Slater Ave., Suite 115; Fountain Valley, CA 92708; 962-4441 or 964-6656.

Festival of Arts, Laguna Beach: More than half a century old, this well-respected, seven-week-long event—which begins in early July and lasts through August—brings some 160 artists and craftsmen to the tree-dotted grounds of Irvine Bowl Park to display and sell their watercolors, oil paintings, sculptures, tapestries, jewelry, and more in open-air booths on the grounds. Meanwhile, at the popular Pageant of the Masters (another part of the event), models re-create famous works of art on stage in two-hour-long "living pictures," accompanied by narration and the music of a 28-piece orchestra. Seats must be reserved well in advance. Performances by the Ballet Pacifica, programs for children, and other entertainment complete the festival, and about 250,000 people attend. A Sawdust Festival and an Art-A-Fair have grown up nearby, in the shadow of this Laguna Beach festival, and make the area even more lively during this period. Details: Festival of Arts; Irvine Bowl Park; 650 Laguna Canyon Rd.; Laguna Beach, CA 92651; 494-1145.

Flight of the Lasers: This two-hour, one-person sailboat race around a five-mile course in Newport Harbor has been a tradition for over 50 years. Thousands line the shores of Newport Harbor to watch. Prizes are awarded to top finishers. Details: Newport Beach Area Chamber of Commerce; 1470 Jamboree Rd.; Newport Beach, CA 92660; 644-8211.

Orange County Fair, Costa Mesa: Held at the Orange County Fairgrounds, this annual event is a bustling hodgepodge of celebrity entertainment, rodeo events, carnival rides, motorcycle races, flower-and-garden shows, arts and crafts exhibitions, commercial exhibits, and more. Details: Orange County Fair; 88 Fair Dr.; Costa Mesa, CA 92626; 751-3247.

AUGUST

Ocean Pacific Professional Surfing Contest, Huntington Beach: Each year, for a week in August, the world's best surfers compete here and draw more than 100,000 spectators. This is a good time to see some terrific wave-riding, and the people-watching is nearly as good. Details: Huntington Beach Community Services Office; 2000 Main St.; Huntington Beach, CA 92648; 536-5486.

SEPTEMBER

Newport Seafest, Newport Beach: Held annually during the third and fourth weeks of September, this ten-day extravaganza celebrates the Southern California way of life through approximately 35 marine and related community events. For details and a schedule of events contact: Newport Harbor

Area Chamber of Commerce; 1470 Jamboree Rd.; Newport Beach, CA 92660; 644-8211. Major events include:

Taste of Newport: The Newport Center Fashion Island mall hosts this three-day festival, which features culinary delights and continuous live entertainment. Sample food, wine, and beer offered by over 40 of the area's top restaurants.

Sand Castle Contest: Clubs, organizations, families, and businesses vie for trophies by sculpting dragons, castles, cars, and much more intricate creations during this 3-hour-long competition. In the past, participants have even gone to the trouble to dye their creations in an assortment of colors. Not surprisingly, thousands show up at Newport Beach's Corona del Mar State Beach to watch.

Catalina Festival of Art, Avalon: Held annually on the third weekend in September, this festival fills two or three city blocks along Front Street (aka Crescent Avenue) in downtown Avalon, on Catalina Island, with arts and crafts exhibits. This is an exceptionally pleasant time of year on the island: The summer crowds have largely dispersed, while the weather is, if anything, more pleasant than ever. Details: Catalina Island Chamber of Commerce; Box 217; Avalon, CA 90704; 213-510-1520.

International Street Fair, Orange: The Plaza Square area is taken over by this event every year from Friday through Sunday of Labor Day weekend. The streets around the square are closed off, and large banners rename them for the duration— American Street, Italian Street, and German, Swedish, Mexican, Vietnamese, and Japanese Streets. Local residents in appropriate national costumes dish out savory platters full of the appropriate national foods, and entertainers amuse visitors with music and folk dances. Details: International Street Fair; Box 927; Orange, CA 92666; 532-6260.

OCTOBER

Halloween Festival, Anaheim: The oldest nighttime parade in the United States, staged the Saturday before Halloween, features marching bands, floats, equestrian units, and a few celebrities. Concurrently and during the preceding days, the city hosts a festival of rides and games and an annual pancake breakfast. Details: City of Anaheim Parks and Recreation Department; Box 3222; Anaheim, CA 92805; 999-5191.

DECEMBER

Christmas Festivities, Disneyland: This may be the park's most beautiful season. Main Street is festooned with greenery, and hundreds of poinsettias bloom in Town Square and the Central Plaza, while a 60-foot Christmas tree decorated with 3,000 colorful lights and 2,800 ornaments embellishes the atmosphere further. Carolers in 19th-century English garb stroll the grounds and, on 2 nights early in the season, there's a solemn and impressive candlelight ceremony involving a procession, Christmas music sung by a 1,000-voice choir, and a reading of the Christmas story by a well-known actor or actress. A special holiday parade is also featured. The week before the holiday ranks among the very best times of year to visit the park. The week afterward, however, is one of the busiest, so wise guests will plan accordingly. Details: Disneyland Guest Relations; Box 3232; Anaheim, CA; 999-4565.

Newport's Christmas Boat Parade, Newport Beach: First held in 1908, this event draws about 200 boats each evening, all of them decked out with Santa Clauses and angels and other holiday characters, and enough Christmas lights to illuminate a score of oversize Christmas trees. Reflecting in the inky waters of Newport Harbor—which hosts the celebration on the seven nights preceding Christmas Eve—all those little colored stars make up a spectacle worthy of the Magic Kingdom. Area waterfront restaurants book reservations for this period up to a year in advance. Details: Newport Harbor Area Chamber of Commerce; 1470 Jamboree Rd.; Newport Beach, CA 92660; 644-8211.

HOW BIG ARE THE CROWDS?

Crowds at Disneyland vary greatly from weekends to weekdays as the charts below illustrate. The information listed should assist in making a decision on when to visit the park. Keep in mind that choosing a least crowded time of year to visit may also mean that some of Disneyland's most entertaining parades and special events (the Main Street Electrical Parade and fireworks exhibitions, for example) might not be on the schedule.

WEEKDAYS
(Mondays through Thursdays)

Least Crowded	Average Attendance	Most Crowded
1st week in January to President's week	Memorial Day week	President's week
Last week in February to 3rd week in March	Labor Day week	Week before Easter Sunday
3rd week in March to week before Easter		Beginning of summer to Labor Day weekend
Week after Easter Sunday		Thanksgiving weekend (Thursday to Sunday)
Two weeks after Easter Sunday to Memorial Day week		Christmas Day to New Year's Day
End of Labor Day week to Columbus Day		
Columbus Day to Thanksgiving		
Thanksgiving weekend to week before Christmas		
Week before Christmas		

WEEKENDS
(Fridays, Saturdays, Sundays)

Least Crowded	Average Attendance	Most Crowded
Last week in February to 3rd week in March	1st week in January to President's week	President's week
	3rd week in March to the week before Easter	Week before Easter Sunday
	Week after Easter Sunday	Two weeks after Easter Sunday to Memorial Day
	Labor Day Week	Memorial Day week
	End of Labor Day week to Columbus Day	Beginning of summer to Labor Day weekend
	Columbus Day to Thanksgiving weekend	Thanksgiving weekend (Thursday to Sunday)
	End of Thanksgiving weekend to week before Christmas	Christmas Day to New Year's Day
	Week before Christmas	

PLANNING AHEAD

Although it takes time to plan a trip, the increased enjoyment that results from custom-tailoring a vacation to your personal tastes makes the effort worthwhile.

The planning will go most smoothly if it's done in an organized manner. First, collect as much information as you can about the sites and attractions to be visited from the sources of information mentioned below. Then peruse these materials before beginning to make any definite plans. Especially if youngsters are going along, allot plenty of time for sports and the beach and, above all, don't try to see and do too much in too short a period.

INFORMATION: For information about special events and performance times, the latest ticket prices, operating hours, and other Disneyland specifics contact Disneyland Guest Relations; 1313 South Harbor Blvd.; Anaheim, CA 92803; 999-4565.

For other area information, contact the following organizations:

● **Anaheim Area Visitor and Convention Bureau**; Box 4270; Anaheim, CA 92803; 999-8999. It's also possible to stop by in person at the office at 800 West Katella Avenue. For a recorded message detailing current area activities, phone 635-8900.

● **Greater Los Angeles Visitors and Convention Bureau**; 515 South Figueroa St.; Los Angeles, CA 90071; 213-624-7300.

● **San Diego Convention and Visitors Bureau**; 1200 Third Ave., Suite 824; San Diego, CA 92101-4190; 619-232-3101.

Inside Disneyland: Park employees can answer questions on just about any subject, and what they don't know they're almost always happy to help you find out. Furthermore, people at both City Hall (on the west side of Town Square) and Carefree Corner (at the north end of Main Street on the east side of the avenue) can field questions about goings-on inside the park. The Disneylanders at Carefree Corner—who in their day have successfully confronted questions as varied as "When does Aunt Martha's plane arrive?" and "What time is the 3 o'clock parade?"—can also discuss Southern California attractions, transportation, and lodging.

RESERVATIONS: Scheduling activities down to the tiniest detail is not necessary when planning a vacation in Southern California. For visits during the busy July and August season, however, make lodging reservations as far in advance as possible to get your choice of accommodations—at least six months ahead if you can, since area hotels run 95 to 97 percent full during these months. For visits at other times of year, check with the Anaheim Area Visitor and Convention Bureau (previous column) to see what conventions are scheduled to be in town when you want to travel. Some of these can crowd facilities enough to warrant altering your plans.

WHAT TO PACK: Southern California isn't *so* laid back that you need no more than a bathing suit, but it isn't an environment that demands formal fashions either. Casual wear will suffice in all but the most formal restaurants, and men usually can wear sports jackets without ties even there. Bathing suits are an obvious must if you plan to take advantage of your hotel's swimming pool (most establishments have them) or go for a walk on one of those long, surf-pounded, Pacific beaches. It's also a good idea to bring along a beach towel. Tennis togs or golf gear may be necessary if you plan to hit the courts or the course. The weather in summer can be hot, but because Southern California air conditioning is usually overefficient, bring a lightweight sweater or jacket to wear indoors.

In winter, warm clothing is a must for evening; during nighttime visits to the park at Christmastime, a down jacket may be appropriate. Always pack for unexpected contingencies by including something to keep you comfortable should the weather turn unseasonably warm or cool. Dressing in layers is the best idea, since this enables you to add or subtract from your attire as weather conditions dictate.

DO YOU NEED A CAR? Southern California is considered America's prime automotive area, but if you're staying in Anaheim for only a couple of days, visiting only Disneyland, and lodging in a nearby hotel, it's not absolutely necessary to have a car. Several airport transportation companies provide service between Anaheim lodging places and the major airports. For details see "Transportation to the Airports" on page 37. Most hotels have shuttle buses to transport you to and from the park. Many hostelries are within walking distance, and there are connecting sidewalks throughout the area. Local taxis are available to get you around when you don't feel like walking.

If you're staying for more than two days, however, you will almost surely want to see a bit more of the area than just a small corner of Anaheim, and although bus transportation does exist, it's far more convenient to have wheels of your own.

SHOULD YOU BUY A PACKAGE?

The wide variety of Southern California vacation packages can easily confuse even the savviest traveler. Every offering contains so many different components that it's difficult to compare one with another.

Most packages save money over the amount that their various elements would total if purchased separately. Another advantage of packages is the convenience of having all the details and elements arranged.

Finding the very best package is mainly a matter of deciding just what sort of vacation you want, and then shopping around for the package that best fits the bill. The various sections of this book describe many of the Southern California activities and attractions that surround Disneyland in enough detail so that it should be relatively easy to choose just what you want to add to your Disneyland visit.

Don't select a package that includes elements that don't interest you—remember, you're paying for them. Also remember that the real value of such so-called extras as welcome cocktails, souvenir keychains, and descriptive brochures is negligible.

Disneyland is a component in a wide variety of package tours available from nearly every carrier serving the Los Angeles/Orange County area, including Delta Air Lines, the Official Airline of Disneyland.

As the Official Airline, Delta is the only airline that has a number of rooms at the *Disneyland* hotel specifically allocated for its use. Delta is, therefore, a good means of access to hard-to-book accommodations. These rooms are available as part of Delta Dream Vacation® packages (800-872-7786), which also have the added attraction of saving visitors some money on airfares.

The following hotels and tour operators include Disneyland in their packages.

● **Walt Disney Travel Company, Inc.;** 1441 South West St.; Anaheim, CA 92802; 520-5050. Packages offered by this Disney subsidiary are particularly good because the company is in the best position to handle any problems that may arise on the spot. They also offer "Magical Smiles" vacation packages (520-5080). Their offices, at the *Disneyland* hotel, are open Mondays through Fridays from 7 A.M. to 7 P.M.; Saturdays and Sundays from 8 A.M. to 5 P.M.

● **Anaheim Hilton;** 777 Convention Way; Anaheim, CA 92802; 750-4321 or 800-223-6904

● **Anaheim Marriott;** 700 West Convention Way; Anaheim, CA 92802; 750-8000 or 800-228-9290

● **Anaheim Plaza;** 1700 South Harbor Blvd.; Anaheim, CA 92802; 772-5900 or 800-228-1357 from North America

● **Grand;** One Hotel Way; Anaheim, CA 92802; 772-7777 or 800-421-6662

● **Howard Johnson's;** 1380 South Harbor Blvd.; Anaheim, CA 92802; 776-6120 or 800-854-0303; 800-422-4228 from California

● **Jolly Roger Inn;** 640 West Katella Ave.; Anaheim, CA 92802; 772-7621 or 800-854-3184

● **Magic Lamp/Magic Carpet;** 1016 West Katella Ave.; Anaheim, CA 92802; 772-9450

● **Penny Sleeper Inn;** 1441 South Manchester Ave.; Anaheim, CA 92802; 991-8100 or 800-854-6118

● **Saga Inn;** 1650 South Harbor Blvd.; Anaheim, CA 92802; 772-0440 or 800-422-4402

● **Stovall's Inn;** 1110 West Katella Ave.; Anaheim, CA 92802; 778-1880 or 800-854-8175

SHOULD YOU USE A TRAVEL AGENT?

Good travel agents who know Disneyland and its surrounding area well, and who understand your tastes and vacation goals, can be a great help in planning a trip. Not only will they have a good sense of the various types of Anaheim accommodations, but they also should save you the trouble of shopping around for the lowest airfare, arranging for rental cars, and other travel-related needs.

We advise you to look for a travel agent in the same way you'd seek out a doctor, lawyer, or other professional. Recommendations from friends who share your tastes and whose judgment you respect usually go a long way. It's also possible to work

directly with the Walt Disney Travel Company (a corporate subsidiary of The Walt Disney Company); its personnel will work with consumers as cheerfully as they work with travel agents, and they are able to book airline tickets and rental cars as well as rooms—with or without a package deal. The firm's office in the *Disneyland* hotel is open Mondays through Fridays.

It is important to note that the *Disneyland* hotel and all other major Anaheim motels and hotels pay direct commissions to travel agents, as does the Walt Disney Travel Company, so there should be no extra fees charged to you.

SAMPLE SCHEDULES

For those folks lucky enough to live in the Los Angeles/Orange County area, Disneyland is a local attraction offering the opportunity to return again and again. Nonetheless, there are strategies even area residents use to avoid the crowds, and these are outlined in the "Special Tips" section of our *Essential Guide to the Magic Kingdom* chapter.

But for those travelers making a special trip to Southern California, you should really spend at least two to three days in and around the Magic Kingdom to see it properly. Furthermore, if you are planning an extended stay, use that extra time to explore other attractions in the area. The sample schedules described below provide some sense of the available options:

One-day visit: This is far from our most enthusiastic suggestion, but if your itinerary allows only one day in Anaheim, by all means spend the entire time at Disneyland. You'll find that you'll make most effective use of that day by looking at the "Suggested Disneyland Itineraries" in *An Essential Guide to the Magic Kingdom*.

Two-day visit: Get to the park early on the first and second days. Spend the morning of the second day in the Magic Kingdom, have lunch there, but when things look like they're crowding up, head back to your hotel (remember to have your hand stamped before exiting and to keep your Passport), change into your golf, tennis, or beach attire and stretch your muscles a bit (see *Sports*). Leave yourself enough time for a refreshing shower and then go back to the Magic Kingdom. The evening, especially when the park is open late, is a great time to see some of the most popular attractions that you may have missed— e.g., Big Thunder Mountain Railroad or the Haunted Mansion.

Three-day visit: Follow the program outlined above for the first two days. On the morning of the third day arrive at the park early and go back to your favorite attractions. In an attraction such as Pirates of the Caribbean, the Audio-Animatronics figures are so enticing and the attention to detail throughout so amazing that you can't possibly catch it all the first time—or the second or third for that matter. Take a break for lunch and then in the early afternoon do some shopping when the stores tend to be least crowded. Souvenirs of Disneyland are always appreciated by the folks back home.

After you've stored your purchases in lockers at the Lost and Found on Main Street, it's a perfect time to take in some live entertainment like the Golden Horseshoe Jamboree (make reservations as soon as you arrive in the park, as this is a very popular attraction). Then enjoy dinner at the *Blue Bayou* restaurant in New Orleans Square and then, take a turn on the dance floors at Carnation Plaza Gardens or Tomorrowland Terrace.

Four-day visit: Leave Disneyland and spend a morning sportfishing with the Dana Point fleet (see *Sports*), about 30 to 35 miles south of Anaheim. If deep-sea fishing is not your thing, head for Long Beach to see the *Queen Mary* or drive to Laguna Beach to see the galleries and boutiques and, in season, the summer arts festival (described in "When to Go," earlier in this chapter). If there's time remaining, visit Buena Park's Movieland Wax Museum and Knott's Berry Farm, where Mrs. Knott's chicken dinners became famous (see *Anaheim*).

Five-day visit: This allows a day for Los Angeles. Start at the Los Angeles County Museum of Art and the La Brea Tar Pits next door, or the Los Angeles Children's Museum, a hands-on, crawl-through sort of place. Lunch at the kiosks at the Farmers Market. In the afternoon, visit Universal Studios. You can dine at a variety of restaurants (and thereby avoid rush-hour traffic) or drive the short distance into downtown Los Angeles to Olvera Street and eat at one of the sidewalk Mexican restaurants and then check out the shops (see *In All Directions*).

Longer visits: Once you've had a chance to become somewhat familiar with Disneyland and its nearest surroundings, it's also possible to combine your trip with a broader vacation itinerary. From your base in Southern California there are several logical routes that can lead you to interesting and exciting places to tour, which will significantly expand and enhance your vacation (see *In All Directions*).

HOW TO GET THERE

Most visitors who come to Disneyland arrive by car. That's partly because so many visitors drive down just for the day or a weekend, and partly because, for many travelers from distant points, Disneyland is just one stop on a broader tour of California. However, you may want to investigate travel by bus or by train. And if you're traveling any significant distance, it may actually cost less to fly than to drive. Here are the leading transportation alternatives.

BY CAR

The following are the fastest, most direct routes to Disneyland from 27 leading cities. These are far from the only recommended routings; more scenic and leisurely routes do exist. If you wish to map out something different on your own, assume you'll drive no more than 350 to 400 miles a day— a reasonable distance that won't wear you out so you can't enjoy your stay.

Atlanta: I-20 west to Birmingham, AL, U.S. 78 west to Memphis, I-40 west to Barstow, CA, I-15 south, S.R. 91 west, S.R. 57 south, Katella Ave. west, Harbor Blvd. north to entrance. 2,176 miles (approx. 43 hours).

Boston: I-90 west, I-84 west to Scranton, PA, I-91 south, I-80 west to Youngstown, OH, I-76 west, I-71 south, 270 west and south around Columbus, OH, I-70 west, I-55 south through St. Louis, I-44 west to Oklahoma City, I-40 west to Barstow, CA, I-15 south, S.R. 91 west, S.R. 57 south, Katella Ave. west, Harbor Blvd. north to entrance. 3,025 miles (approx. 60 hours).

Calgary: P.R. 2 south, U.S. 89 south, U.S. 287 south, I-15 south, S.R. 91 west, S.R. 57 south, Katella Ave. west, Harbor Blvd. north to entrance. 1,535 miles (approx. 31 hours).

Chicago: I-5 south through St. Louis, I-44 west to Oklahoma City, I-40 west to Barstow, CA, I-15

south, S.R. 91 west, S.R. 57 south, Katella Ave. west, Harbor Blvd. north to entrance. 2,101 miles (approx. 43 hours).

Cleveland: I-71 south, 270 west and south around Columbus, OH, I-70 west, I-55 south through St. Louis, I-44 west to Oklahoma City, I-40 west to Barstow, CA, I-15 south, S.R. 91 west, S.R. 57 south, Katella Ave. west, Harbor Blvd. north to entrance. 2,392 miles (approx. 48 hours).

Dallas: I-20 west, I-280 north around Ft. Worth, U.S. 81/287 west to Amarillo, TX, I-40 west to Barstow, CA, I-15 south, S.R. 91 west, S.R. 57 south, Katella Ave. west, Harbor Blvd. north to entrance. 1,440 miles (approx. 29 hours).

Denver: I-70 west to Salina, UT, U.S. 89 south to Sevier, UT, I-70 west, I-15 south, S.R. 91 west, S.R. 57 south, Katella Ave. west, Harbor Blvd. north to entrance. 1,025 miles (approx. 21 hours).

Detroit: I-75 south to Cincinnati, I-71 south, I-264 south around Louisville, KY, I-65 to Nashville, I-40 west to Barstow, CA, I-15 south, S.R. 91 west, S.R. 57 south, Katella Ave. west, Harbor Blvd. north to entrance. 2,551 miles (approx. 51 hours).

Houston: I-10 west, I-410 north around San Antonio, I-10 west to San Bernardino, CA, S.R. 91 west, S.R. 57 south, Katella Ave. west, Harbor Blvd. north to entrance. 1,575 miles (approx. 32 hours).

Las Vegas: I-15 south, S.R. 91 west, S.R. 57 south, Katella Ave. west, Harbor Blvd. north to entrance. 258 miles (approx. 5 hours).

Miami: I-95 north, Florida's Turnpike north, I-75 north, I-10 west, I-12 west around New Orleans, I-10 west, I-610 north around Houston, I-10 west, I-410 north around San Antonio, I-10 west to San-Bernardino, CA, S.R. 91 west, S.R. 57 south, Katella Ave. west, Harbor Blvd. north to entrance. 2,778 miles (approx. 56 hours).

Montreal: P.R. 40 west, P.R. 401 west to Detroit,

I-94 west to Gary, IN, I-80 west, I-55 south through St. Louis, I-44 west to Oklahoma City, I-40 west to Barstow, CA, I-15 south, S.R. 91 west, S.R. 57 south, Katella Ave. west, Harbor Blvd. north to entrance. 2,921 miles (approx. 58 hours).

New York City: George Washington Bridge west, I-80 west to Youngstown, OH, I-76 west, I-71 south, 270 west and south around Columbus, OH, I-70 west, I-55 south through St. Louis, I-44 west to Oklahoma City, I-40 west to Barstow, CA, I-15 south, S.R. 91 west, S.R. 57 south, Katella Ave. west, Harbor Blvd. north to entrance. 2,802 miles (approx. 56 hours).

Philadelphia: I-76 west, I-70 west, I-55 south through St. Louis, I-44 west to Oklahoma City, I-40 west to Barstow, CA, I-15 south, S.R. 91 west, S.R. 57 south, Katella Ave. west, Harbor Blvd. north to entrance. 2,719 miles (approx. 54 hours).

Phoenix: I-10 west to San Bernardino, CA, S.R. 91 west, S.R. 57 south, Katella Ave. west, Harbor Blvd. north to entrance. 343 miles (approx. 7 hours).

Portland: I-5 south, Harbor Blvd. south to entrance. 964 miles (approx. 19 hours).

Reno: I-80 west to Sacramento, I-5 south, Harbor Blvd. south to entrance. 515 miles (approx. 10 hours).

Sacramento: I-5 south, Harbor Blvd. south to entrance. 379 miles (approx. 8 hours).

St. Louis: I-44 west to Oklahoma City, I-40 west to Barstow, CA, I-15 south, S.R. 91 west, S.R. 57 south, Katella Ave. west, Harbor Blvd. north to entrance. 1,823 miles (approx. 36 hours).

Salt Lake City: I-15 south, S.R. 91 west, S.R. 57 south, Katella Ave. west, Harbor Blvd. north to entrance. 674 miles (approx. 13 hours).

San Diego: I-5 north, Harbor Blvd. south to entrance. 92 miles (approx. 2 hours).

San Francisco: I-80 east to Oakland, I-580 east, I-5 south, Harbor Blvd. south to entrance. 394 miles (approx. 8 hours).

Seattle: I-5 south, Harbor Blvd. south to entrance. 1,142 miles (approx. 23 hours).

Toronto: P.R. 401 west to Detroit, I-94 west to Gary, IN, I-80 west, I-55 south through St. Louis, I-44 west to Oklahoma City, I-40 west to Barstow, CA, I-15 south, S.R. 91 west, S.R. 57 south, Katella Ave. west, Harbor Blvd. north to entrance. 2,586 miles (approx. 52 hours).

Tucson: I-10 west to San Bernardino, CA, S.R. 91 west, S.R. 57 south, Katella Ave. west, Harbor Blvd. north to entrance. 476 miles (approx. 10 hours).

Vancouver: P.R. 99 south, I-5 south, I-405 around Seattle, I-5 south, Harbor Blvd. south to entrance. 1,288 miles (approx. 26 hours).

Washington, D.C.: I-66 west, I-81 south, I-40 west to Barstow, CA, I-15 south, S.R. 91 west, S.R. 57 south, Katella Ave. west, Harbor Blvd. north to entrance. 2,659 miles (approx. 53 hours).

AUTOMOBILE CLUBS: Any one of the nation's leading automobile clubs can come to your aid in the event of breakdowns en route, and provide insurance covering accidents, arrest, bail bond, lawyers' fees for defense of contested traffic cases, and personal injury, plus trip-planning services—not merely advice, but also free maps and route-mapping assistance. No two programs are quite the same; fees range from around $35 to $50 annually for the most reputable clubs, which include the following:

- **Allstate Motor Club**; 1500 Shure Drive; Arlington Heights, IL 60004; 800-347-8880
- **American Automobile Association**; 1000 AAA Heathrow, FL; 800-336-4357
- **Amoco Motor Club**; Box 9040; Des Moines, IA 50369-0001; 800-334-3300
- **Ford Auto Club**; Box 224688; Dallas, TX 75222-4688; 800-348-5220
- **Gulf Motor Club**; 6001 North Clark St.; Chicago, IL 60660; 800-633-3224
- **CIGNA Road and Travel Inc.**; Box 13901; Philadelphia, PA 19101; 800-523-4816
- **Montgomery Ward Auto Club**; 200 North Martingale Rd.; Schaumburg, IL 60194; 800-621-5151
- **Motor Club of America**; 484 Central Ave.; Newark, NJ 07107; 800-435-7622
- **United States Auto Club Motoring Division**; Box 660460; Dallas, TX 75266; 800-348-5058

ROAD MAPS: Those who aren't members of a travel or automobile club should peruse Rand McNally's *Road Atlas* (about $14.95 in bookstores). It is also possible to obtain free maps from individual state tourist boards.

BY TRAIN

A few years ago, Anaheim was added to Amtrak's network of California stations; the station is located at 2150 East Katella Ave., just two miles from Disneyland's main gate. For reservations and information call 800-USA-RAIL. The *San Diegan*, the train that runs between Los Angeles and San Diego, stops at Anaheim; the train operates about eight times daily. Two trains run daily between Santa Barbara (about 80 miles north of Los Angeles) and San Diego. Trains operating on this line do not drop checked baggage at Anaheim.

Union Station in Los Angeles is served by a number of trains from the rest of the state, the South, and the Midwest. To get to Anaheim, it's possible to make a connection with the *San Diegan*, described above. Those preferring to rent a car can use the major car rental agencies' direct-dial phones (to their downtown offices) available at Union Station. Among the trains arriving in Los Angeles are:

- **Coast Starlight:** Originating in Seattle, this train—one of the 2 most heavily used long-distance trains in the Amtrak system—makes stops in Portland and Eugene, Oregon; and Sacramento, Oakland, and San Jose, California. Daily. Seattle to L.A., about 32 hours.
- **Desert Wind:** Departing Chicago daily, this train stops in Omaha and Lincoln, Nebraska; Denver, Colorado; Salt Lake City, Utah; and Las Vegas, Nevada. Total trip time from Chicago to L.A. is about 47 hours; getting to Los Angeles takes about 29½ hours from Denver; about 14 hours from Salt Lake City; and about 7 hours from Las Vegas.

BY AIR

Los Angeles International Airport is one of the busiest in the world. There are approximately 1,100 departures and arrivals by nearly 65 commercial airlines each day. Delta Air Lines alone, as the Official Airline of Disneyland, carries more than three million passengers into Los Angeles on nonstop flights from 87 cities, direct flights, and connecting flights from 150 additional cities. Delta offers a special style of service for all passengers, along with special meals and The Fantastic Flyer® program for kids. Other major carriers include American, Continental, Pan Am, TWA, United, and USAir. Though Anaheim lies about 45 minutes to the southeast, most Disneyland guests who come by plane arrive at LAX, as this airport is generally known.

Orange County's John Wayne Airport, located considerably closer to Anaheim in Santa Ana, recently completed construction of a new terminal and parking structure. This expansion means that the airport is now able to handle more traffic than in past years. As a result, more airlines now offer flights to this convenient airport. Long Beach Airport is also close by, but only a few airlines serve it on a nonstop basis.

Which airport you use and which airline you decide to fly will depend largely on where you live, when you'll be traveling, and which airline can get you there when you want to go—at the best possible price and with the most direct route. It is usually possible to find the same fare to John Wayne/Orange County Airport, so the major consideration is whether a nonstop flight is available.

HOW TO GET THE BEST AIRFARE: There was a time when it cost a finite, predictable number of dollars to get from one city to another. No longer. Nowadays, the fare is governed not only by when you go and how long you stay, but also by the airline that will transport you. Each one has its own set of restrictions and rules governing who can qualify for its very lowest fares. So it's more important than ever to shop around. Here are some suggestions.

● Find out the names of all the airlines serving your destination, and then call them all (or ask your travel agent to do so)—more than once if your route is complex. Tell the airline's reservation clerk how many people are in your party, and emphasize that you're interested in economy. Ask if you can get a lower fare by slightly altering the dates of your trip, the hour of departure, or the duration of your stay—or, if you live halfway between two airports, by leaving from one rather than the other.

● Watch your local newspapers for ads announcing new or special promotional fares.

● When you have to change planes en route, try

● San Joaquin: Three trains daily provide service between the San Francisco Bay area and the San Joaquin Valley, with stops at Oakland and Fresno. At the terminus in Bakersfield, a bus transports connecting passengers to Union Station in Los Angeles. The trip takes about six hours from San Francisco to Bakersfield.

● **Southwest Chief:** Daily service from Chicago is provided by this train, which stops in Kansas City, Missouri; Topeka, Kansas; and Albuquerque, New Mexico; among other cities. From Chicago to L.A., about 40 hours; 30 hours from Topeka; and about 16 hours from Albuquerque.

● **Sunset Limited:** Service is provided from New Orleans on Mondays, Wednesdays, and Saturdays, with stops in Houston, San Antonio, El Paso, Tucson, and Phoenix. About 42 hours for the trip from New Orleans to L.A.

BY BUS

Buses make sense if you're not coming from too great a distance or if you have plenty of time, if there are only two or three in your party, or if cost is a major consideration.

Following the merger of Greyhound and Trailways, there is now only one bus terminal in Anaheim. The Greyhound terminal (635-5060) is located at 2080 South Harbor Boulevard, about three-quarters of a mile south of Disneyland.

Taxis can transport you from the terminal to your lodging place or Disneyland.

The following sample trip times are for runs directly to Anaheim and require no change of bus.
Phoenix ....about 10 hours
San Diego ....about 2½ hours
San Francisco...........................about 9 hours

For travel from most other destinations, a change of vehicles in Los Angeles will probably be required.

to stick with one airline: Its own agents will probably know their routings and discounted fares better than those of a competitor—and there's less chance of luggage getting misdirected.

● Try for a night flight for low night-coach fares.

● Fly weekends on routes heavily used by business travelers, and midweek on routes more commonly patronized by vacationers.

● Plan and pay as far ahead as possible. Most carriers guarantee their fares, which means you won't have to pay extra if fares have gone up since you purchased your ticket. If, however, you have *not* paid for your ticket, you *will* be required to pay the extra charge. Similarly, if you change dates of travel or flight times and your ticket has to be rewritten, you'll have to pay the new fare. If fares have come down in price since you paid for your ticket, the difference will be refunded to you by the airline, even if you've already paid the higher fare in full. Be sure to watch the newspaper ads and to call the airline to check for new, lower fares since you have to request the refund.

WHICH AIRLINE FLIES FROM YOUR CITY?

More than two dozen airlines serve Los Angeles, Orange County's John Wayne Airport, and Long Beach Airport from almost 100 different cities nonstop. The list that follows was correct at press time. Schedules do change, however, and flights are occasionally dropped or added. So be sure to double-check as close to your departure date as possible. A (2) indicates that the flight lands at John Wayne Airport. A (3) indicates the flight lands at Long Beach Airport.

Acapulco, Mexico	DL
Albuquerque, NM	DL, WN
Aspen, CO	UA
Atlanta, GA	DL, EA
Austin, TX.	CO
Bakersfield, CA.	DL, AA, UA, PQ
Baltimore, MD	US
Boise, ID	UA
Boston, MA.	AA, UA, TW, NW
Bullhead City, AZ/Laughlin, NV	YW
Bullhead City, AZ/Laughlin, NV(2)	YW
Burbank, CA.	YW, 7V
Burbank, CA(3).	AS
Calgary, Alberta	DL, AC
Charlotte, NC	US
Chicago, IL	AA, UA, ML
Chicago, IL(2)	AA, UA
Chicago, IL(3)	UA
Cincinnati, OH.	DL
Cleveland, OH	US, CO

Concord, CA	US
Dallas/Ft. Worth, TX	DL, AA
Dallas/Ft. Worth, TX(2)	DL, AA
Dallas/FT. Worth, TX(3)	AA
Dayton, OH	US
Denver, CO	CO, UA
Denver, CO(2)	CO
Detroit, MI	NW
El Centro/Imperial, CA	DL
El Paso, TX.	WN
Eugene, OR.	US
Fresno, CA.	DL, UA, US, AA
Fresno, CA(2)	DL, UA
Grand Canyon, AZ	JT
Guadalajara, Mexico	DL, MX, AM
Honolulu, HI.	DL, AA, CO, UA, HA, NW, TW
Houston, TX.	CO
Houston, TX(2)	CO
Indianapolis, IN	US
Inyokern, CA.	AA
Ixtapa/Zihuatanejo, Mexico	DL
Kahului, Maui, HI.	DL, UA
Kansas City, MO.	US, UA, YX
La Paz, Mexico	AM
Las Vegas, NV	DL, HP, AA, CO US, UE, QD, TW
Las Vegas, NV(2).	HP, AL
Las Vegas, NY(3).	HP
Leon-Guanajuato, Mexico	AM
Los Angeles, CA(2)	DL, AA, TW, UA
Los Cabos, Mexico	AM, JR, AS
Mammoth Lakes, CA	7V

Mazatlan, Mexico......................DL, MX	San Antonio, TX ....CO
Medford, OR ....US	San Diego, CA...................DL, AA, YW
Memphis, TN.. ....NW	TW, UA, US, AS
Mexico City, Mexico ......DL, MX,LR, AM	San Diego, CA(2)....................NW, YW
Miami, FL ....AA, EA	San Francisco, CA... ....DL, AS, UA,
Milwaukee, WI ....NW, YK	US, AA, CO, NW, WN
Minneapolis/St. Paul, MN ....NW	San Francisco, CA(2).............US, AA, UA
Minneapolis/St. Paul, MN(2) ....NW	San Francisco, CA(3)...................AS, UA
Monterey, CA ....DL, US, UA	San Jose, CA. ....DL, US, AA, AS
Monterey, CA(2)...............................DL	San Jose, CA(2)........................AA, US
Nashville, TN.................................AA	San Jose, CA(3).........................AS, HP
New Orleans, LA.. ....DL, UA	San Luis Obispo, CA.................DL, AA
New York, NY/Newark, NJ........AA, CO,	Santa Barbara, CA...............DL, AA, UA
TW, UA, MG	Santa Maria,CA.........................DL, AA
Oakland, CA.. ....US, AS, UA, AA	Santa Rosa, CA ....UA
Oakland, CA(2) ....US, UA	Seattle/Tacoma, WA......DL, AS, US, UA,
Oakland, CA(3).................................AS	CO, NW
Ontario, CA...........................DL, PQ	Seattle/Tacoma, WA(2) ....NW, AS
Ontario, CA......................................UA	Stockton, CA ....US, UA
Orange County, CA ....DL, AA, YW	Stockton, CA(2)................................UA
Orlando, FL.......................................DL	Tampa/St. Petersburg, FL ....US
Oxnard, CA...............................UA, AA	Toronto, Ontario ....AC
Palm Springs, CA ....DL, AA, TW, UA	Tucson, AZ ....DL, US
Palm Springs, CA(2) ....DL	Tucson, AZ(2) ....US
Philadelphia, PA.. ....TW, UA, US	Vancouver, British Columbia ......DL, CP
Phoenix, AZ......................DL, US, WN	Washington, DC ....AA, US, UA, TW
Phoenix, AZ(2)...........................US, HP	Yuma, AZ ....DL
Phoenix, AZ(3)...................................HP	
Pittsburgh, PA ....US	
Portland, OR ....DL, AS, UA	
Portland, OR(2) ....AS	
Portland, OR(3)..................................AS	
Puerto Vallarta, Mexico ....DL, MX	
Reno, NV..........................DL, US, UA	
Sacramento, CA............DL, US, AA, UA	
Sacramento, CA(2) ....US, AA, UA	
Sacramento, CA(3)..........................HP	
St. Louis, MO ....TW	
St. Louis, MO(2) ....TW	
Salt Lake City, UT ....DL	
Salt Lake City, UT(2)......................DL	

ABBREVIATIONS—AA: American Airlines. AC: Air Canada. AM: Aeromexico. AS: Alaska Airways. CO: Continental. CP: CP Air. DL: Delta. EA: Eastern Airines. HA: Hawaiian Air Lines. HP: America West Airlines. JR: Aero California. JT: Iowa Airways. LR: Lasca. MG: MGM Grand. ML: Midway. MX: Mexicana. NW: Northwest. PQ: Pacific Coast Airlines. QD: Grand Airways. TW: Trans World Airlines. UA: United. UE: Air LA. US: USAir. WN: Southwest Airlines. YW: Stateswest Airlines. 7V: Alpha Air.

HOW TO CUT TRAVEL COSTS

Between inflation and the rising cost of operating a car, vacations are becoming increasingly more expensive. Yet prudent planning can trim costs and save the annual getaway from becoming an economic casualty.

Lodgings: The most important rule is not to pay for more than you need—or can realistically afford. Budget chains don't offer many frills, but they are usually clean and contain all the essentials. The best guide to these economical accommodations is the *National Directory of Budget Motels*, revised annually and available for $3.95, plus $1 postage and handling, from Pilot Books; 103 Cooper St.; Babylon, NY 11702; 516-422-2225.

If swimming pools and other such optional amenities are important, you'll probably prefer to stay in less austere chain establishments. You even can save here occasionally by checking the cutoff ages for children—the age at which there is a charge for youngsters sharing their parents' rooms. Most of the hotels and motels in the Anaheim area allow children under 12 to stay free. Some have a cutoff of 17 or 18, so it's a good idea to check when making reservations.

Food: The budget-minded should try to have hot meals in coffee shops or fast-food outlets, which are less costly than establishments with waitress service. If you want to try a fancy place, don't go at dinner but at lunchtime, when the same entrées usually cost less. Carry sandwich fixings and have lunches alfresco, when possible. Beach picnics are great in Southern California; Disneyland even has a small picnic area just outside the main gate. You can also save significantly by looking for lodging places that include kitchen facilities. The savings on food, especially where a large family is concerned, may more than cover the additional cost of accommodations. In Anaheim proper, there are a number of establishments that offer kitchen facilities. These accommodations rent quickly, so it's a good idea to make your reservations as far in advance as possible.

- **Admiral's Cove**; 1028 West Ball Rd.; 774-1650
- **Anaheim Stadium TraveLodge**; 1700 East Katella Ave.; 634-1920
- **Best Western Apollo:** 1741 South West St.; 772-9750
- **Best Western Stardust:** 1057 West Ball Rd.; 774-7600
- **Islander**; 424 West Katella Ave.; 778-6565
- **Magic Lamp**; 1030 West Katella Ave.; 772-7242
- **Park Vue**; 1570 South Harbor Blvd.; 772-5721
- **Penny Sleeper:** 1441 South Manchester Ave.; 991-8100
- **Tropicana**; 1540 South Harbor Blvd.; 635-4082

If there aren't too many people in your family or traveling group, guesthouses and tourist homes may be a very good buy. Since these hostelries generally assess extra charges for more than two people in a room, regardless of age, rooms that are inexpensive for a couple may prove less economical for a whole family. For a list of such accommodations, consult *Bed & Breakfast U.S.A.* by Betty Rundback and Nancy Kramer ($10.95; E.P. Dutton). For more detailed information, see *Transportation and Accommodations*.

Transportation: As always, it pays to shop around. But when you do, be sure to add the cost of local transportation to your computations. When calculating the cost of driving, consider your car's gas mileage, the current price of gasoline, the distance you plan to cover, and the expense of accommodations and food en route. And when you compare that estimate to the cost of going by bus, train, or plane, don't overlook the cost of getting from the airport or train or bus terminal to your motel, and the cost of renting a car at your destination, if you plan to do that. Keep in mind that discount fares, which can prove so inexpensive for a couple traveling together, may be less advantageous for a family than a regular economy fare, which generally offers discounts for children traveling with their parents. Be sure to look into packages since they usually include transportation, accommodations, and even a rental car.

Disneyland was designed by artists who had spent their lives framing scenes in camera viewfinders. So it's not surprising that almost every square foot of the place seems as amazingly photogenic as it is. If you instinctively reach for your camera while strolling through Disneyland, it's because the park was especially planned with that in mind. Millions of photographs are snapped here every year.

There are so many terrific images to be snatched that almost every camera in good working order can get a few for you. It will help considerably, however, to take note of these few hints:

● Don't shoot closer than 4 feet from your subject, and don't try for a flash picture when you're standing more than 12 feet away. The former will turn out fuzzy, and the latter will be dark, since flash light doesn't reach more than a dozen feet away. (Important: Flash photography is prohibited inside all Disneyland attractions.)

● Fill the frame with as much of your subject as possible. Remember, especially when photographing people, that pictures are more interesting when the subject appears large in the picture.

● Hold the camera steady as you squeeze the shutter.

● Don't shoot into the sun. Cameras with electric eyes assume that there is more light on the subject than there actually is and adjust shutter openings accordingly—leaving the subject dark. A better idea is to stand so that the light is falling directly on the object you want to photograph—that is, coming from the side or from behind you.

● Check the camera's batteries and battery contacts regularly.

● Be sure to use film that is fresh. Check the expiration date printed on the film boxes when making film purchases. Keep film as cool as possible—don't leave it in a hot car for a long period of time.

● Blow dust off your lenses or wipe them with soft lens tissues to keep specks off your pictures. Also, blow dust out of the inside of the camera periodically.

● For movies or videotapes, remember that the most effective results are obtained when you have a basic theme, such as "A Walk Through Adventureland," or something similar. Never shoot directly into the sun (for the reasons noted above), and check carefully before you film to make sure that your subject matter is fairly evenly lighted. When you pan, do it smoothly and slowly, and don't rush through a scene; give every image about 5 seconds. Use a zoom lens sparingly, remembering that it easily can become too much of a good thing.

● If you suspect that your camera is not working properly, visit the Kodak Camera Center on the east side of Main Street to have it inspected. Minor repairs can be made there.

RENTAL CAMERAS: Among Disneyland's best bargains are the rental cameras offered at the Kodak Camera Center on Main Street. The rental fee is $5, plus a returnable deposit from $30 to $95, depending upon the equipment you choose. VHS and 8mm video cameras are also available for a $40 fee, with a $1,000 refundable deposit. All deposits can be made in cash or with an American Express, MasterCard, or Visa card.

Outside Disneyland, Anaheim Camera Supply (855 South Harbor Blvd., a half mile from the main gate; 778-3115) rents 35mm single-lens reflex cameras and a variety of lenses, VHS video camcorders, and some Polaroid cameras. Deposits, payable in cash or by credit card (MasterCard, Visa, or Discover), are required. The deposit is small for California residents, but hefty for other renters (for insurance purposes).

CAMERA REPAIRS: Repairs of a minor nature can be handled by the Kodak Camera Center on Main Street. For anything more than a simple problem, your best bet is to rent a camera and get the factory-authorized shop in your hometown to do the necessary work on your own camera when you get home.

FILM PROCESSING: Same-day processing service available through Fox Photo Film Processing. Pickups are made every hour, beginning at park opening, and deliveries are made every hour. Processing only takes about two hours, so you can take today's photographed memories home tonight.

THE BEST PHOTOS

HOW TO PHOTOGRAPH FIREWORKS: To get acceptable images, it's necessary to have a camera with a manually adjustable shutter speed and aperture. Using color negative film (Kodak ASA 400), put the camera on a tripod, or brace it firmly in some other way; set the aperture at f8 and the shutter speed at B, and hold the lens open for three to five seconds at each burst, covering the lens with your hand between explosions.

HELPFUL HINTS

Traveling can be hard work, but a little know-how can smooth the way and make a vacation much more relaxing. Here are some hints for getting the most out of your trip and your visit to Disneyland.

HINTS ON TRAVELING WITH CHILDREN

When you tell your kids that a Disneyland vacation is planned, the response is apt to be overwhelming. So it will take all your savvy to keep your youngsters relatively calm until you arrive.

PLANNING: By far the best way to cope with excited youngsters is to allow them to participate in some part of the planning of the upcoming Disneyland trip. Not only will it heighten their enjoyment after they arrive, but also it will provide visitors of all ages with a realistic sense of what to expect. Give every child a small part of the trip's preparations as his or her responsibility—what attractions to see in what order, where to have lunch each day, what other activities to include in your Southern California visit, etc. Just writing for brochures and pamphlets can be a very important job for a youngster, and make him or her feel more a part of the general undertaking.

EN ROUTE: Certain techniques can stave off children's tiresome "Are-we-there-yets?" until you walk through the main gate. One ploy is to set up a series of intermediate goals to which they can look forward, if you're traveling by car. Younger kids might anticipate getting to the bottom of a child-size suitcase, stuffed with well-loved toys and games.

Also, be sure to pack snacks to quiet rumbling stomachs at those inconvenient times when there's not a decent restaurant in sight. Most important of all, plan for plenty of breaks en route.

If you're flying, try to time your departure and return flights for off-peak hours and off-seasons, when chances are better that an empty seat or two will be available. During takeoffs and landings, encourage babies to suck on bottles, pacifiers, or even thumbs to keep ears clear, and supply small children with chewing gum or hard candy. Remember that newborn babies (those only a couple of weeks old) probably should not fly, since their lungs may not be able to handle the altitude. Check with your doctor to be sure. As the Official Airline for Disneyland, Delta tries to make flying fun. There is a special program just for kids, ages 2 to 12, who fly on Delta. The Fantastic Flyer Program® means that children will receive a complimentary Mickey Mouse visor, a copy of the Fantastic Flyer magazine, with games, puzzles, prizes, and other treats. Ask a flight attendant for details.

IN ANAHEIM: Several Anaheim restaurants offer children's menus. See *Good Meals, Great Times* for a listing.

IN THE HOTELS: During the summer, both the *Disneyland* hotel and the *Anaheim Hilton* offer special kids' programs in sports and arts and crafts at no charge for the children of guests. Children have to be signed in and out of activities by their parents.

INSIDE DISNEYLAND: Having kids along is about as easy as it can be. And in the park itself, the smiles that break out on the faces of the little ones as they greet Mickey, Minnie, and the other characters, or steer a motorboat or car, or gaze in wonderment at all those moving dolls in It's a Small World will repay you a thousandfold for any fuss and bother en route.

Favorite attractions: When traveling with young children, you will want to substitute some of the attractions listed in the Disneyland itineraries in our *Essential Guide to the Magic Kingdom* with a few others. For example, Casey Jr. Circus Train, the Motor Boat Cruise, and the Autopias are mainly for young children with their parents; the Storybook Land Canal Boats and It's a Small World charm young children and older folks alike. (Teenagers, however, might be less

enchanted.) In Fantasyland, young children will delight most in the bright colors and the dazzling special effects. Snow White's Scary Adventures may be too frightening for some young children, but the guest waiting area does set the mood, so you might want to check your youngster's reaction before you board. Other youngsters have been known to get upset inside the Haunted Mansion, but neither of these attractions is likely to truly terrify anyone, and most kids enjoy them enormously.

Strollers: These can be rented for $5 (plus a returnable $5 deposit) at the Stroller Shop, to the right as you enter the main gate. If yours disappears while you're inside an attraction, just take back your claim ticket and you can get another.

Baby care: The Baby Center is important to know about. For tots, it has child-size flush toilets that can only be described as cute—and are conveniently functional as well. In addition, there are pink and blue changing tables, a limited selection of juices and strained baby foods for sale at a nominal fee, and facilities for warming both food and bottles. A special room with comfortable chairs is available for nursing mothers. The decor there (and in the rest of the Baby Center) is soothing, and the hubbub of the rest of the park seems a million miles away. A stop here for diaper changing constitutes a restful break for both parent and child alike—although changing tables are available in most ladies' rest rooms as well.

Where to buy baby care items: Disposable diapers and baby bottles are sold at the Emporium on Main Street.

Lost children: When a child suddenly disappears or fails to show up on time, it's reassuring to know that Disneyland's security force and all Disneylanders are carefully trained to follow specific procedures with a lost child. The child is taken to Lost Children, adjacent to Central First Aid, where there are Disney movies and a variety of books to amuse lost youngsters. The child's name is registered in the lost children's log book there, and in the one at City Hall. The telephone number for Lost Children is 999-4210. If you're calling from inside the park, dial only the last four digits.

HINTS FOR OLDER TRAVELERS

Southern California can overwhelm an elderly traveler not accustomed to freeways and busy traffic, and even Disneyland can be disorienting with its many sights and sounds. Yet as one newly married nonagenarian, away from home for the first time in her life, once exclaimed, "What a beautiful world it is!" The rewards of a visit here warrant the advance planning required to make a stay go smoothly. Here are a few ways to insure those good times. For answers to your specific questions, contact the Anaheim Senior Citizen Center at 280 East Lincoln Ave.; 533-1981; or 1800 West Ball Rd.; 535-8210.

- Join a tour. Travel agents can help find one that best suits your interests. Visitors who come in groups should allow plenty of time to return to their buses at the end of a day. One good tactic is to save Main Street's sights—such as The Walt Disney Story featuring "Great Moments with Mr. Lincoln," the Penny Arcade, and the Main Street Cinema—for the end of the day. If you arrive at the main gate too far in advance of the group's meeting time, you can spend the extra minutes at those attractions. Town Square is an easy 10- or 15-minute walk, at most, from the bus parking area.

- Inside the Magic Kingdom, group tours also are a good idea for individual travelers. These guided walks cover the whole park, and the price includes general admission to Disneyland for the day, the services of a guide throughout the three-hour tour, and then the run of the park for the rest of the day. For details, contact Disneyland Guest Relations; 1313 South Harbor Blvd.; Anaheim, CA 92803; 999-4565.

- The week before Christmas and the weekdays in spring and fall are ideal. Remember that Tuesdays, Wednesdays, and Thursdays are generally the quietest days of the week, and that Saturdays are always the busiest. If you must visit on a weekend, choose a Sunday.

- Read Disneyland literature carefully before arrival, so the park's layout is as familiar as possible.

- In the park, don't be shy about asking for advice or directions from Disneyland employees. They're happy to help out.

- Eat early or late to avoid crowds at mealtimes.

- Protect yourself from the sun. Wear a hat and sunscreen.

- If you do visit in summer, don't allow yourself to get overheated. Take frequent rest stops in the shade, and get out of the midafternoon heat by pausing for a snack in a cool restaurant or snack stand. If you feel faint, speak to a Disney employee or go to a first aid center.

- Don't push yourself. After all, half the fun of Disneyland is just sitting on a park bench underneath some shady tree and watching the people go by.

- Remember that sightseeing takes energy, and only healthy meals can provide it. Don't try to save money by scrimping on food. Prices for meals at Disneyland are quite reasonable. Outside the park,

LOST ADULTS

Traveling companions do occasionally get separated. If someone in your party disappears all of a sudden, or fails to show up at an appointed meeting spot, head for Lost Children, next to Central First Aid just off Main Street, or check in at City Hall. (The two offices keep in close contact.) City Hall also has a message book where members of a group can leave notes for each other during the day.

some restaurants offer discounts for senior citizens. These include the *Four Seasons* cafeteria at 1363 South Anaheim Boulevard (776-6140), which offers a $2.95 lunch special; and the *Sizzler* family restaurant at 888 South Brookhurst Street (772-8812), which offers discounts throughout the day Mondays through Wednesdays, and from 2 P.M. to 5 P.M. Thursdays through Sundays.

Senior Fun Days at Disneyland: Sundays through Fridays from September through June, specially priced Passports are available to those age 60 and up. Plan accordingly.

HINTS FOR THE HANDICAPPED

Disneyland is more accessible to the handicapped than ever before, and as a result makes a very good choice as a vacation destination. But advance planning is still a must: *Access to the World* by Louise Weiss ($16.95; Facts on File; 460 Park Ave. South; New York, NY 10016) provides useful, detailed information on general matters relating to travel by the handicapped or disabled. The *Disneyland Disabled Guest Guide*, offering information on rest rooms and park attractions accessible to the handicapped, is a good planning tool as well (see "Inside Disneyland," later in this section).

TOURS: The Society for the Advancement of Travel for the Handicapped (The Penthouse; 26 Court St.; Brooklyn, NY 11242; 718-858-5483) has a number of member travel agents who are knowledgeable about tours for the handicapped and can help arrange individual and group trips. (Send $1 and a self-addressed, stamped envelope to receive a copy of their listings.) In addition, a number of groups sponsor package tours that include Disneyland:

● **Evergreen Travel Service**; 4114 198 SW, Suite 13; Lynnwood, WA 98036; 206-776-1184 or 800-435-2288

● **Flying Wheels Travel**; Box 382; 143 West Bridge St.; Owatonna, MN 55060; 507-451-5005 or 800-535-6790

GETTING THERE: Probably the most effective means of assuring a smooth trip are plenty of advance contacts for every phase of the trip.

Traveling by train: All new and rebuilt Amtrak equipment operating in and to California has special facilities to aid handicapped travelers, including grab bars in the toilets, specially equipped sleeper compartments, and seats with an adjoining empty space for a wheelchair. Wheelchairs or electric carts are available at all major stations, including both the Los Angeles and Anaheim stations. Both stations have wheelchair-lift devices. Many other stations in the western part of the United States have been similarly fitted out.

Blind and handicapped passengers are entitled to a 25 percent discount on regular one-way fares; companions must pay full fare, however, and most round-trip excursion fares are lower than the discounted fares for the handicapped. Seeing-eye and hearing-ear dogs are allowed to ride with passengers at no charge.

Battery-powered, standard-size wheelchairs are permitted in coaches. Fuel-powered and oversize chairs must be stored in the baggage car for the duration of the trip. (Note, however, that not all trains stopping at Anaheim carry baggage cars, so check in advance.) Always be sure to phone the train stations and reservations center well before your departure date to arrange for any special facilities or services you may need.

Additional information about train travel for elderly and handicapped travelers is included in Amtrak's free "Travel Planner" booklet, which is available by calling 800-USA-RAIL.

Traveling by plane: Fortunately, times have changed in the way that airlines deal with handicapped travelers. Vacationers are occasionally allowed to board aircraft in their own wheelchairs—provided the chair is narrow enough for the plane's aisles; more often, the passenger is transferred to a narrower airline chair at the loading gate and his or her own is packed away in the luggage compartment. Wheelchair passengers are usually helped on board before other passengers, and deplaned after everyone else. If you have a tight connection, it's especially important to notify airline attendants in advance. The use of an airline wheelchair to make these connections also must be arranged ahead of time. Again, don't fail to alert airline personnel, at the time you make your reservation, of any special needs you may have.

Note that airlines' policies on motorized wheelchairs vary, depending on the type of chair and the carrier. So check well in advance. All airlines now permit seeing-eye dogs aboard aircraft, though some may require the animal to be muzzled. Canes and crutches, unless collapsible, must be stowed during takeoffs and landings, but will be returned to passengers upon request during the flight. Again, let the carriers know in advance about what's coming.

For more helpful hints on traveling by air, obtain copies of *Fly Rights: A Guide to Air Travel in the United States*, available for $1 from the Government Printing Office (Washington, DC 20402-9325; include the brochure's stock number, 050-000-00-513-5; call 202-783-3238 to check availability); and *Access Travel: Airports*, available for $1.25 from the National Clearing House of Rehabilitation Train-

HINTS FOR SINGLE TRAVELERS

There's so much to see and do in Disneyland that the park can be as enjoyable for solo travelers as it is for couples, families, and groups. College students will encounter peers all over the park as well. (On the other hand, single men and women who want to continue to vacation solo won't have any problems preserving their privacy.)

Outside Disneyland, Southern California offers plenty of opportunities for striking up friendship, or at least conversation. In Anaheim proper, the wood-paneled bar at *El Torito's Who-Song & Larry's Cantina*, at 2020 East Ball Road (956-4880), is as active as they come. Anyone who likes people-watching can have a field day studying who's moving in on whom—and that's true even when the place is nearly empty. *Sgt. Preston's Yukon Saloon* in the *Disneyland* hotel, at 1150 West Cerritos Avenue (778-6600), offers drinks, a good show, live entertainment, and the opportunity to mix—or not to mix—as you choose.

Probably the liveliest areas for singles are Newport Beach, the Balboa Peninsula, and Balboa Island—a half hour's drive to the south. Disneyland employees can often be found here after work at spots like the *Cannery* at 3010 Lafayette Avenue in Newport Beach (675-5777). *T.G.I. Friday's,* the restaurant and bar at 601 Anton Boulevard in the South Coast Plaza area of Costa Mesa (540-2227), is frenetically active, especially after performances at the Orange County Performing Arts Center or the South Coast Repertory Theater.

---

ing Materials (Oklahoma State University; 816 West Sixth St.; Stillwater, OK 74078-0435; 405-624-7650; include the code number, 108-X).

Traveling by bus: A handicapped vacationer and a companion may travel together on Greyhound with a single adult ticket; the only requirement is a written statement from a doctor confirming the necessity for such aid. Nonmotorized folding wheelchairs are carried with no additional charge. Motorized chairs are not accepted.

GETTING AROUND ORANGE COUNTY: Avis, Hertz, and National (the official car rental agency of Disneyland and Walt Disney World) all have a limited number of hand-control cars available for rent in Southern California, mostly at Los Angeles International Airport.

Though slightly less convenient, it's also possible to get around by public transportation. Some 40 percent of the buses operated by the Orange County Transit District, the public bus company that serves Orange County, have lifts so that wheelchair travelers can board them easily. Many routes pass Disneyland. The company also operates a Dial-A-Ride Service (638-9000).

Sightseeing tour buses are another option. Though none have lifts for wheelchairs, all have storage facilities for collapsible chairs, making this a possibility for travelers who have a companion to help them on and off the bus. Starline-Gray Line (213-463-3131) tours Hollywood, Beverly Hills, and San Diego; Co-Ordinators Tours (771-7600) travel to the *Queen Mary* and *Spruce Goose* in Long Beach, Sea World, Los Angeles, the San Diego Zoo, and Tijuana, Mexico; Specialty Fun Bus (635-1390) travels to points in Southern California, San Diego, and Tijuana. Pacific Coast Sightseeing Tours (978-8855) offers a popular trip to Knott's Berry Farm, among its many Southern California packages.

ANAHEIM LODGING: The following motels and hotels have at least one room equipped for the handicapped with extra-wide doorways, grab bars in the bathroom for shower or bath and commode, and sinks at wheelchair height, plus ramps at curbs and steps to provide wheelchair access. (See *Transportation and Accommodations* for further information on lodging.) Rates range from expensive ($65 and up for doubles), to moderate ($45 to $64), to inexpensive (under $45).

- **Aloha TraveLodge**; 505 West Katella Ave.; 774-8710. Inexpensive to moderate.
- **Anaheim Hilton**; 777 West Convention Way; 750-4321. Expensive.
- **Anaheim Marriott**; 700 West Convention Way; 750-8000. Wheelchair access is also provided to the indoor-outdoor swimming pool and the hydrotherapy pool, and elevator buttons are at wheelchair height. Expensive.
- **Anaheim Stadium TraveLodge**; 1700 East Katella Ave.; 634-1920. Special features include a

clothes-rack bar that can be lowered so it can be reached from a sitting position. Moderate.

- **Candy Cane Inn**; 1747 South Harbor Blvd.; 774-5284. Moderate to expensive.
- **Castle Inn**; 1734 South Harbor Blvd.; 774-8111. Moderate.
- **Disneyland**; 1150 West Cerritos Ave.; 778-6600. Elevator controls are lowered for wheelchair access and doorknobs are all at wheelchair height. Expensive.
- **Pan Pacific**; 1717 South West St.; 999-0990. Expensive.
- **Hampton Inn**; 300 East Katella Way; 772-8713. Expensive.
- **Holiday Inn of Anaheim**; 1850 South Harbor Blvd.; 750-2801. Expensive.
- **Howard Johnson's**; 1380 South Harbor Blvd.; 776-6120. Expensive.
- **Jolly Roger Inn**; 640 West Katella Ave.; 772-7621. Expensive.
- **Park Place Inn**; 1544 South Harbor Blvd.; 776-4800. Expensive.
- **Ramada Maingate**; 1460 South Harbor Blvd.; 772-6777. Expensive.

INSIDE DISNEYLAND: For blind guests, a tape recorder with cassette describing the park is available at City Hall. Seeing-eye dogs are allowed in almost all places in the park except on extremely active attractions such as Space Mountain, the Matterhorn, and Big Thunder Mountain Railroad.

For hard-of-hearing guests, there are volume-control telephones available all around the park.

Wheelchair guests, displaying a "disabled" placard, who request directions from park employees (when passing through the auto toll plaza) will be directed to the handicapped parking section near the main gate ticket booths. Remember to request the *Disneyland Disabled Guest Guide* at the main gate turnstiles. It describes accessibility to Disneyland's shops, restaurants, and attractions, and tells where to find the wheelchair entrances. It also can be obtained by writing to Disneyland Guest Relations; 1313 South Harbor Blvd.; Anaheim, CA 92803. Wheelchairs also can be rented at the Stroller Shop just inside and to the right of the main gate turnstiles.

Attractions: Generally speaking, the conventional waiting areas are not accessible to wheelchairs, and handicapped guests enter attractions at some other point. These entrances are described in the *Disneyland Disabled Guest Guide*. If the handicapped guest is traveling in a party of two, both guests may enter the attraction through the special entrance point. If there are three or more in your group, at least one person will have to wait in line.

In all cases, handicapped guests should be escorted by someone who can provide any necessary help. In the list below, the attractions marked (C) are accessible to those who are completely wheelchair bound, while those marked (P) require that the guest be lifted in and out of the chair, and those marked (W) require that the guest be able to walk a few steps. Those marked (I) are inaccessible to wheelchair guests.

- **Adventureland:** Enchanted Tiki Room (W), a few steps up a small stairway; Jungle Cruise (P); Swiss Family Treehouse (I).
- **Critter Country:** Davy Crockett's Explorer Canoes (I); Country Bear Vacation Hoedown (C); Teddi Barra's Swingin' Arcade (C).
- **Frontierland:** Frontierland Shootin' Arcade (C); Golden Horseshoe Jamboree (C); Big Thunder Mountain Railroad (W), about 10 to 15 feet from loading area to seat; *Mark Twain* Steamboat (C); Sailing Ship *Columbia* (W), a few steps up a stairway; Rafts to Tom Sawyer Island (I); Mike Fink Keel Boats (P).
- **Fantasyland:** Sleeping Beauty Castle (I); Snow White's Scary Adventures (P); Pinocchio's Daring Journey (P); Dumbo the Flying Elephant (P), only for guests light enough to be lifted onto the elephants; Skyway to Tomorrowland (I); Casey Jr. Circus Train (P); Disneyland Railroad (P); Story-book Land Canal Boats (P); It's a Small World (P); Motor Boat Cruise (P); Fantasyland Autopia (P), need to be able to push the pedals; Matterhorn Bobsleds (P); Alice in Wonderland (P); Mr. Toad's Wild Ride (P); Peter Pan's Flight (W), need to be able to walk down a ladder in case of emergency; King Arthur Carrousel (P); Mad Tea Party (P).
- **Main Street:** Disneyland Railroad (W), recommend using the Tomorrowland or New Orleans station, only certain trains; The Walt Disney Story (C); Main Street Vehicles (P); Main Street Cinema (C); Penny Arcade (C).
- **New Orleans Square:** Pirates of the Caribbean (P); Disneyland Railroad (P); Haunted Mansion (P).
- **Tomorrowland:** Starcade (must be able to stand); Space Mountain (W); considerable distance; Mission to Mars (C); Skyway to Fantasyland (I); Disneyland Railroad (P), only certain trains, and locking wheelchair required; Star Tours (P); Captain EO (C); Tomorrowland Autopia (P), need to be able to push the pedals; Submarine Voyage (I); Disneyland Monorail System (C), collapsible wheelchairs required; PeopleMover (I); Rocket Jets (W), need to walk about 25 steps; CircleVision (C).
- **Disneyland Monorail System:** This attraction is not easily accessible to wheelchair guests, particularly those with electric chairs. Wheelchair guests must be able to be lifted into the train or walk a few steps.

Restaurants: Nearly all food locations are completely accessible to wheelchair guests, with the following exceptions and qualifications:

- **Main Street:** The *Plaza Pavilion* has a short flight of steps at the entrance.
- **Frontierland:** At *River Belle Terrace*— otherwise accessible—the stanchions that mark off the cafeteria line are spaced too closely together to permit wheelchair passage. Tom Sawyer Island and consequently the snack stands there are not accessible.

Shops: Nearly every shop in the park is completely accessible to wheelchair guests. Exceptions include Patented Pastimes on Main Street which is a bit small to allow easy maneuverability, and One of a Kind antiques, which is too cramped.

OTHER INFORMATION

BARBER SHOPS: Lord Jim's Barber Shop; 700 West Orangewood, Suite A; 971-5530; is about three blocks from Disneyland.

BEAUTY SHOPS: The closest to Disneyland is Keiko's, in the *Disneyland* hotel; 1150 West Cerritos Avenue; 991-6960. Other choices include The Coral Tree, in the *Marriott* hotel; 700 West Convention Way; 750-6573; and the Orangewood Beauty Salon, about three blocks from the park, 700 West Orangewood, Suite C; 971-5625; next door to Lord Jim's, above.

CAR CARE: Those who belong to auto and travel clubs should call their club-sponsored towing service in the event of problems. The Anaheim AAA is at 150 West Vermont Ave., 774-2392. Another AAA station in the area is Anaheim Hills; 5500 East Santa Ana Canyon Rd.; 921-2850.

RELIGIOUS SERVICES: One of the most interesting places to attend services is the Crystal Cathedral; 12141 Lewis St.; Garden Grove; 971-4000. Completed in 1980, it is huge—one of the largest houses of worship in the world—but unlike some others it is not oppressive. The entire structure is made of glass, so the sky is visible all around. The pipe organ is the biggest in the western United States and the minister, Robert Schuller, is credited by Muriel Humphrey with giving her husband, the late Senator Hubert Humphrey, the strength to live out his remaining days. One unusual feature of the church is that two 90-foot doors open so people can take part in the service without ever leaving their automobiles. This has been called a typical California phenomenon, and is a throwback to the days when Schuller began his ministry preaching in a drive-in theater 30 years ago. Services are held on Sundays in the small Chapel-in-the-Sky on the grounds at 8 A.M., and at 9 A.M., 11 A.M., and 6:30 P.M. (7 P.M. in summer) in the cathedral proper. (For further information, see *Anaheim*.)

Baptist: The Garden Church; 8712 East Santa Ana Canyon Rd. (Anaheim Hills); 282-1899. Services are on Sundays at 9:30 A.M.; Sunday school at 10:45 A.M.; Bible study on Tuesdays at 7 P.M.

Catholic: The Church of St. Boniface; 120 North Janss at Harbor Blvd.; 956-3110; is about two miles from Disneyland. Masses are held on Saturdays at 5 P.M. (in English), 6:30 P.M. (Vietnamese), and 8 P.M. (Spanish), and on Sundays at 7 A.M. (English), 8 A.M. (Spanish), 9:30 A.M. and 11 A.M. (English), 12:30 P.M. (Spanish), 5 P.M. (English), and at 7 P.M. (Spanish). Daily masses are held at 6:30 A.M., 8 A.M., and 5:30 P.M. (English), and at 7 P.M. (Spanish).

Christian Science: The First Church of Christ Scientist; 918 North Citron St.; 535-0631. Services are at 10 A.M. on Sundays and at 8 P.M. on Wednesdays. Sunday school is at 10 A.M.

Episcopal: St. Michael's Episcopal Church; 311 West South St.; 535-4654; is about seven blocks from Disneyland. Services are held on Sundays at 8 A.M. and 10 A.M., and Wednesdays at 7:30 P.M.

Jewish: The Temple Beth Emet; 1770 West Cerritos Ave.; 772-4720; a ten-minute walk from Disneyland, has services at 8 P.M. on Fridays, 9:15 A.M. on Saturdays.

Lutheran: Prince of Peace Church; 1421 West Ball Rd.; 774-0993. Located two miles from Disneyland, has services on Sundays at 8 A.M. and 10:30 A.M. Sunday school is at 9:15 A.M.

United Methodist: The West Anaheim United Methodist Church; 2045 West Ball Rd; 772-6030; about three miles from Disneyland, has Sunday services at 10:30 A.M. Sunday school is at 9 A.M.

LIQUOR: Though liquor is now being served in the Magic Kingdom for the first time in more than 30 years, don't get the idea that spirituous libations are easy to come by. In an effort to compete more

among Disneylanders and other guests, so if you lose something, don't fail to check before you leave the park. The Lost and Found office is located on Main Street behind the Market House.

MAIL: Postcards are for sale in gift shops all over Anaheim, and in many Disneyland shops and souvenir stands, including Carefree Corner on Main Street—which is, incidentally, a good spot to buy special occasion cards as well. Don't forget to arrange for your mail at home to be held by the post office or picked up by neighbors while you're on vacation.

Postage stamps: For sale in the park at the following locations:

- Newsstand to the left of the ticket booths at the park entrance
- Souvenir stands, located on either side of Main Street, near the train station
- Postage machines are located inside the Camera Center (Main Street), and the Premiere Shop (Tomorrowland)

Mailboxes: There are 20 of these olive-drab mail depositories inside Disneyland. Cards and letters are picked up and delivered to the post office once a day and postmarked Anaheim, not Disneyland. Locations are as follows:

- Just outside the main gate, at the Newsstand
- On the main gate side of each of the tunnels into the park
- In Town Square, just outside the Walt Disney Story and just outside City Hall
- On Main Street, outside the front door of the Emporium; outside the Disney Clothiers; and outside the front door at Carefree Corner
- On the east and west sides of the Central Plaza
- In Adventureland at the Adventureland Bazaar
- In Critter Country at the Indian Trading Post and at Teddi Barra's Swingin' Arcade
- In Frontierland outside Frontierland Menagerie and Silver Spurs Supplies
- In Fantasyland at Briar Rose Gifts and at the Fantasyland Souvenir Stand, near the Matterhorn
- In Tomorrowland at the Star Trader, and at Tomorrowland Terrace

Post Office: The closest U.S. post office is Holiday Station, about three blocks from the park; 1180 West Ball Rd.; Anaheim; 533-8700. It is open from 8:30 A.M. to 5 P.M. Mondays through Fridays.

MONEY: Cash, traveler's checks, personal checks, American Express, Visa, and MasterCard are accepted as payment for admission to Disneyland, for merchandise purchased in shops, and for meals (except for food carts, where only cash is accepted). Checks must be imprinted with the guest's name and address, drawn on a U.S. bank, and accompanied by proper identification—that is, a valid driver's license and a major credit card such as American Express, Carte Blanche, Diners Club, MasterCard, or Visa. (Oil company credit cards and department store charge cards are not acceptable identification for check-writing purposes.)

The Bank of America: This small, old-fashioned branch of the Southern California giant, decorated with antiques, can really help out in a

effectively with off-premises restaurants and clubs for corporate gatherings, beer, wine, and champagne are now available on Disneyland turf, but only after dark and at corporate parties for 500 or more. So, for all intents and purposes, a casual drink is still not available in the Disney domain. Liquor may, however, be purchased at nearby liquor stores, restaurants, and bars; the liquor store closest to Disneyland, is Wonderland Liquors; 1178 West Katella Ave.; Anaheim; 535-0127. The legal drinking age in California is 21.

LOCKERS: Coin-operated lockers are available just outside the main gate. There are token-operated lockers inside the park at the Lost and Found on Main Street behind the Market House. Tokens cost 75¢ each. New tokens (or quarters in the case of the outside lockers) must be inserted every time you open and relock one. The ready availability of these storage facilities makes it convenient to do your shopping in midafternoon, when the stores are relatively empty and the attractions are busy, and to then stash purchases when you want to return to the attractions, during the less-congested late afternoon or evening hours.

LOST AND FOUND: At any given time, a survey of the shelves of Lost and Found might turn up cameras, umbrellas, strollers, handbags, lens caps, cigarette lighters, sunglasses, prescription glasses, suitcases, and even hair dryers; once, a wallet containing $1,700 in cash was turned in. Hub caps, false teeth, crutches, radios, and jewelry also have turned up. If you find something, you'll be asked to fill out a card with your name and address; if the item isn't claimed within 90 days, you have the option of keeping it. Items not claimed by their finders are eventually sold to employees and the proceeds donated to charity. The system has a way of encouraging honesty

MEDICAL MATTERS: Blisters are the most common complaint received at Central First Aid, at the north end of Main Street near Carefree Corner, the Plaza Inn, and the Baby Center. So be forewarned and wear comfortable, well-broken-in shoes for your Disneyland visit.

If you have a more serious medical problem in the park, contact any Disneyland employee. He or she will get in touch with Central First Aid to make any necessary arrangements.

Those with chronic health problems should be sure to carry copies of all their prescriptions, and before leaving home ask family physicians for the names of Southern California colleagues.

Prescriptions: Try Sav-on Drugs located about two blocks from Disneyland, not far from the intersection of Katella and Euclid; 1660 West Katella Ave.; Anaheim; 530-0500. Hours are 9 A.M. to 9:30 P.M. Mondays through Saturdays, 9 A.M. to 7 P.M. on Sundays.

The nearest 24-hour pharmacy is in Bellflower, about 20 miles away from Anaheim, at the Kaiser-Permanente Hospital; 9400 East Rosecrans Ave.; 213-920-4321.

Refrigerator facilities for insulin: At Disneyland, insulin that must be refrigerated can be stored for the day at Central First Aid on Main Street. Outside the park, there are refrigerators in lodging

places with kitchen facilities (see "How to Cut Travel Costs"), as well as in the suites of certain other area facilities—among them the *Conestoga*, the *Disneyland* hotel, the *Anaheim Plaza*, the *Holiday Inn*, the *Inn at the Park*, *Hyatt Regency Alicante*, the *Jolly Roger Inn*, the *Quality* hotel, the *Sheraton-Anaheim*, the *Grand*, the *Anaheim Marriott*, the *Castle Inn*, *Howard Johnson's*, *Ramada Maingate*, *Apollo Inn*, and *Anaheim Inn*.

---

pinch. Open from 9 A.M. to 4 P.M. every day that the park is open, including Saturdays and Sundays, it can:
- Cash personal checks upon presentation of the proper identification (as outlined above)
- Cash traveler's checks in dollar and foreign currency denominations
- Exchange foreign currency
- Give cash advances on MasterCard and Visa credit cards, with a $50 minimum, in amounts as large as the guest's credit limit allows
- Sell Bank of America traveler's checks, and provide refunds for lost checks
- Assist in wire transfers of money from a hometown bank to the Bank of America
- There is a charge for cashing non-Bank of America checks.

American Express Cardmember services: American Express has an Express Cash machine near the *Disneyland* hotel's monorail station. American Express cardholders can cash personal checks of up to $1,000 with a personal American Express card (up to $5,000 with a Gold Card) at the American Express Travel Agency in the Main Place Mall; 2800 North Main St., Suite 600; Santa Ana; 541-3318. This office also exchanges foreign

currency, can replace lost cards within 24 hours (first call 800-528-4800), as well as lost American Express traveler's checks (first call 800-221-7282), and arrange emergency fund transfers. Hours are 10 A.M. to 9 P.M. weekdays, 10 A.M. to 7 P.M. Saturdays, 11 A.M. to 6 P.M. Sundays. There are six Cardmember's Check Dispensers at the Los Angeles airport. To use these, you need a personal identification number, which must be arranged through American Express in advance.

Other major credit cards: Cash advances on MasterCard and Visa credit cards can be arranged at the Bank of America, according to the limits outlined above; or through Western Union. The Western Union office in Anaheim, located at 616 North Anaheim Blvd.; 535-2291; is open from 8 A.M. to 6 P.M. each weekday, until 3 P.M. Saturdays, and is closed on Sundays.

To report lost Visa or MasterCard credit cards, guests in the Disneyland area should call 800-556-5678. Among the banks in Anaheim that sell Visa and MasterCard traveler's checks are:
- Union Federal Savings and Loan; 511 South Harbor Blvd.; 991-3720
- Wells Fargo Bank; 420 South Harbor Blvd.; 956-1920

PETS: Except for seeing-eye dogs, no animals are allowed in the Magic Kingdom. Those who are traveling with their family pet can board it for the day in Disneyland's air conditioned kennel, where there are large, airy, individual enclosures ($5 per day, including food). Enclosures are disinfected between arrivals. Just outside the kennel, there's a 494-square-foot exercise area. (The lawn here is resodded about every two years.) All pet owners must put their animals into the cages and take them out again, since Disneyland personnel do not handle the animals. Cheetahs, non-poisonous snakes, ocelots, parrots, guinea pigs, and other animals have been accommodated here, as well as cats and dogs.

Note that in busy seasons there is usually a 1½ hour-long rush period, which starts about 30 minutes before park opening. You may be subject to some delay in arranging your pet's accommodations.

Outside Disneyland: Some hotels and motels in the Anaheim area accept well-behaved, and preferably small, pets; most of these hotels do not allow guests to leave pets in the room unattended. These include the following:
- **Space Age Lodge**; 1176 West Katella Ave.; 776-0141
- **Anaheim Marriott**; 700 West Convention Way; 750-8000
- **Hampton Inn**; 300 East Katella Way; 772-8713
- **Residence Inn**; 1700 South Clementine St.; 533-3555

SHOPPING FOR NECESSITIES: It's a rare vacationer who doesn't leave some essential at home, so it's always useful to know where to find certain everyday items.

Health aids and toiletries: Gift shops in all the big hotels stock essentials, but they usually cost more than in conventional retail shops, so try to shop elsewhere. One good source is the Sav-on Drugs closest to Disneyland; 1660 West Katella Ave.; 530-0500.

Inside Disneyland, aspirin, suntan lotions, lozenges, and similar sundries are available at the Newsstand at the main gate, at the Emporium on Main Street, at the Davy Crockett's Pioneer Mercantile, at the Marché aux Fleurs, Sacs et Modes hat shop in New Orleans Square, and at Star Trader in Tomorrowland. You'll also find a variety of personal items inside Fantasyland at Geppetto's Arts and Crafts.

Newspapers: In Anaheim proper, your best bets are hotel gift shops. The *Anaheim Marriott*; 700 West Convention Way; 750-8000; stocks *The Wall Street Journal*, *Barron's*, *USA Today*, and, on Sundays, *The New York Times*, in addition to local papers. The *Grand*; One Hotel Way; 772-7777; and Castle Sundries in the *Disneyland* hotel; 1150 West Cerritos Ave.; 778-6600; stock *The Wall Street Journal*, as well as local papers. For a more varied selection, you must leave Anaheim. The World Book and News Company; 1652 North Cahuenga Blvd.; Hollywood; 213-465-4352; carries papers from as many as 38 states, including *The New York Times*, *The Washington Post*, the

Chicago Sun-Times, and others, plus magazines, paperback books, and foreign periodicals from as far afield as Europe and the Middle East. It's open around the clock.

Books: For a better selection of reading matter than is generally found in hotels, try Waldenbooks in the Anaheim Plaza Shopping Center; 500 North Euclid St.; 956-3510; and B. Dalton Bookseller in the City Shopping Center off the 22 Freeway on City Drive; 634-8603. If you're staying in Newport Beach, your best bets are the B. Dalton Bookseller (644-0041) and the Doubleday Book Shop (640-5312) in the Newport Center Fashion Island Mall.

Cigarettes: Inside Disneyland, the places to buy smokable items are the Market House on Main Street, the Marché aux Fleurs, Sacs et Modes in New Orleans Square, Crocodile Mercantile in Critter Country, and the Star Trader in Tomorrowland.

TELEPHONE: Local calls from most pay phones in Southern California cost 20¢. However, most hotels in the same area charge 75¢ for local calls made from your room. So call from outside your hotel or use a public pay phone whenever possible. For long-distance calls, policies vary from hotel to hotel, but charges are always higher than they would be for direct-dial calls made from a pay phone. Generally speaking, if you plan to talk for a long period of time, your conversation will cost least if you call your party, talk just long enough to let them know where you are, and have them direct-dial you back. Using a telephone credit card or calling collect is second best.

TIME AND WEATHER PHONE: In Anaheim, call 853-1212 for the exact time; for the best local weather forecast, call the Los Angeles weather number (213-554-1212).

TIPPING: The standard gratuities around Anaheim are about the same as in any other city of its size. Expect to tip bellboys 75¢ per bag; $1 per bag is considered generous. It's customary to give cab drivers a 15 percent tip, especially on longer trips, and in restaurants, 15 percent to 20 percent is the norm, depending on the establishment.

TRANSPORTATION AND ACCOMMODATIONS

Until you've actually been to Southern California, it's not unusual to assume that all the most appealing attractions are situated within a few short miles of one another. That's only partly true. For though distances may be relatively short, driving time can really add up if destination and route are not planned with care. So it's important to pick a lodging place that's convenient to all the sites you'll be visiting, and you may even want to move around a bit to make your trip most efficient.

This chapter provides a broad overview of the transportation options within Southern California—rental cars, buses, taxis, tours, and, yes, even freeways. It also offers some advice on places to stay around the area—not only in Anaheim proper, but also in Buena Park, Newport Beach, Orange, Garden Grove, Los Angeles, and San Diego. We've tried to provide a reasonable variety of styles of accommodations, from the spiffily contemporary to the opulently old-fashioned, and we've spanned the spectrum of prices, too; some stopping places we note are quite

expensive while others are strictly no-frills accommodations at more reasonable prices for budget-minded travelers. A careful perusal of the offerings that follow should help save valuable time and money.

(Unless otherwise noted, phone numbers are in area code 714.)

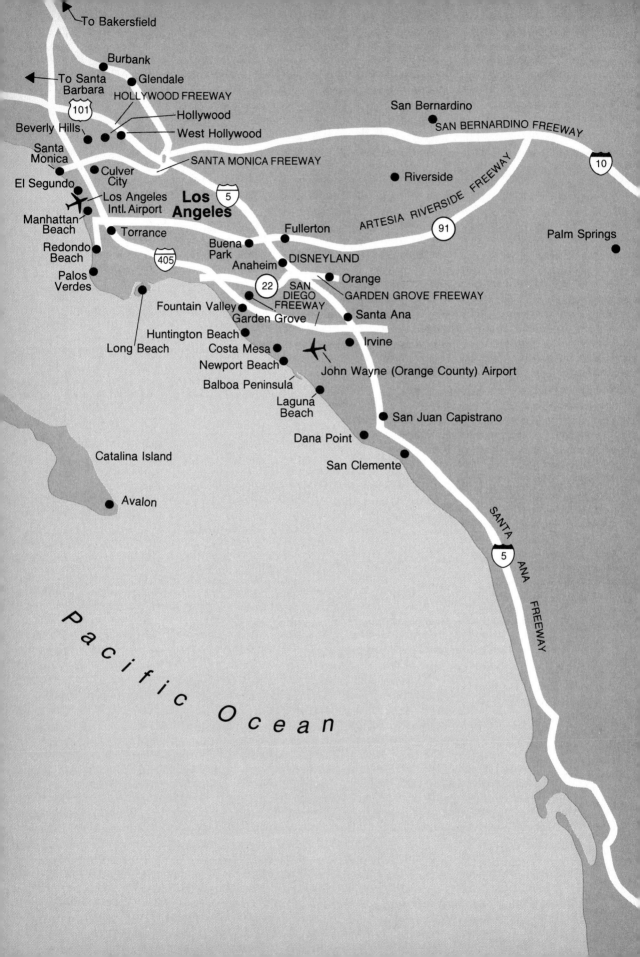

GETTING AROUND

Southern California is an amalgamation of small communities that have grown until their borders touched, where city limits have become irretrievably blurred. Anaheim is bordered by Fullerton and Placentia to the north, the city of Orange to the east, Santa Ana to the southeast, Garden Grove to the southwest, and Buena Park to the northwest.

South of Anaheim you will encounter the communities of Huntington Beach, Costa Mesa, Newport Beach, Irvine, Laguna Beach, San Juan Capistrano, San Clemente, and, about 75 miles (1½ hours) from Anaheim, San Diego.

The towns of Riverside, San Bernardino, and Palm Springs are roughly to the east.

Proceeding west, there are Long Beach, Palos Verdes, Redondo Beach, Torrance, Manhattan Beach, El Segundo, Los Angeles International Airport, and Culver City. Traveling north through Los Angeles are Beverly Hills, Hollywood and West Hollywood, Santa Monica, Glendale, and Burbank. The San Fernando Valley is farther north and a bit inland. Malibu is about the same distance from Anaheim as the San Fernando Valley, but on the coast. Santa Barbara lies about 1½ hours away, and Bakersfield is to the north and slightly east.

All of these communities are connected by an extraordinary group of limited-access highways which, in Southern California, are called freeways.

Disneyland is located in the city of Anaheim. Many of the other area attractions are in nearby towns—Garden Grove, Buena Park, Fountain Valley—or even farther away in Los Angeles or along the coast. Most of the driving to be done requires using a combination of surface streets and freeways; but once one is familiar with a few names and numbers, navigating shouldn't be too difficult.

SOUTHERN CALIFORNIA FREEWAYS: Even if you like to drive, driving on the freeways here is not exactly pure pleasure. Still, these roadways are well marked and (in the best of times) quite fast, and driving them is by far the most convenient way to see Southern California.

For a stranger, the best way to get from one spot to the next is to ask directions. Be sure to write them down and trace the route on a road map before heading down the freeway entrance ramp. When making note of the directions, don't fail to get some idea of the distances between one turnoff and the next. Also remember to get both the names and the route numbers of the freeways to be followed. The proper names of most roads change frequently depending on where you are. For instance, I-5—called the Santa Ana Freeway in Orange County—becomes the Golden State Freeway in the Los Angeles area. Once on the highway, it can be very difficult to get on track again if you go astray.

It is also useful to have some idea of the overall layout of the freeways. There are several that run parallel to the Pacific coast. These are intersected by other freeways running due east and west. And though this scheme is pretty clear as stated here, it is complicated by still other freeways that seem to squiggle willy-nilly across the map. Nor does it help matters much that the roads' names are sometimes misleading (the San Diego Freeway, for instance, does not go to San Diego).

North-south freeways: I-5, which runs from Vancouver to San Diego, is the principal inland route. Near Hollywood, it sprouts I-405 (the San Diego Freeway). This road bulges toward the coast and rejoins I-5 at Irvine, south of Anaheim.

East-west freeways: Of the roads that intersect these two principal north-south arteries, one of the closest to Disneyland is Rte. 22, known as the Garden Grove Freeway, which begins near the ocean in Long Beach and runs across the southern border of Anaheim.

Rte. 91, which is known as the Artesia Freeway on the west side of I-5 and the Riverside Freeway on the east side, lies about eight miles north of Rte. 22.

The next east-west route to the north is I-10, which is called the Santa Monica Freeway from its beginnings near the Pacific shore in Santa Monica to just east of downtown Los Angeles. At this point, it makes a jog north and then turns east again, becoming the San Bernardino Freeway. I-10 is located about 12 miles north of Rte. 91.

North of I-10—anywhere from two to eight miles depending on your location—is U.S. 101. This comes from Ventura (up north), and then heads due east across I-405. It is called the Ventura Freeway on the west; at a point a few miles beyond the intersection with I-405, it makes a jog south, becomes the Hollywood Freeway, and eventually crosses I-5.

ANAHEIM-AREA SURFACE STREETS: Disneyland is bounded by Harbor Boulevard on the east, West Street on the west, Ball Road on the north, and Katella Avenue on the south. Many of the city's hotels and motels, restaurants, and coffee shops are located on or just off these streets. Slanting through Anaheim, more or less bisecting the city, is the Santa Ana Freeway (I-5). This is the main route north to Los Angeles or south to San Diego. Ball Road, near Harbor Boulevard, is the most convenient place to pick up this freeway going north. Katella Avenue, which runs between Harbor Boulevard and State College Boulevard, is the most convenient entrance to the southbound Santa Ana Freeway.

RUSH HOURS: The freeways are always busy, but they're *really* congested—miserably bumper to bumper—during commuting hours, from 6 A.M. to 9 A.M. and from 3 P.M. to 6 P.M. Avoid these periods whenever possible, and allow at least 50 percent more driving time when you can't.

CAR RENTAL FEES

	ALAMO	AVIS	BUDGET	DOLLAR	HERTZ	NATIONAL	THRIFTY
One day							
Subcompact	$22.89	$28		$32	$32.93	$35.95	$28.99
Compact	$25.89	$31	$32.99	$34	$34.93	$35.95	$28.99
Intermediate	$26.89	$31	$37.99	$36	$37.93	$41.95	$31.99
Weekend (per day)							
Subcompact	$13.99	$17.80		$18	$19.96	$22.95	$21.99
Compact	$14.99	$19.90	$29	$18	$21.96	$22.95	$21.99
Intermediate	$16.99	$19.90	$32	$21.90	$24	$27.95	$24.99
One week							
Subcompact	$ 89.99	$ 98		$129	$118	$139.99	$149.99
Compact	$ 93.89	$108	$169	$139	$129	$139.99	$149.99
Intermediate	$108.89	$123	$189	$149	$144	$169.99	$165.99

- At press time there were wide variations in the way Anaheim-area rental agencies classified cars. For example, a car the size of a Chevrolet Cavalier is considered "Compact" by some agencies, while others price it at the "Intermediate" level. Be sure to be specific about car, make, and model when making reservations.
- To help ensure availability of the car of your choice, place your reservations as early as possible.
- Extras, such as automatic transmission and collision damage insurance, as well as whether the car is returned to the original outlet, may affect the rental charge. Prices were accurate at press time, but may be different at the time you call.
- Weekend rates generally apply from noon Thursdays until noon Mondays, with a minimum two-day charge.

CAR RENTALS: There are at least 20 car rental agencies in the Anaheim area alone, and there are wide variations in the prices charged and the selection of cars available. To get the best deal it's imperative to shop around for the most competitive prices.

Many of the firms offer unlimited mileage programs; some offer special convention rates. It's also important to figure the cost of collision damage waiver (CDW) insurance in all price calculations; it can vary enough from agency to agency to make a difference in the overall cost of longer rentals. (Note that most vacation packages that include a rental car do not include CDW; if you choose not to take it, the agency may require a large deposit.) Also be aware that an increasing number of credit cards offer free collision damage coverage simply for charging the rental to their card, and that some of these even provide *primary* coverage. That means your credit card company may deal with the rental company directly in the event of an accident, rather than compensate you through reimbursal. This sort of coverage is a very strong incentive to charge your rental to the card that offers the most extensive coverage.

The larger Anaheim-area car rental firms include:
- **Alamo:** 800-327-9633
- **Avis:** 800-331-1212
- **Budget:** 800-527-0700
- **Dollar:** 800-800-4000
- **Hertz:** 800-654-3131
- **National:** 800-227-7368
- **Thrifty:** 800-367-2277

If luxury is not important, look into Ugly Duckling Rent-a-Car, 2940 Randolph Ave., Costa Mesa (545-3825). Nationwide Rent-A-Car (502 South Harbor Blvd.; 535-2245) also has a fleet of American-made and foreign used cars of 1979 to 1987 vintages, in various sizes, from compacts to 15-passenger vehicles. The company will pick you up at your Anaheim hotel and take you to its offices to handle paperwork. When you turn the car in, the company will deposit you back at your hotel or, with bag and baggage, at one of the terminals of the Airport Coach buses.

To celebrate a special occasion, contact the Luxury Line Rent-A-Car office in Beverly Hills (300 South La Cienega Blvd.; 213-659-5555 or 800-826-7805), one of the few car rental agencies that rent truly deluxe vehicles to individuals. You can pick up a Rolls Royce or Mercedes sedan or convertible, a Cadillac Seville or a Lincoln Town Car, a Corvette or a Porsche 928 or a Volkswagen Rabbit convertible. Rates range from $500 a day plus 50¢ a mile for the Rolls, down to about $70 a day plus 100 free miles per day for the VW Rabbit convertible.

MAPS: Most gas stations sell (usually for about $2) local maps detailed enough to find tourist attractions, major roads, and many minor streets. The small maps that car rental companies give out when you pick up a car also can be helpful. If you intend to do enough driving to warrant the investment, buy *The Thomas Brothers' Orange County Street Guide and Directory* ($13.95), or the combined Los Angeles—Orange County edition

($22.95). These books, available at local bookstores and some hotel gift shops, are so detailed that they can provide directions to a specific block.

TAXIS: Yellow Cab of Anaheim provides 24-hour service. Fare is $1.90 at the flag drop, $1.60 each mile thereafter for one to five persons (535-2211).

BUS TRANSPORTATION: Orange County Transit District operates buses throughout the area every day (but with limited weekend service). Several bus lines stop at Disneyland. Exact-change fares are 85¢, transfers are free. Senior citizens pay 10¢, except during weekday rush hours (from 6 A.M. to 9 A.M., and from 3 P.M. to 6 P.M.) when the fare is 40¢. Dial-A-Ride (638-9000) is also available. This door-to-door van ride, which is designed for short trips within specific neighborhoods, is only available for seniors and handicapped; vehicles with wheelchair lifts can be requested. The fare is 90¢, the blind ride free. However, all public transportation generally involves considerable waiting and considerable transferring, and may not prove truly convenient.

To get farther afield without your own wheels, the best bet is to sign up for a bus tour. Several companies in the area offer these: Pacific Coast Sightseeing (978-8855), Starline-Gray Line Tour Company (213-463-3131), and Co-Ordinators (771-7600) are among them. Visitors staying in the Los Angeles hotels can use Starline-Gray Line Tour Company (213-463-3131). Hotel and motel desks can provide information about schedules and prices, sell you the proper tickets, and notify the sightseeing tour company to pick you up.

TRANSPORTATION TO THE AIRPORTS: Los Angeles International Airport is 45 minutes (at the best of times) from Anaheim. Airport Coach buses (714-491-3500 or 800-772-5299) and Airport Cruiser (714-761-3345) provide frequent scheduled service between Los Angeles International and Anaheim hotels. Airport Coach and Airport Cruiser buses both stop in front of each airline terminal just outside the baggage claim area. After claiming your luggage, proceed outside the terminal building to the red "bus stop" signs on the center island. Airport Coach buses can be identified by the words "Disneyland/Anaheim" displayed above the windshield. Airport Cruiser buses can be identified by the words "Disneyland/Buena Park" displayed above the windshield. At the John Wayne Airport, after claiming your luggage, proceed to the red "bus stop" zone to the right of the John Wayne statue outside the baggage claim area. Airport Coach buses can be identified by the words "Disneyland/Anaheim" displayed above the windshield.

Airport Coach provides frequent scheduled service daily to and from John Wayne Airport (about 20 minutes from Anaheim) and designated area hotels. After claiming your luggage, proceed to the red "bus stop" zone to the right of the John Wayne statue outside the baggage claim area. Airport Coach buses can be identified by the words "Disneyland/Anaheim" displayed above the windshield.

To return to the airports, check with your hotel front desk the day before departure for bus schedules and reservation information.

SuperShuttle also serves both airports. At Los Angeles International, proceed to the nearest courtesy phone or pay phone and contact SuperShuttle at 213-417-8988 for pickup. (The courtesy phone has specific dialing instructions.) The van picks up passengers at the outer island within 15 minutes. For guests arriving at John Wayne Airport, 24-hour advance reservations are required; call 714-973-1100. Upon arrival, use the courtesy phone to request pick-up. A van will arrive within 15 minutes at the curb outside the terminal.

For passengers returning to John Wayne Airport, check with hotel front desk personnel for return schedules the day before departure.

Green Flag Airport Shuttle (714-641-6666) is another option for both airports. Reservations are required 24 hours in advance.

TO AND FROM THE AIRPORTS

	Airport Coach Airport Shuttle	Green Flag	SuperShuttle	Airport Cruiser
From Los Angeles International Airport to Disneyland	$12.75/adult	$45 for one, plus $5 per additional person	$12 per person	$13/adult
From John Wayne Airport to Disneyland	$8/adult	$25 for one, plus $5 per additional person	$13 per person	

All fares are one-way. Prices were accurate as we went to press, but are subject to change.

ANAHEIM-AREA MOTELS AND HOTELS

There are no accommodations inside Disneyland itself. The *Disneyland* hotel is, however, owned by The Walt Disney Company.

But Disneyland is literally ringed with hotels and motels, ranging from local representatives of national chains to "mom-and-pop" operations, with each one promising that it alone offers the only rooms in the area of any true distinction. Actually, most area lodging places provide predictable U.S. motel fare: two double beds, plush carpet, a color TV, and a private bath. Most have modest restaurants or are so near to eateries that it doesn't really matter. Most are about equally convenient to Disneyland.

So in choosing a place to stay, price should probably be the primary consideration. Decide how much money you want to spend, then check to see which hostelry offers the most for your dollar.

Motels are usually the least expensive. Some in the area were built during the late 1950s, and despite countless refurbishings over the years, still show their age. In recent years, several new motels have been built, and while most simply sell a room with a view of the parking lot, they offer good value. Some motels specialize in suites (often a desirable option for a family). Others may have family units which can be particularly handy if you have small children, since the second bedroom has no outside access at all.

Hotels, their high-rise towers scraping against the sky, usually cost more. But they are also livelier and offer more of that ephemeral quality called "atmosphere." Their public spaces are better designed and more attractively laid out. The grounds are generally well-landscaped, and swimming pools tend to be larger. Many establishments have their own spa facilities, or offer access to other sports facilities—a local health club or the courts at Tennisland, for instance. The guestrooms may have views over Disneyland or Anaheim, toward the mountains or the ocean. The towels are generally thicker and larger than in most motels, and small complimentary amenities such as shampoo, fancy soaps, and bubble bath are frequently found in the rooms. Beauty and barber shops, tour desks and concierges, and the like are nearly ubiquitous.

When comparing the cost of accommodations, remember to take into consideration any potentially hidden costs, such as transportation to Disneyland or parking. Some establishments provide free van or minibus service to the park (a necessity for those without their own vehicles and a convenience for everyone else). Some hotels charge for parking and some don't. Most charge an additional fee when more than two adults occupy a room, but the cutoff age at which children are billed as extra adults does vary. (Some hotels consider 17-year-olds as children, and others start charging for them as grown-ups above age 12.) Sometimes payment is only according to the number of beds required. Similarly, many establishments offer discounts for senior citizens, although some do not. Charges for rollaways and cribs vary widely. Most of the time, the extra costs don't seem to amount to much individually, but they can really add up over the course of a few days. So before selecting a lodging place, be sure to figure the total charges with your family's specific needs in mind.

In the following selection of some of the most attractive or most advantageously priced Anaheim accommodations, all the establishments accept major credit cards unless otherwise noted. Rates were correct at press time, but are subject to change. "In season" refers to the Christmas and Easter holidays and the months of June through August. Many establishments offer packages, sometimes through the Walt Disney Travel Company; for details see "Should You Buy a Package?" in *Getting Ready to Go*. In the same chapter, "Other Information" tells which hotels and motels permit pets, and "Helpful Hints" provides a list of lodging places that offer facilities for the handicapped. For more information about conference facilities, see the *Meetings and Conventions* chapter. And for more information about the individual establishments' restaurants, see "Anaheim" in *Good Meals, Great Times*.

ANAHEIM HILTON: A three-story atrium lobby brings the outdoors into this hotel, which opened in 1984. And its 14-story modern glass exterior reflects the Anaheim Convention Center, just steps away. This is Southern California's largest hotel, with 1,600 rooms, including 100 suites. The rooms and suites on the upper floor comprise the Towers level, which has more elaborate decor and furnishings, its own concierge, VIP check-in and check-out, and a special VIP lounge and bar. Tower guests also receive complimentary continental breakfast, and in-room amenities include soaps, lotions, robes, electric shoe buffers, and scales. The hotel's fifth floor is a rooftop recreation center featuring a heated swimming pool, four spas, and acres of sun decks and rose gardens. Special provisions for handicapped travelers include 46 specially fitted guestrooms and suites, braille elevator buttons, reserved parking, and phones for the hearing impaired. There are good convention facilities here (see *Meetings and Conventions*), a café open 20 hours a day, three specialty restaurants, an intimate lobby bar, a sports bar, plus a nightclub with recorded music, videos, and a large dance floor. Other services include beauty and barber shops, gift shops, foreign currency exchange, a self-service post office, and a

the Matterhorn, and Space Mountain. Disneyland ticket media is sold at the front desk. The restaurants are some of the best in Anaheim. The large, roughly key-shaped pool, part outside and part inside, is palm shaded, has a large supply of lounge chairs, and is equipped with a hydrotherapy pool. The lobby was expanded by 40 percent in 1990, and has a new marble floor and front desk. Rooms, which come with either one king-size bed or two doubles, cost $160 (from $400 for suites) for two (no charge for children under 18 sharing their parents' room) year-round, plus $10 per additional adult and $10 for rollaways. Special packages and discounted weekend rates are available. Parking for registered guests costs $4 per day. The facilities for handicapped guests are excellent—wide doors, grab rails, hand-held shower heads, braille buttons low enough for wheelchair-bound people to reach in the elevators. The hotel, located a couple of long blocks from Disneyland, provides complimentary shuttle transportation to the park on a green-and-beige trolley-on-wheels that kids love. Airport Coach service to the Orange County, Long Beach, Ontario, and Los Angeles airports is available, and there's a capable concierge who can book tours and tickets and answer just about any question. Details: Anaheim Marriott; 700 West Convention Way; Anaheim, CA 92802; 750-8000 or 800-228-9290.

business center. The Sports and Fitness Center has exercise equipment and weight machines, an indoor pool, spa, basketball gym, aerobics classes, co-ed sauna, steam baths, and massage. Rates for a double room range from $150 to $170 (inquire about special packages), plus $20 per extra adult (no charge for children, regardless of age, when sharing their parents' room); no charge for cribs or rollaways. Details: Anaheim Hilton and Towers; 777 Convention Way; Anaheim, CA 92802; 750-4321 or 800-222-9923.

ANAHEIM MARRIOTT: This hotel, opposite the Anaheim Convention Center, is a really delightful place—well kept, stylish, attractive (but not gaudy), comfortable, well run, and recently renovated to the tune of $13 million. Of the 1,039 rooms located in the two towers (one 17 stories, the other 19 stories) and two 4-story wings, most have balconies, and all have been redecorated. Rooms facing Disneyland provide views over Big Thunder Mountain,

ANAHEIM PARKSIDE: This four-story establishment, located about half a mile east of Disneyland near Interstate 5 on Freedman Way, offers 227 cheerfully decorated guestrooms. In addition to the heated swimming pool, the hotel offers such amenities as a spa, laundry facilities, in-room coffee and tea, room service, valet service, free parking, a gift shop, in-room movies, and complimentary transportation to and from Disneyland, as well as local airport transportation bus terminals. *Le Restaurant* offers continental dining. *Claudine's* poolside lounge serves imported wine, in addition to other beverages. Banquet and meeting facilities are available. Some guestrooms are equipped for handicapped travelers. Rates are $80 in season for doubles with either two queen- or one king-size bed (no charge for children under 18 sharing their parents' room) and $75 the rest of the year, plus $10 per extra adult and $10 for rollaways; no charge for cribs. Rates are discounted for senior citizens. Details: Anaheim Parkside; 100 West Freedman Way; Anaheim, CA 92802; 520-9696, or 800-824-5459.

ANAHEIM PLAZA: A hotel with high-rise amenities but a rambling two-story layout is something of a rarity in this area. But that's the distinction of this property just across the street from Disneyland. Currently, there are 300 guestrooms and 8 suites, in seven low-rise buildings. Guestrooms are decorated in soft pastels and are generally furnished with one king or two double beds. Some rooms are equipped for handicapped travelers. About half have balconies overlooking the palm- and shrub-dotted grounds. Don't miss the salad and dessert bar at the hotel's restaurant. Towels are large and fluffy, and there is a range of special complimentary toiletries in the bathrooms. The pool is Olympic-size, a delight for lap swimming, and there's an adjacent spa. In addition, there's a car rental office, a tour desk that will arrange sightseeing, a Disney-run gift shop, baby-sitters and a physician on call, and convention facilities. The hotel's free shuttle to Disneyland operates hourly, but the park is an easy walk from the hotel. Rates are $92 to $107 for doubles and $200 and up for suites year-round (no charge for children under 18 sharing their parents' room), plus $10 per extra adult. No charge for cribs. Details: Anaheim Plaza Resort; 1700 South Harbor Blvd.; Anaheim, CA 92802; 772-5900 or 800-228-1357 in North America.

ANAHEIM TRAVELODGE SUITES: This four-story property, located three-and-a-half long blocks south of Disneyland, offers good rates for its 100 suites. There are petite suites (one room with separate living and sleeping areas), two-room suites with separate living and sleeping rooms, and honeymoon suites with in-room spas. Non-smoking guest quarters are available, and some suites are equipped for handicapped travelers. Amenities include refrigerators, microwaves, remote-control color television sets with movie channels, and clock radios. There's also a heated pool and spa. Complimentary continental breakfast is served daily, and there's a free shuttle to Disneyland and the convention center. Transportation to the airports is provided by various airport bus companies. Rates for petite suites range seasonally from $58 to $88; two-room suites cost from $63 to $108. Family suites sleep eight and run $73 to $123.(Inquire about special rates.) Details: Anaheim Travelodge Suites; 2141 South Harbor Blvd.; Anaheim, CA 92802; 971-3553 or 800-526-9444.

CANDY CANE INN: There's a lot to like about this moderately priced, two-story motel, located just down the street from Disneyland's main entrance. This is one of the area's newest motels, and it is well designed and nicely landscaped. All 175 rooms offer ceramic-tiled bathrooms, and separate dressing and vanity areas. There also are a gift shop, guest laundry and valet services, a swimming pool, a kids' wading pool, and a gazebo-covered spa. Complimentary continental breakfast is served. Sightseeing, airline ticket reservation services, and FAX services are available, and there's a small meeting facility and conference room. Transportation to local airports can be arranged. Some rooms are equipped for handicapped guests. Rates for a double with two queen-size beds range (according to season) from $54 to $99 (no charge for children under 18 sharing their parents' room), plus $10 for rollaways; no charge for cribs. Details: Candy Cane Inn; 1747 South Harbor Blvd.; Anaheim, CA 92802; 774-5284 or 800-345-7057.

CASTLE INN: This 200-room, four-story property, one of the newest lodging places in the area, resembles a castle with all its turrets, towers, and heraldic symbols. A drive inside the entrance reveals a more standard motel layout (guestrooms surround and overlook the parking lot). Still, it's a good value and is less than a block from Disneyland's main entrance. Rooms contain either a king- or two queen-size beds, and such amenities as a VCR, color television set, and a refrigerator. Suites (including some with in-room steambaths) are available. There's a heated pool and whirlpool outside. Valet service is provided, and there's a laundry. Some rooms are equipped for the handicapped. Rates range seasonally from $68 to $78 for a regular room, and from $88 to $118 for a two-room family suite with three queen-size beds; plus $10 for rollaways, $6 for cribs. Details: Castle Inn; 1734 South Harbor Blvd.; Anaheim, CA 92802; 774-8111 or 800-521-5653.

CONESTOGA: Though only about a block off the beaten track and truly in the immediate vicinity of Disneyland, this 252-room establishment still seems pleasantly out of the way. It also offers a lot for its cost. Its pervasive Old West atmosphere stops just short of being too much, with a main building that might almost be at home on the streets of Dodge City. The trio of themed eating and drinking spots here is remarkably handsome for a chain establishment. Rooms, decorated in soft mauve and blue tones are comfortably modern. The food from room service is charged at the hotel's coffee shop prices (no extra fee for delivery). There are free shuttles to Disneyland, and Airport Cruiser and Airport Coach buses stop here.

There's also a small gameroom, a heated pool with adjacent spa, and space for conferences and meetings. Also, guests get a discount at Tennisland, located next door (see *Sports*). Room rates are $99 to $109 for doubles year-round (no charge for children under 16 sharing their parents' room) and $89 to $99 for singles, plus $10 for rollaways. No charge for cribs. Details: Conestoga; 1240 South Walnut Ave.; Anaheim, CA 92802; 535-0300, 800-321-3530 in California, or 800-321-3531 from the continental United States.

DISNEYLAND: This huge establishment (and the only one in Anaheim owned by The Walt Disney Company) would be a destination in its own right, even if it were not located right next door to Disneyland. Occupying 60 acres that have been landscaped so lavishly that you hardly suspect you're in the heart of Anaheim, it boasts a man-made marina where pedalboats can be rented for a pleasant afternoon on the water, a 165-foot-wide waterfall that you can actually walk underneath, a pool full of exotic Japanese koi fish to feed, a nighttime Dancing Waters show, a pleasant resort atmosphere, extensive convention facilities, the most extensive gameroom of any hotel in the area (it looks like a Monte Carlo casino), and a whole raft of shops, restaurants, entertainment spots, and sports facilities. The hotel is also

directly connected (via speedy monorail) to Disneyland—an enormous convenience for hotel guests that allows quick trips to the hotel's swimming pools when the park gets too crowded; a Disneyland Passport or hand stamp is required. The hotel's monorail station sells admission media.

The hotel has three swimming pools, all big enough for exercise purposes, two with a sandy beach and the other the largest at any Anaheim hotel. The Sierra Pool has special hours just for lap swimming (adults only) from 7 A.M. to 9 A.M. daily. On summer evenings, the Youth Club provides supervised activities, games, Disney videos, and snacks for children ages 4 to 12. Hotel guests also have privileges at the ten-court tennis club, Tennisland. Tennis lessons can be arranged through the Tennisland pro (see *Sports*).

The hotel has 1,132 rooms and suites located partly in two-story villas which are actually sections of the establishment's original building, and partly in three high-rise towers. Most tower rooms have two double beds and many can accommodate up to five persons (one of them on a rollaway) quite easily. All the tower rooms have small balconies big enough to accommodate a chair, say, to watch the Dancing Waters show. The 11-story Sierra Tower looks toward Disneyland on one side and the colorful hotel marina on the other. The 13-story Bonita Tower and the 11-story Marina Tower have rooms with marina views as well, but only on one side. Guests on the opposite side look over parking lots or city rooftops. The villas have private patios or sun decks and grassy lawns, and some Oriental Garden rooms can accommodate six.

Besides the monorail, there is free ground transportation to the main gates of Disneyland via trams that run from the Travelport immediately underneath the monorail station. You do pay for parking here ($7 overnight for hotel guests; others $1 per half-hour for first 2 hours, $2 per hour thereafter; $12 maximum for 24 hours). Airport Coach buses bound for the Orange County, Ontario, Long Beach, and Los Angeles airports make regular stops at the hotel. There are reservations desks for various airlines and bus companies, as well as the Walt Disney Travel Company, which offers a full range of travel services. Auto rentals, baby-sitter referrals, and safe deposit boxes are also available through the hotel. Rates in season for doubles are $120 to $215 (about $20 less off-season), depending on the room's view and location, plus $15 for rollaways. Suites go for $400 and up. Details: Disneyland Hotel; 1150 West Cerritos Ave.; Anaheim, CA 92802; 714-778-6600 or 407-W-DISNEY (934-7639).

DOUBLETREE: One of the newer establishments in the area, this 461-room high-rise is located in the city of Orange, a little over two miles from Disneyland. The City Shopping Center, with 100 stores and restaurants, and the Crystal Cathedral are in the immediate neighborhood. The spacious lobby is very attractive and inviting, and the hotel's restaurants and two bars are also located on the ground floor. Outside, there's a nicely landscaped pool and spa area, with two lighted tennis courts adjacent to the pool. A special "Concierge Floor" provides additional amenities such as complimentary bathrobes, shoeshine equipment, a hair dryer, various business publications, and other conveniences. Some rooms are equipped for handicapped guests. The hotel provides complimentary shuttle service to Disneyland and to John Wayne/Orange County Airport. Year-round rates for doubles are $129 for a standard room, $144 for a Concierge Floor room, plus $10 per extra adult and $10 for rollaways; no charge for cribs or for children under 18 sharing their parents' room. Parking is free. Details: Doubletree; 100 The City Drive; Orange, CA 92668; 634-4500 or 800-528-0444.

GRAND: The big square lobby, with antique-white furniture upholstered in soft violet hues, is pleasantly bright and cheerful. Guests prefer the park views from some of the 240 rooms with queen-size beds. Kids like the video-game enclaves which, though located just off the main corridor to the meeting rooms, still seem discreetly out of the way. There are a swimming pool, two whirlpool spas, and an exercise room, as well as a playground designed primarily for small children (children should be escorted). Among the hotel's restaurants is the popular *Grand Dinner Theatre*. A 20-passenger minibus takes guests to Disneyland free of charge. The hotel is a terminal for Airport Coach and Airport Cruiser buses, which provide scheduled transportation to the major airports. Eight rooms are specially equipped for the handicapped. Rates are $90 to $110 for doubles, depending on the season and the room's location, plus $10 for rollaways. No charge for cribs or for children under 18 sharing their parents' room. Details: Grand; One Hotel Way; Anaheim, CA 92802; 772-7777 or 800-421-6662 .

HAMPTON INN: This five-story, 136-room property is located about a mile from Disneyland. The interior is modern and comfortable, and complimentary continental breakfast is served in the well-designed lobby. Local phone calls, an in-room movie channel, parking, and transportation to Disneyland and the Convention Center are also complimentary. Non-smoking rooms are available as is one hospitality suite (a guestroom with added space and facilities to accommodate a small meeting). Some rooms are equipped for handicapped guests. There is a pool. This is one of the few lodging places in the area that allows pets (call ahead). Year-round rates (for up to four people in a room) range from $77 for a room with 2 double beds to $82 for a "king study" with a king-size bed and queen-size sofa bed, plus $5 for rollaways; no charge for cribs. Details: Hampton Inn; 300 East Katella Way; Anaheim, CA 92802; 772-8713 or 800-426-7866.

HOLIDAY INN: While not particularly attractive architecturally, this twin-tower, 312-room establishment does offer a traveler advantageous rates for its pleasantly decorated rooms—most with two double beds, and some with one king. Non-smoking rooms are available. And there is a medium-size rectangular swimming pool and a wading pool for kids; a coffee shop called the *Pickford*, open daily for breakfast, lunch, and dinner; a lounge with live entertainment; and a conference room. Shuttle service is provided to Disneyland, and Airport Cruiser buses stop here. There are four rooms equipped for handicapped travelers. Rates are $89 for doubles year-round (no charge for children under 19 sharing their parents' room), plus $10 for rollaways; no charge for cribs. Details: Holiday Inn of Anaheim; 1850 South Harbor Blvd.; Anaheim, CA 92802; 750-2801, 800-624-6855 directly to the hotel, or 800-HOLIDAY to Central Reservations.

HOWARD JOHNSON'S: This property is a surprising place. For one thing it looks more like a condominium complex than a hotel because of the way the 318 rooms are arranged in the establishment's several buildings—four with two stories, one with four, and a seven-story tower. For another, the hostelry seems exceptionally well-built, well-maintained, and carefully planned, and it's full of nice touches. All the hotel buildings are constructed of concrete and fitted with double-paned windows, so that rooms are quiet even though the complex backs on a freeway. Rooms were recently upgraded during a $2 million renovation, which included the addition of mini–refrigerators and coffeemakers to the guestrooms. There is a *Bob's Big Boy* restaurant on the premises. The grounds are secluded and full of fountains and palms, and there are two swimming pools; a wading pool and a spa; a gameroom with 12 electronic games and 4 pinball machines; a gift shop, and two guest laundries in addition to valet service. In all the rooms, beds are extra-long, and bathrooms have two sinks; in about a third of the rooms, the bathrooms are equipped with black-and-white television sets. The 15 rooms for the handicapped have extra space in the bathrooms, grab bars, and easy-to-grip door-knobs. The management provides free transportation via trolley car to Disneyland, and Airport Coach and Airport Cruiser buses stop here.

For all this, the prices are quite reasonable. Rates are $65 to $88 for doubles year-round, depending on room location (no charge for children under 18 sharing their parents' room), plus $7 per additional adult and $7 for rollaways; no charge for cribs. Details: Howard Johnson's; 1380 South Harbor Blvd.; Anaheim, CA 92802; 776-6120; 800-422-4228 from California, 800-854-0303 from the rest of the United States, and 800-874-6120 from Canada.

HYATT REGENCY ALICANTE: This hotel is distinguished by its 17-story atrium (the largest in the western United States). The towering atrium, which connects the hotel to the adjoining Plaza Tower office complex, encloses palm trees, fountains, and greenery. It houses the *Café Alicante*, the *Atrium Bar*, and specialty shops. The hotel also has a family-style restaurant that serves Italian cuisine, and a lounge with live entertainment. Travelers bound for Disneyland should note that although the hotel's address is Garden Grove, it is situated at the corner of Harbor Boulevard and Chapman Avenue, just a mile from the park. The 17-story hotel has 400 guestrooms, decorated in a pale peach and gray-green color scheme, available with either a king-size bed or two double beds. Imported marble and oak furnishings complement the rooms' modern interior design. There are also 17 spacious suites with living and dining rooms, wet bars, entertainment consoles, and balconies overlooking the gardenlike atrium courtyard. The hotel's recreational facilities are located on its attractively landscaped, 25,000-square-foot, third-story roof. Here you'll find a pool, a raised spa, two tennis courts, a gameroom, and an exercise room. There are 12 rooms specially equipped for handicapped travelers. Many room phones are designed for hearing-impaired guests and there are braille elevator buttons. Complimentary transportation is provided for guests to Disneyland. Several transportation companies provide service to the major airports. Rates are $145 for doubles (with a weekend rate of $89), $225 to $895 for suites, plus $20 for each additional adult (no charge for children under 18 occupying their parents' room); no charge for rollaways or cribs. Details: Hyatt Regency Alicante; 100 Plaza Alicante; Harbor Boulevard and Chapman Avenue; Garden Grove, CA 92640; 971-3000 or 800-972-2929.

INN AT THE PARK: Situated on four acres just a block and a half south of Disneyland, with especially pretty grounds that have a "just grown" look—neat and well kept, but natural and almost homey in feel—with boulders scattered among the shrubs and palms. The good-size swimming pool is particularly inviting on a sunny afternoon, thanks to an attractive deck area, an abundance of chaise lounges and chairs, and a brass-colored fence that matches the rails on the balconies of the white, 14-story tower, where the 500 guestrooms are located. Accessible via a glass-walled elevator, these overlook the pool and nearby Garden Grove's Crystal Cathedral on one side, Disneyland

on the other. There are queen-size beds in single-bedded rooms, double beds in two-bedded rooms, and king-size beds in the rooms with adjacent living rooms. Adjoining the tower is the structure that houses the main lobby, several good Disney-operated shops, the hotel lounges, the restaurants, plus most of the hotel's meeting and convention facilities.

Free shuttles are available to Disneyland, and various airport transportation companies provide service between the hotel and Los Angeles and John Wayne/Orange County airports. And there's a gameroom with 11 electronic games and 4 pinball machines. Room rates are $115 to $145 for doubles year-round, and $225 to $425 for suites. There is a $15 charge for each additional adult, but children under 17 staying in the room with a parent are free. There is no charge for cribs. Details: Inn at the Park; 1855 South Harbor Blvd.; Anaheim, CA 92802; 750-1811 or 800-421-6662.T

JOLLY ROGER INN: Another surprising place that is a particularly good value. Even though the property occupies one corner of what is probably Anaheim's busiest intersection, the inn has a

secluded air. This is accomplished mostly by the positioning of the public buildings as buffers for the worst of the noise. With the addition of a new building in 1989, there are now 250 rooms, and the older rooms have all been redecorated. There's also a splendidly romantic Indoor Pool Suite, which consists of sleeping quarters (with a king-size bed) done up in light woods, wicker, and pastels, and an adjoining private 12-by-14-foot plunge pool walled in by mirrors. Some rooms are equipped for handicapped travelers. Guests share the outside pools (two of them), the kids' wading pool, and the spa. There's a convenient (but less than compelling) coffee shop that serves breakfast, lunch, and dinner; a dining room decorated with marine antiques, open usually for lunch and always for dinner; and a lounge that features live entertainment and dancing. Also on the premises are a beauty shop, liquor store, and a dress shop. And there's the usual courtesy shuttle to Disneyland and to an airport transportation bus stop. Best of all, the staff is friendly and the atmosphere definitely family-oriented. Rates for a room occupied by up to four people range seasonally from $55 to $70 for the Courtyard building and from $70 to $90 for the Bali Hai and Harbor buildings; plus $8 for rollaways; no charge for cribs. Details: Jolly Roger Inn; 640 West Katella Ave.; Anaheim, CA 92802; 772-7621 or 800-854-3184.

PAN PACIFIC, ANAHEIM: This property has 2 high-rise towers—one 15 stories, one 14 stories—slightly juxtaposed to create a central atrium where the lobby is located. The 502 rooms (including 12 suites and 26 equipped for handicapped travelers) all have two extra-long double beds or a king-size bed plus a fold-out twin sofa bed in the sitting area, making it a particularly comfortable place for families. Non-smoking rooms are available. It's just across the street from Disneyland and a one-minute walk from the monorail and tram at the *Disneyland* hotel. On the third floor, a huge landscaped recreation deck includes a split-level sun deck, swimming pool, whirlpool spa, and snack bar. Several lanai units with private patios have direct access to it. On the ground floor are

the hotel's two restaurants, as well as the bar, which offers nightly entertainment and dancing. Rates for doubles are $115 to $149 (check availability of special rates), plus $10 per extra adult. No charge for cribs or for children under 12 sharing their parents' room. Details: Pan Pacific, Anaheim; 1717 South West St.; Anaheim, CA 92802; 999-0990 or 800-821-8976.

QUALITY HOTEL AND CONFERENCE CENTER: This light brown, nine-story high rise opposite the Anaheim Convention Center, two long blocks south of Disneyland, has 284 guestrooms. The lobby is furnished in French Provincial style. The guestrooms are decorated in autumn colors, and some of them are designated non-smoking rooms. What's more, all rooms have balconies, and those high enough have fine views. Some rooms and suites are equipped for handicapped guests. The swimming pool is large and rectangular. The hotel has a café, a restaurant, and an adjoining lounge with live entertainment that is open nightly for drinks and dancing. There is also a salon, a gift shop, and, for the kids, a video game area. Free shuttles take guests to Disneyland and direct bus service is available to Los Angeles and Orange County airports. Conference facilities are available. Room rates are $75 to $95 for doubles in season, $67 to $87 the rest of the year (no charge for children under 18 sharing their parents' room), plus $10 for additional adults and $10 for rollaways; no charge for cribs. Details: Quality Hotel and Conference Center; 616 Convention Way; Anaheim, CA 92802; 800-777-1455, 750-3131, or 800-228-5151.

RAMADA MAINGATE: This 467-room establishment is located across from Disneyland on Harbor Boulevard. Rooms are located in 2 towers (one of nine stories, the other eight stories high). Many of the rooms are designated non-smoking, and seven rooms are equipped for handicapped travelers. The hotel is served by a family-style restaurant called *Millie's Country Kitchen*. Other facilities include a pool and spa, a gameroom, and a gift shop; parking is free. Rental car service is available, as are room service, babysitting referrals, complimentary shuttle service to Disneyland, and free pick-up and drop-off at an Airport Cruiser or Airport Coach terminal. The hotel has meeting and banquet facilities for up to 300. Rates for rooms (which may be occupied by up to 5 people) range from $89 to $109; plus $10 for rollaways. Details: Ramada Maingate; 1460 South Harbor Blvd.; Anaheim, CA 92802; 772-6777 or 800-447-4048.

RAMADA INN: Located about a mile from Disneyland, closer to Anaheim Stadium than to the park proper, this establishment makes up in atmosphere, decor, and overall quality what it lacks in proximity to the Magic Kingdom. The 240 guestrooms with separate dressing areas were recently redecorated in beige and burgundy tones. Even the lobby, with its couches and chairs arranged in a couple of conversational groupings, is especially pleasant—a rarity among two-story motels. The pool is a good size, and there's a spa alongside it. Kids enjoy the grassy play area. There's also a coffee shop/restaurant complex and a cocktail lounge with patio seating. The hotel operates hourly complimentary shuttles to the park, and transports guests to the Convention Center and Anaheim Stadium on request. The year-round rate for a room with either one king-size or two queen-size

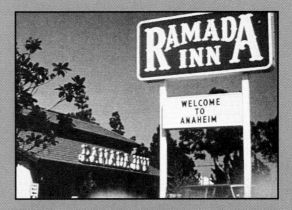

beds is $74 ($55 on weekends); no charge for rollaways; no charge for cribs or for children under 18 sharing their parents' room. Details: Ramada Inn Anaheim/Disneyland; 1331 East Katella Ave.; Anaheim, CA 92805; 978-8088, 800-228-0586, or 800-2-RAMADA for Ramada's Central Reservations.

RESIDENCE INN: This delightful, 200-suite lodging place, owned by Marriott, is on a side street about two blocks from Disneyland. At first glance, its two- and three-story, terracotta-colored stucco buildings with red tile roofs might be mistaken for a condominium complex. The grounds are beautifully maintained and adorned with hibiscus, bougainvillea, and park-style benches, and there's a sport court for tennis, basketball, or volleyball. Inside, the lobby is spacious and homey, with comfortable couches, chairs, cocktail tables, a fireplace, and a television set. Complimentary continental breakfast is served. There's an attractive swimming pool and spa area, and a guest laundry. Because this hotel is designed for long-term (as well as short-term) guests, suites are spacious and feature a breakfast bar, and a fully equipped kitchen with a dishwasher. Three floor plans are available. A one-room studio suite, with two queen-size beds and a pull-out sofa, costs $129 for a night's stay; a one-level suite with a separate bedroom (containing two double beds) and a pull-out sofa in the living room costs $139; and a bi-level penthouse suite (with sleeping areas upstairs and downstairs, 2 bathrooms, and 2 television sets) costs $159. There's no charge for cribs, but a rollaway costs $10. Lower long-term rates are available. Non-smoking suites are offered, and some suites are equipped for handicapped travelers. Some pets are accepted (call ahead). Special features and services include a mini-market, safe-deposit boxes, valet service, meeting rooms for up to 50 people, free shuttle to Disneyland and the Convention Center, and free hors d'oeuvres Mondays through Thursdays from 5 P.M. to 7 P.M. Details: Residence Inn; 1700 South Clementine St.; Anaheim, CA 92802; 533-3555 or 800-331-3131.

SHERATON-ANAHEIM: With its turrets, towers, and Tudor design, this 493-room establishment looks a bit like a fortress. The grounds include two courtyards, a rose garden, a fish pond, even a waterfall. The hotel's 460 rooms and 33 suites are done in soft colors; 20 rooms are exclusively for non-smoking guests. The rooms—all large, with two queen-size beds or one king—have cable television. Among the suites, one of the most intriguing is the Turret Suite, located in a round tower and furnished with a king-size bed, plus a wet bar.

There is a concierge-served level with the VIP Le Club that offers personalized services such as airline and restaurant reservations, charge phones, a selection of periodicals and games, and a wide-screen television set. The hotel boasts a free-form swimming pool, a lounge open nightly for entertainment and dancing, laundry facilities, room service, and valet service, and conference rooms. The ground-transportation system includes direct transfers to Los Angeles International Airport and a shuttle that provides free transportation to Disneyland throughout the day. Rates are $95 to $135 for doubles during the summer, $80 to $125 the rest of the year (no charge for children under 18 when sharing their parents' room), plus $15 for each additional person and $15 for rollaways; no charge for cribs. Suites, including the Turret Suite, cost $285 year-round. Details: Sheraton-Anaheim; 1015 West Ball Rd.; Anaheim, CA 92802; 778-1700 or 800-325-3535.

STOVALL'S BEST WESTERN HOTELS: Two of the older properties in this group of seven (under the same owner) are built of blue-trimmed white stucco and look like 1960s versions of space stations set up to host conventions of astronauts. Stovall's Inn is well known locally for its topiary gardens—bushes and trees wired and trimmed in the forms of camels, elephants, bears, and rabbits. Most of the inns offer free shuttles to Disneyland. Airport Cruiser buses stop at Stovall's Inn and Airport Coach buses stop at all the properties.

Anaheim Inn: This is a newer building, a typical beige stucco Stovall property, and sits just across the street from the park. There are 88 rooms, decorated in earth tones, in a 3-story layout with elevators. Two rooms are fitted for handicapped travelers. There's a pool, a spa, saunas, and a guest laundry. Rates run $75 to $85 for doubles in season, $55 to $65 the rest of the year (no charge for children under 18 sharing their parents' room), plus $8.50 for a rollaway; no charge for cribs. Details: Anaheim Inn; 1630 South Harbor Blvd.; Anaheim, CA 92802; 774-1050 or 800-854-8177.

Apollo Inn: Except for walls and floors that are on the thin side, this 136-room establishment is perfectly comfortable, if a bit dated in appearance, like most of the older Stovall lodging places. You'll find a coffee shop, a swimming pool with an adjacent breakfast lounge area, a kids' wading pool, a spa, two saunas, and 14 rooms equipped for handicapped guests. There are elevators to all rooms above the second floor. Rates are $70 to $80 for doubles in season, $50 to $60 the rest of the year (no charge for children under 18 sharing their parents' room), plus $8.50 for a rollaway; no charge for a crib. Details: Apollo Inn; 1741 South West St.; Anaheim, CA 92802; 772-9750 or 800-854-8175.

Best Western Galaxy: There are 98 rooms at this property adjoining the *Cosmic Age*. There's a guest laundry, a rectangular swimming pool, a spa, an especially good-size wading pool, and family suites—two-bedroom units with two double beds in one room and one double bed in another. Rates for a room with two double beds are $50 to $60; $105 for a family suite in season; less the rest of the year (no charge for children under 18 sharing their parents' room); plus $8.50 for rollaways; no charge for cribs. Details: Best Western Galaxy Motel; 1735 South Harbor Blvd.; Anaheim, CA 92802; 772-1520 or 800-854-8177.

Cosmic Age Lodge: Right next door to Disneyland, this 156-room, two-story Stovall property boasts a gameroom and a large, rectangular swimming pool. Some rooms are set up for handicapped travelers. Rates are set at $70 to $80 for doubles in season, $50 to $60 the rest of the year (no charge for children under 18 sharing their parents' room), plus $8.50 for rollaways; no charge for cribs. Details: Cosmic Age Lodge; 1717 South Harbor Blvd.; Anaheim, CA 92802; 635-6550 or 800-854-8177.

Park Place Inn: This three-story, 199-room establishment is the newest Stovall property, just across the street from Disneyland. The lobby is large and fashionably decorated in Southwestern desert hues of beige and pink, and the Southwestern motif is also reflected in the furnishings and wall hangings. Just off the lobby is a small gift shop with Disney souvenirs. There's also a pool with an adjacent spa, and 2 elevators make it easier to reach the top 2 floors. Some rooms are equipped for handicapped guests. Rates for doubles in season are $75 to $85 for a room with a king-size bed and pull-out sofa or 2 queen-size beds; and from $70 to $80 for 2 double beds. There's no charge for children under 18 sharing their parents' room, no charge for cribs; rollaways cost $8.50. Details: Park Place Inn; 1544 South Harbor Blvd.; Anaheim, CA 92802; 776-4800 or 800-854-8175.

Stovall's Inn: The one Stovall property with a bar, this establishment also has two swimming pools, each with an adjacent spa, several rooms equipped for handicapped guests, and a banquet room that holds 200. There are 290

rooms. Rates are $70 to $80 for doubles in season, $50 to $60 the rest of the year (no charge for children under 18 sharing their parents' room), plus $8.50 for rollaways; no charge for cribs. Details: Stovall's Inn; 1110 West Katella Ave.; Anaheim, CA 92802; 778-1880 or 800-854-8175.

Space Age Lodge: This 100-room property boasts a parallelogram-shaped pool. Rates are $68 to $78 for doubles in season, $48 to $58 the rest of the year (no charge for children under 18 sharing their parents' room), and $8.50 for rollaways; no charge for cribs. Details: Space Age Lodge; 1176 West Katella Ave.; Anaheim, CA 92802; 776-0141 or 800-854-8175.

TRAVELODGE AT THE PARK: This five-story, 260-room establishment, located about half a mile north of Disneyland's main entrance, has one of the best landscaped pool areas in Anaheim. Other facilities and services include complimentary transportation to Disneyland and an Airport Coach terminal, free in-room movies, car-rental service, free parking, tour service, a gift shop, a restaurant, and a lobby bar. Eight rooms are specially equipped for handicapped travelers. Meeting rooms accommodate from 20 to 200 persons. Rates for doubles are $89 in season, $79 the rest of the year, plus $10 for each extra adult (no charge for children under 18 sharing their parents' room), $10 for rollaways; no charge for cribs. Senior citizen discounts are available. Details: Travelodge at the Park; 1221 South Harbor Blvd.; Anaheim, CA 92805; 758-0900 or 800-545-7275.

ORANGE COUNTY HOTELS

Of the cities other than Anaheim where you might lodge while visiting Disneyland, one of the most obvious choices is Buena Park, situated just northwest of Anaheim and accessible via the Santa Ana Freeway (I-5). That's because of its proximity to so many other attractions; the two-block area where most are located is, like Disneyland, completely surrounded by hotels and motels. On the whole, the properties here are a notch below those in Anaheim. But there are still some first class accommodations, and they generally cost a tad less than rooms in similar establishments in Anaheim.

For upscale accommodations, lodging in Orange County's coastal areas is a good idea. **Note:** Since coastal hotels do not generally offer the kind of regularly scheduled shuttle service available around Anaheim and Buena Park, it's advisable to have your own car when you stay there.

Here's a selection of some of the better lodging places in both areas. Rates, which were correct at press time, are for two adults unless otherwise noted.

BUENA PARK: This 350-room, nine-story high-rise hotel is located just behind Knott's Berry Farm. The guestrooms are decorated in peach tones with plush carpeting. Rooms have balconies (albeit small ones), and there's a good-size swimming pool—nicely landscaped with shrubs and trees, and surrounded by chaise lounges and umbrella-shaded tables. The hotel has a coffee shop, a specialty restaurant, a nightclub called *Shoe Bops* that features 1950s and 1960s music, and a top-floor banquet room that offers a fine view of Orange County. There's also a gameroom. Direct bus service is available to the Los Angeles and Orange County airports. Year-round rates are $85 to $95 for standard doubles, $95 to $105 for "Executive Service" doubles (no charge for children under 12 sharing their parents' room), plus $5 per extra adult and $10 for rollaways; no charge for cribs. Details: Buena Park; 7675 Crescent Ave.; Buena Park, CA 90620; 995-1111; 800-422-4444 from California; 800-854-8792 from the rest of the United States; and 800-325-8734 from Canada.

EMBASSY SUITES: This hacienda-style hotel, located just one block north of Knott's Berry Farm, has several features that make it attractive to family travelers. All 203 rooms are actually suites with a bedroom (one king or two double beds) and a separate living room with a double hide-a-bed. There's a telephone and a color TV set in each room. Also, all rooms offer galley-type kitchen facilities and conference-dining tables. Rooms are arranged attractively around an open-atrium courtyard with Spanish-style fountains, pool, and spa. There is a gift shop and a restaurant that is open for lunch and dinner. There are two hours of free cocktails (and billiards) nightly in the lounge, and complimentary, American-style, cooked-to-order breakfasts. One of the nicer aspects: The hotel maintains a no-tipping policy. There are three suites with special facilities for the handicapped. SuperShuttle service is available to the Los Angeles and Orange County airports, and the hotel's courtesy limousine will take guests to Disneyland. Rates are $109 to $124 for a double year-round, $10 for each additional adult. Children 12 and under are free when staying in their parents' room. There is no charge for cribs, and special packages and weekend rates are available. Details: Embassy Suites; 7762 Beach Blvd.; Buena Park, CA 90620; 739-5600 or 800-362-2779.

FOUR SEASONS: This luxurious, 285-room, high-rise hotel, located across the street from the Newport Center Fashion Island shopping complex, is set on about five acres of landscaped gardens overlooking Newport Harbor and the Pacific Ocean. The hotel is managed by Four Seasons Hotels, the same company that manages such elegant hostelries as San Francisco's *Clift* hotel and the *Pierre* in New York. From its lovely beige lobby to its extra-spacious, luxuriously appointed guestrooms (all with balconies), this hotel is marked by a refined California elegance. Antiques and fine works of art abound in the public areas. Outdoors, you can dine casually by the beautifully landscaped pool and spa area, or enjoy a game of tennis on one of two lit courts. Other facilities include two restaurants, a lounge and cocktail bar, and a health club. Guestrooms include such amenities as twice-daily maid service, bathrobes, and a spacious vanity/dressing area separate from the bath. There are non-smoking floors, as well as rooms for handicapped guests. Rates for doubles are $210 to $270 (no charge for children under 16 sharing their parents' room), plus $25 per extra adult, $12 for parking; no charge for cribs or rollaways. Suites start at $300. Details: Four Seasons; 690 Newport Center Dr.; Newport Beach, CA 92660; 759-0808 or 800-332-3442.

DANA POINT RESORT: This 350-room, Cape Cod Victorian-style resort has a picture-perfect setting high on a bluff overlooking the 2,500-slip Dana Point Yacht Harbor, the Pacific Ocean, and Doheny State Beach. Surrounding the resort are 42 lushly landscaped acres of park and lawn and an abundance of flowers. The hotel's lobby and other public areas are noteworthy for the truly artistic, exotic floral arrangements created by in-house florist Michael Berbae. The ocean views from the guestrooms, the restaurant, and the two lounges are splendid. Guestrooms are decorated in seafoam green, ocean blue, and pastel sand colors. Amenities include terraces, twice-daily maid service, live plants, two phones, and lounging robes. Some rooms are equipped for handicapped guests. There are 17 suites. Recreational facilities include two pools, three spas, a health club and Nautilus gym, a masseuse, croquet, kite flying, bicycle riding, and lawn games. Basketball courts, par course jogging trails, and a playground are just steps away. Dana Point is the perfect spot for whale watching (in season), parasailing, deep-sea fishing, sailing, and windsurfing. The concierge can help guests arrange activities. Children's programs are offered daily during the summer and on weekends year-round. There's complimentary transportation to the San Juan Capistrano Amtrak depot, from where trains go to Anaheim. Rates for doubles are $170 to $280 (inquire about money-saving packages, which include whale watching, tennis, and more); no charge for children under 16 sharing their parents' room; $20 per extra adult; $20 for cribs or rollaways. Details: Dana Point Resort; 25135 Park Lantern; Dana Point, CA 92629; 661-5000 or 800-533-9748 .

NEWPORT BEACH MARRIOTT: The charms of this 600-room establishment are many, but foremost are the views of Balboa Bay and the Pacific Ocean, the eight tennis courts (lit for night play), two good-size swimming pools and two spas, and the location across the street from Newport Center Fashion Island, with its 150 boutiques, department stores, and restaurants. The hotel also boasts a very fine restaurant with an open-air terrace overlooking Newport Harbor, plus a couple of pleasant bars. A concierge is available to help with reservations for airlines, car rentals, tours, and other travel plans. The hotel also offers a gift shop, free transportation to the John Wayne/ Orange County Airport, and the following facilities: complimentary underground parking

for 600 cars, a health club with saunas (free to hotel guests), a gameroom, and a beauty shop. Guestrooms are located in two towers (one tower has a top-story cocktail lounge with a fabulous view of the Pacific Ocean), and in two low-rise wings; they come with double, queen-, or king-size beds. Some rooms are equipped for handicapped travelers, and pets are permitted. Rates are $149 to $169 for doubles and $250 and up for suites (no charge for children under 13 sharing their parents' room), plus $10 per additional adult year-round. No charge for cribs or rollaways. A number of packages are also available (see *Sports*). Details: Newport Beach Marriott Hotel & Tennis Club; 900 Newport Center Dr.; Newport Beach, CA 92660; 640-4000 or 800-228-9290 to Central Reservations.

HYATT NEWPORTER: This local landmark resort hotel was built on what was a family-owned ranch until the early 1960s. The hotel's rose-beige exterior has French doors and windows that carry out a California-Mediterranean theme. The resort has 410 guestrooms. There are several distinctive room settings: Some rooms surround a courtyard and have golf and bay views; terrace rooms surround the lower pool and garden, and have views of Newport Bay; rooms in the main building have convenient access to the hotel's public areas and upper pools; and rooms in the Balboa Building overlook the golf course. For true luxury, there are four villas, each equipped with three bedrooms, three baths, a fireplace, and a private yard with swimming pool. Recreational opportunities abound: There's a nine-hole golf course, a jogging-and-exercise trail, three large swimming pools, three spas, volleyball and shuffleboard courts, a health and fitness center, and about 26 acres of landscaped grounds. Guests also have privileges at the adjoining private John Wayne Tennis Club, which has 16 courts lit for night play. The hotel also has several shops, more than a dozen meeting and banquet rooms, and an entertainment lounge. There are three restaurants. One offers indoor dining as well as outdoor patio service. An intimate dining room with seating for 30 has an extensive wine cellar. The third restaurant features Northern Italian cuisine and entertainment in the form of singing waiters and waitresses. There is complimentary transportation to Balboa Island, to Fashion Island, and to the John Wayne/Orange County Airport, where you can take the Airport Coach or Airport Cruiser bus to the *Disneyland* hotel. Rates are $135 to $169 year-round for doubles, $300 to $450 for suites (no charge for children under 18 sharing their parents' room), plus $25 per extra adult using existing facilities and $15 for rollaways; no charge for cribs. Villas cost $650. Details: Hyatt Newporter; 1107 Jamboree Rd.; Newport Beach, CA 92660; 729-1234 or 800-233-1234 to Central Reservations.

MORE SOUTHERN CALIFORNIA LODGINGS

There are some truly world class places to stay outside Orange County. The following are especially worth checking into when you leave the Disneyland area for forays into other sections of Southern California.

AROUND LOS ANGELES

FARMER'S DAUGHTER: Located just across the street from the Farmers Market, this three-story motel (with an elevator) puts you right in the heart of a very busy part of L.A. There's a swimming pool and a restaurant, and the 66 rooms have refrigerators and either two double beds or a single queen-size one. Starline-Gray Line tour buses take guests to Disneyland; the cost is about $54 per adult (including park admission). Motel rates are $70 during the summer and $58 the rest of the year, plus $3 per additional person regardless of age; no charge for rollaways; cribs are not available. There are no rooms specially equipped for the handicapped. Details: Best Western Farmer's Daughter; 115 South Fairfax; Los Angeles, CA 90036; 213-937-3930.

BILTMORE: Named a historical landmark by the city's Cultural Board in 1969, this four-star grand old hotel underwent a multimillion-dollar renovation just a few years ago. The results were quite

spectacular. In the main galleria, recessed lighting illuminates the vaulted ceiling and friezes designed by Italian muralist Giovanni Smeraldi in the 1920s. The lobby (previously the music room) features a working marble fountain, tapestries, silks, overstuffed furniture, and antique tables. Three distinctive trompe l'oeil murals were commissioned for the lobby and the court café. There are 700 extra-spacious guestrooms and all are luxuriously appointed with traditional and French furnishings, writing desks, armoires, plush carpeting, and matching tile. The hotel, which overlooks garden-like Pershing Square in downtown Los Angeles, has some fine restaurants on the premises including *Bernard's*. There is also a health club with an indoor pool. Some guest quarters are equipped for handicapped travelers. There is SuperShuttle service ($11 per person) to the Los Angeles Airport, and Starline-Gray Line tour buses bring guests to Disneyland (about $54 for adults, including admission to the park). Rates are $205 to $275 for doubles, and $400 and up for suites (no charge for children under 18 sharing their parents' room) year-round, plus $30 per extra adult (charge includes rollaway); no charge for cribs. Ask about special weekend packages starting at $99 per night. Details: The Biltmore; 506 South Grand Ave.; Los Angeles, CA 90071; 213-624-1011 or 800-245-8673.

CENTURY PLAZA: The centerpiece of Century City, an ultramodern city-within-a-city built on property that once was Tom Mix's ranch and, later, Twentieth Century-Fox Studio's back lot. The tall buildings of this development west of Beverly Hills, between Olympic and Santa Monica boulevards, stand like great exclamation marks against the West Los Angeles skyline. The hotel is actually comprised of two buildings connected by an elegant marble corridor which houses a portion of the hotel's $4 million art collection. One is a half-moon-shaped edifice, 19 stories high, with 750 recently renovated rooms with king-size or double beds, and oak armoires to conceal the color television sets, and large, private balconies. The other building, a 30-story tower, has 322 extra-spacious, 570-square-foot guestrooms. Tower rooms have marble baths, wet bars, and private balconies. There is a special children's program for Tower guests, including a box of welcome toys at check-in and milk and cookies at bedtime. The hotel also boasts several good

restaurants, and two good-size outdoor swimming pools, with an adjacent landscaped sun deck. Hotel guests have access to the facilities of a nearby health club. Starline-Gray Line tours to Disneyland (about $54, including transportation to the park, general admission, and unlimited use of attractions) are available as well. Across the street, and accessible via an underground passageway, is the ABC Entertainment Center, home of the Shubert Theater, a handful of dining spots, and four movie houses. The Century Plaza is a popular spot for conventions. Double rooms cost $210 to $240 in the main building, $260 to $300 in the tower. Details: Century Plaza; 2025 Ave. of the Stars; Los Angeles, CA 90067; 213-277-2000 or 800-228-3000.

HYATT REGENCY LONG BEACH: Located 15 miles south of downtown Los Angeles and 30 minutes from Disneyland, its 521 rooms have great views of the beach or the harbor. There is a large rectangular pool with an adjacent ten-foot spa. Fifteen rooms are designed for handicapped travelers, with oversize bathrooms, grab rails, and wide entrance doors. Rates are $150 for doubles year-round (no charge for children under 18 occupying their parents' room); rollaways are $10 and cribs are free. Details: Hyatt Regency Long Beach; 200 South Pine Ave.; Long Beach, CA 90802; 213-491-1234 or 800-233-1234.

MIKADO BEST WESTERN: This 58-room, two-story establishment is located between Laurel and Coldwater canyons in one of the most scenic sections of Los Angeles. Rooms are nicely decorated, and have two double beds or a single king- or queen-size bed. The tiled, kidney-shaped swimming pool is quite handsome; a spa is nearby. Rates are $85 to $95 for doubles with slight seasonal variations, plus $10 per additional person (no charge for children under 12) and $20 for rollaways; cribs are $10. There are no rooms specially equipped for the handicapped. Details: Mikado Best Western; 12600 Riverside Dr.; North Hollywood, CA 91607; 818-763-9141 or 800-528-1234.

SAFARI INN: While not particularly convenient to Disneyland, this establishment in Burbank is a good bet if you're planning to visit the Burbank Studios, and the spacious location in the valley gives a feeling of openness that is not found in many other establishments discussed here. There are 103 rooms in a two-story main building and another three-story structure with an elevator, plus a swimming pool, spa, cocktail lounge, and restaurant. Rates range from $58 to $80 year-round, plus $10 per additional person (no charge for infants), $10 for rollaways, and $4 for cribs. There are no rooms equipped especially for handicapped travelers. Details: Safari Inn; 1911 West Olive Ave.; Burbank, CA 91506; 818-845-8586 or 800-782-4373.

SHERATON UNIVERSAL: Location is the reason to stay in this 446-room hotel on the grounds of Universal Studios: When you lodge here, though you're about an hour from Disneyland by freeway, you're at the official hotel of Universal Studios, and you're well positioned for forays into downtown Los Angeles, Westwood, and the suburbs on the northern end of metropolitan Southern California—that is, Beverly Hills, Santa Monica, Malibu, and the like. Rooms in the 20-story tower have views of the San Fernando Valley and the Hollywood Hills; those in the three-story Lanai Wing are close to the pool, the spa, and the nearby sauna and gameroom. All guestrooms are fitted out with all sorts of nice touches (fresh flowers, baskets of luxury soaps) and there is a full-service concierge in the hotel lobby. There are also rooms equipped for handicapped travelers. The hotel has a guest laundry, valet service, various shops, and several eating and drinking spots. Transportation is available to the Los Angeles Airport via SuperShuttle (about $12 per person), and Starline-Grayline tour buses will take you to Disneyland. The fare, which includes park admission, is about $54 for adults. Room rates are $160 to $230 year-round, depending on the type of bed and the floor you occupy (no charge for children under 17 sharing their parents' room), plus $25 per extra adult, $25 for rollaways, and $10.50 a night for parking; no charge for cribs. Details: Sheraton Universal; 333 Universal Terrace Pkwy.; Universal City, CA 91608; 818-980-1212 or 800-325-3535.

An outdoor swimming pool is right on the premises. Some rooms are equipped for handicapped travelers. Transportation is available to the Los Angeles Airport ($11.50 per person), and there are tours to Disneyland (cost is about $54 for adults). Rates are $175 to $210 for doubles year-round, depending on the floor and the view (no charge for children under 18 when sharing their parents' room), plus $25 for additional adults, and $16.50 for parking; no charge for cribs or rollaways. Details: The Westin Bonaventure; 404 South Figueroa St.; Los Angeles, CA 90071; 213-624-1000 or 800-228-3000.

BEVERLY HILLS & WEST HOLLYWOOD

BEVERLY HILLS: The stargazing at this comfortable, 268-room enclave on a dozen palm-dotted acres is about as good as exists in Southern California—not only around the swimming pool (the largest in Beverly Hills), but also in the famous *Polo Lounge*, a favorite of movie moguls for lunch or cocktails. There's plenty of charm, too: The three-story main building was constructed in Spanish colonial style just before World War I, and the rooms are individually decorated with walnut, oak, and mahogany furniture. Private balconies or patios and gas fireplaces characterize many of the suites and some 21 bungalows. Twin, queen-, and king-size beds are available. Recreation facilities include two tennis courts (with lights for night play) and a handful of chic boutiques, and 21 private poolside cabanas (with telephones) that may be rented during the day. The hotel has some rooms specifically designed for handicapped guests. Rates are $230 to $320 for doubles year-round and $395 to $3,100 per night for one- to four-bedroom suites, plus $25 per additional occupant regardless of age; no charge for rollaways or cribs. Details: Beverly Hills; 9641 Sunset Blvd.; Beverly Hills, CA 90210; 213-276-2251 or 800-283-8885.

BEVERLY RODEO: This small, four-story hotel is quite comfortable and a bit less expensive than some nearby establishments, despite its convenient location, right in the middle of Rodeo Drive, in the heart of Beverly Hills, and despite the fact that all the rooms have been completely redecorated in the last few years. Rates are about $170 for two, year-round, plus $15 per additional over age 12 (maximum of three to a room); cribs and rollaways are free. Details: Beverly Rodeo; 360 North Rodeo Dr.; Beverly Hills, CA 90210; 213-273-0300 or 800-356-7575.

REGENT BEVERLY WILSHIRE: This 363-room, eight-story hotel has two distinct buildings. The original Wilshire structure on Wilshire Boulevard was lavishly renovated to the tune of $65 million. The lobby has a new floor of French and Italian marble, in addition to marble-lined columns, a restored bronze and crystal chandelier, and hand-wrought sconces. Guestrooms feature period

UNIVERSAL CITY HILTON: This 24-story glass tower, designed by architect William Pereira, is located next to Universal Studios. Appointments in the 456 guestrooms and suites are luxurious and include marble baths. Some rooms are equipped for handicapped travelers. Other facilities and services include a heated outdoor swimming pool; an exercise room; a whirlpool; banquet, convention, and meeting facilities; valet service; concierge service; a parking garage; a gift shop; and two cocktail lounges. There are two restaurants, including one that is housed under a beautiful glass-domed pavilion. The other, *Hiro*, is an authentic Japanese restaurant with tatami rooms. SuperShuttle provides service to the Los Angeles Airport. Rates for doubles year-round are $170 to $195 (children under 18 are free when sharing their parents' room), plus $20 per extra adult, $20 for rollaways; no charge for cribs. Details: Universal City Hilton and Tower; 555 Universal Terrace Pkwy.; Universal City, CA 91608; 818-506-2500 or 800-HILTONS.

WESTIN BONAVENTURE: This soaring quintet of mirrored-glass towers, located a half mile from the Convention Center in downtown Los Angeles, is a city within a city. Occupying the entire block bound by 4th and 5th Streets and by Flower and Figueroa, it has 1,474 recently renovated guestrooms and some very luxurious suites, 28 reception and meeting rooms, a 25,116-square-foot exhibition hall, one of the largest hotel ballrooms on the West Coast, a variety of pedestrian bridges and walkways, and 23 passenger elevators, a dozen of them enclosed with glass. The lobby, a six-story glass-roofed atrium, features its own one-acre lake and a five-level shopping gallery. There are several eating and drinking spots, including one that curves around the lobby's lagoon; a 34th-floor cocktail lounge that rotates a full circle each hour (and offers a star-spangled city panorama in the process), a restaurant with a view one floor above; a futuristic nightclub called *Fantasia*, with a stainless-steel dance floor; and *Beaudry's*, which serves continental/California cuisine and vintage wines for dinner daily; and the *Flower Street Bar*, which serves a light buffet lunch on weekdays and has a large selection of imported beers and wines.

furniture and fabrics in soft hues of wheat, celery, rose, and peach. Oversize marble bathrooms have glass-enclosed showers and such amenities as a television set, a make-up vanity, bathrobes, and cut-crystal boxes for toiletries. The Beverly Wing (just behind the original structure) was recently renovated as well. The Spa and Fitness Center features exercise equipment and saunas for women and men, and an outdoor pool; Mr. Ko Takata is known for his massages—Swedish and shiatsu—which may be just the thing after a long day at Disneyland. The hotel also boasts a number of fine eating and drinking spots. Transportation to Disneyland, via Oskar J's, is quite convenient. The fare, which includes admission to the park, is about $59 for adults. This also is the Beverly Hills luxury hotel that's most convenient to the area's chicest shops. Room rates start at $325; suites start at $500; no charge for an extra person or for rollaways or cribs. Details: Regent Beverly Wilshire; 9500 Wilshire Blvd.; Beverly Hills, CA 90212; 213-275-5200 or 800-545-4000 for central reservations.

BEL-AIR: This quiet hotel, just north of UCLA, in the most exclusive (and expensive) part of Bel Air, has only 92 rooms. The seclusion of the 11½ acres of landscaped grounds—complete with a pond and a family of swans—isn't for everyone, but fans consider it L.A.'s most fashionable address. And if getting away from it all is what you have in mind, this is the place for you. The rooms have been lovingly and lavishly decorated, and it's hard to imagine a more luxurious stopping place. There's also a swimming pool, restaurant, and bar to keep you diverted. Rates range from $245 to $395 for doubles and $450 to $2,000 for suites year-round, plus $20 for rollaways; no charge for cribs. Facilities designed for handicapped guests have been completed; although there are significant distances to traverse on foot to get around the hotel grounds, these areas are accessible to wheelchairs.

Details: Hotel Bel-Air; 701 Stone Canyon Rd.; Los Angeles, CA 90077; 213-472-1211 or 800-648-4097 from outside California.

L'ERMITAGE: This elegant, eight-story, European-style hotel boasts 112 one- to three-bedroom suites and luxury all the way—as you'd expect for the price, with rates ranging from $275 up to $1,500 a night. Sunken living rooms, fireplaces, wet bars, refrigerators, and automatic dishwashers are just a few of the amenities here, but features vary from one suite to the next. There are conference rooms, a swimming pool, and a private dining room for guests only. Services include complimentary caviar and paté from 5 P.M. to 7 P.M., valet parking, and a chauffeured limousine to Beverly Hills. Details: L'Ermitage; 9291 Burton Way; Beverly Hills, CA 90210; 213-278-3344 or 800-424-4443 from the United States and Canada.

LE PARC: For about the price of an ordinary double room elsewhere in this chic nieghborhood—that is, $165 to $255 for two, year-round—this delightful small hotel will rent a whole suite, with a king-size bed and a sofa bed, a kitchen, a fireplace, a VCR, a private balcony, and an extra-large bathroom. Each suite has three multi-line telephones with conference capabilities. And if that's not enough to lure you here, the large roof-top spa with its lit tennis court, whirlpool, and heated swimming pool may do the trick; there's also a sauna and gym on the hotel's third floor. Valet parking is available. Children under 12 are free, but there are additional charges of $25 per extra adult and $15 for each rollaway; you don't pay extra for cribs. Details: Le Parc; 733 North West Knoll; West Hollywood, CA 90069; 213-855-8888 or 800-424-4443 from the United States and Canada.

AROUND SAN DIEGO

LA COSTA: Located about 30 miles north of San Diego, this sprawling establishment ranks among the best resorts in the country for sports. There are 23 tennis courts, a good many of them lit for night play, and 36 holes of challenging golf. The Golf Academy is headed by Carl Welty, and tennis pros are on hand under the direction of Pancho Segura to help you improve your scores. And afterward you can recuperate in one of the most elaborate health spas in the country. Saunas and steamrooms, Roman pools, Swiss showers that zap you from all sides until every inch of skin is deliciously tingling, mineral whirlpools, herbal wraps, massages, manicures, pedicures, facials, and the like are all available. If you're not worn out from outdoor sports, you can sign up for group exercise classes or work out in the weight room. There are eight restaurants—including one where the menu lists the calorie counts of all the offerings. And there are about 500 rooms and

suites in several wings of the main hotel building along with an assortment of villas and châteaus and other structures around the grounds. All rooms have two queen-size beds. Eight rooms are specifically designed for handicapped guests. Rates start at $215 for two, not including meals, sports, and use of spa facilities; there's a charge of $30 per additional person over age 18; children under 18 are free and you don't pay extra for roll-aways. Valet parking is free for hotel and restaurant guests. Details: La Costa Resort and Spa; Costa Del Mar Rd.; Carlsbad, CA 92009; 619-438-9111 or 800-854-5000.

HUMPHREY'S HALF MOON INN: This lovely, low-slung, Polynesian-style hideaway on Shelter Island has 183 rooms, many with private patios or balconies and fine views over the bay or a marina full of sleek and shining boats; there are 70 suites with kitchens. The heated, Olympic-size swimming pool (and the adjacent whirlpool) are focal points of activity, but the complex also boasts lush gardens, a restaurant, a putting green, bicycles, Ping-Pong, and a three-slip marina; sportfishing facilities are within walking distance. There are no special facilities for the handicapped. Transportation to the airport, train station, and bus depot is provided. Starline-Grayline tour buses also provide transportation to Disneyland; the fare, about $54 for adults, includes park admission. The room rate for 2 people ranges from $85 to $155 year-round (no charge for children under 17 sharing their parents' room), plus $10 per night for each extra adult; cribs are free. Details: Humphrey's Half Moon Inn; 2303 Shelter Island Dr.; San Diego, CA 92106; 619-224-3411 or 800-542-7400.

HANALEI: Centrally located in the Hotel Circle area and convenient to Sea World, this contemporary 8-story high-rise, on ten acres landscaped with palm trees, succulents, and waterfalls, boasts 425 cheerful rooms, decorated in mint and mauve with bleached wood furnishings; 8 of them can accommodate handicapped guests. The hotel has a heated pool; a whirlpool spa; a large gameroom; and a trio of wining-and-dining spots on the premises. Six tennis courts and a nine-hole golf course are next door, and guests enjoy visitors' privileges at the nearby Atlas Health Club: racquetball and tennis courts, a weight room, a masseur and masseuse, and a pool large enough for swimming laps. Starline-Gray Line and other tour bus services go to Disneyland; the fare for adults is about $54 (including admission to the park). Rates are $92 to $125 for doubles year-round (no charge for children under 18 sharing their parents' room), plus $10 per additional adult, $10 for rollaways, and $5 for cribs. Details: Hanalei; 2270 Hotel Circle North; San Diego, CA 92108; 619-297-1101, 800-542-6082 from California, 800-854-2608 from the rest of the United States, and 800-854-6742 from Canada.

LA VALENCIA: This graceful dowager of a Spanish-style hotel, all pink stucco and Spanish archways and located in the jewel-like coastal suburb called La Jolla, has drawn Hollywood's elite for generations. Rudolf Valentino stayed here, and so did Greta Garbo, Lillian Gish, Ramon Navarro, and, more recently, Dustin Hoffman and Bob Hope. Though the hotel isn't on the ocean per se, it does command a glorious view of La Jolla Cove and the Pacific, across the street. The lobby, which occupies the seventh floor—the hotel is built into a hillside—is the kind of room that makes you want to linger, and many guests do. A jigsaw puzzle is set up on one of the tables and there's a piano; you can sit with a glass of premium California wine from the *La Sala* wine bar, and just gaze out through the large windows at one of those incomparable Pacific sunsets. The hotel also has a swimming pool, sun deck, Jacuzzi, a small health spa with exercise equipment and a sauna, and a handful of spots where you can have cocktails or a leisurely meal; the *Whaling Bar* reputedly serves the best Bloody Marys in San Diego, and the tenth-floor *Sky Room*, which has a wonderful ocean view, is great for a relaxed lunch. There are 100 guestrooms. Rates are $135 to $250 year-round for doubles, plus $10 per additional adult. Details: La Valencia; 1132 Prospect St.; La Jolla, CA 92037; 619-454-0771 or 800-451-0772.

SAN DIEGO MARRIOTT: The major asset here is the 26-acre waterfront location, overlooking San Diego Bay and adjacent to the San Diego Convention Center. The two 25-story elliptical mirrored glass towers hold 1,355 guestrooms, most of which have fine views of San Diego Bay. All 681 rooms in one tower have balconies. Sixty-eight suites are available, and several rooms are equipped for handicapped guests. An especially nice feature is the landscaped pool area. Guests who arrive by boat can tie up at the full-service, 446-slip marina, where telephone and cable television hookup, room service, laundry, and valet services are all available. Other recreation facilities include tennis courts and a health club. There are three restaurants, and extensive conference and convention facilities. Starline-Gray Line tour buses go to Disneyland ($54 per adult, including park admission). Rates for doubles are $150 to $190, plus $20 per extra adult (maximum of five to a room); no charge for children under 18; no charge for rollaways or cribs. Details: San Diego Marriott Hotel & Marina; 333 West Harbor Dr.; San Diego, CA 92101-7709; 619-234-1500 or 800-228-9290.

WESTGATE: Many valuable antiques decorate the premises of this deluxe, 19-story establishment in downtown San Diego. But that's only one of the reasons it is considered stylish. All of the 223 rooms (including 11 suites) are handsomely furnished with English Regency and Louis XV and XVI reproduction furniture, and the bathrooms are tiled with marble and fitted out with brass fixtures. The *Fontainebleau Room* ranks among the city's best restaurants. There are no rooms specially equipped for the handicapped. Starline-Gray Line tour buses stop here en route to Disneyland; the fare, which includes park admission, is about $54 for adults. Rates are $144 to $164 year-round (inquire about weekend rates and packages), plus $10 for each additional person over age 18; cribs are free. Details: Westgate; 1055 Second Ave.; San Diego, CA 92101; 619-238-1818 or 800-221-3802.

SPECIAL PLACES

Even in Southern California, that stronghold of look-alike lodging places, it's possible to find several one-of-a-kind hostelries worth traveling the distance to experience and enjoy.

DEL CORONADO: Boasting both the gracious look of the last century and many of the amenities of the present one, this sprawling oceanside establishment, on the Coronado Peninsula just across a bridge from San Diego, is a National Historic Landmark. Twelve U.S. presidents have been guests here, and legend has it that Edward, the Duke of Windsor, met Wallis Simpson here. You will recognize the place immediately by its red roof, turrets, cupolas, and ornate jigsaw-cut wooden trim—all the rage back in 1888, when the hotel first opened its doors just over a century ago. There are all sorts of intriguing touches inside. Just outside the *Prince of Wales Room* is one of the old fire wagons that protected the building before the installation of sprinklers in the early 1900s. The *Crown Coronet Room*, whose Sunday brunch is locally cherished, boasts an Oregon pine ceiling put together with wooden pegs instead of nails. And the lobby, paneled in dark woods and lighted by a Bavarian crystal chandelier, has an old-fashioned Otis birdcage elevator that is still functioning. There are enough similar points of interest in the hotel to fill up a very informative audiocassette, which you can rent in the lobby gift shop for $3 per adult and $2 for students under 18 and senior citizens. There also are all kinds of sports facilities, including two huge swimming pools, spas for men and women, and six lit tennis courts on the premises, plus paddleboats and sailboats for rent on Glorietta Bay right in front of the hotel. Golf is available a half mile away. Guestrooms now total 700—more than half of them in the original building, the others in the modern seven-story Ocean Towers and the three-story Poolside Wing. Several are specially equipped for handicapped guests. All guestrooms were recently renovated, right down to the bathrooms, which now boast new ceramic tile and stylish sinks and fixtures. Rooms in the main building have attractive floral curtains, rose-colored bedspreads, and appropriate Victorian-style furniture. Rates are $145 to $265 for doubles, depending on the room's size, location and view, and suites range from $275 to $470; plus $25 per extra adult, $15 per additional person age 5 to 18 (no charge for children under 5); $8 per day for guest parking; no charge for cribs. Details: Concierge; Hotel Del Coronado; 1500 Orange Ave.; Coronado, CA 92118; 619-522-8000 or 800-HOTEL-DEL.

INDUSTRY HILLS SHERATON: Though just 25 miles and 35 minutes north (nestled between the San Bernardino and Pomona freeways, in the City of Industry) by car from Disneyland, this resort is a world away. The multi-level atrium is really stunning, and the guestrooms are large and well appointed and look less like hotel rooms than bedrooms at home. They all have private balconies with spectacular views of the San Gabriel Mountains and Valley. The real lure, however, is an array of sporting facilities varied enough to warrant all sorts of superlatives beginning with "paradise for the sports lover." The resort boasts not one but two 18-hole golf courses, one of them ranked by *Golf Digest* in the top 25 public courses in the United States (see *Sports*); and there's a lit putting green laid out on a hillside. There are 17 lit tennis courts (including a center court with room for 2,000 spectators), plus a hitting net and facilities for videotaping

(see *Sports*), an equestrian center, a warm-up pool plus a true Olympic-size pool, (and a ten-meter diving platform), a whirlpool spa, steamrooms, and locker facilities. Considering the facilities, the prices are not out of line—$120 to $150 for a double room year-round (no extra charge for children under 15 sharing their parents' room), plus $15 for any rollaways you might require, plus whatever fees you incur for use of the sporting facilities, few of which are included in the basic room rates. Cribs are $15. Several package deals are available. Details: Industry Hills & Sheraton Resort; One Industry Hills Pkwy.; City of Industry, CA 91744; 818-965-0861, or 800-325-3535.

RITZ-CARLTON, LAGUNA NIGUEL: Located on the Southern Orange County coast, this magnificent Mediterranean villa-style resort hotel sits high on a bluff overlooking the Pacific Ocean. The view from the lounge and from many of the 393 guestrooms (all of which have French doors and balconies) is sensational; on a clear day it is possible to see Catalina Island, some 37 miles away. The hotel's marble floors, handwoven area carpets, 19th-century English crystal chandeliers, and 18th-century Belgian tapestries make a visit worthwhile even if you don't plan to stay overnight. In addition to a lovely two-mile stretch of beach (which is open to the public), there are two pools and two spas; an 18-hole golf course designed by Robert Trent Jones, Jr.; several tennis courts; a fitness center (with classes free to guests, lockers, sauna, whirlpool, steamroom, exercise room, massage, and personal care salons); and a volleyball court. The *Dining Room* is one of Orange County's finest restaurants. Rates for doubles range from $185 to $360, depending on location and view, plus $50 per extra adult (no charge for cribs or for children under 18 sharing their parents' room). Suites start at $770. Twelve rooms are equipped for the handicapped. The hotel is a 35-minute drive southeast from Disneyland. Details: Ritz-Carlton, Laguna Niguel; Ritz-Carlton Dr.; Laguna Niguel, CA 92677; 240-2000 or 800-241-3333.

SEAL BEACH INN AND GARDENS: This place is an utter delight, all 22 rooms of it—full of Victorian antiques, old prints, oriental carpets, and vibrant colors. There are brass chandeliers from an old house in New Orleans and stained-glass windows from Scotland. The grounds are ornamented by a red telephone booth from England, by lampposts that stood on the streets of nearby Long Beach in the 1930s, by a 300-year-old iron fountain from France, by a tiny swimming pool, and by gardens that bloom profusely throughout the year. In the *Tea Room*, a lavish complimentary breakfast, prepared by the inn's chef, is served on tables covered with lace cloths. And in the library next door, you can play chess, checkers, or Scrabble™. Most guestrooms have built-in bookcases and kitchens that are fully equipped, right down to tea cups. Some of the larger rooms are furnished to accommodate more than two people. Rates are $98 for Cottages, rooms which face the street; and $108 for the Garden Cottage. There are 12 Royal Villas, which cost $145 to $155. These are charming suites with handcarved tables, satin bedspreads, and lace curtains. For a real treat, inquire about the inn's "Chocolate Love-in Package" or the "Gondola Getaway Package." Extra guests, regardless of age, cost $10 each. Children are welcome, but given the value of the antiques, it's probably not a good place to bring curious toddlers. The inn is located a short walk from the beach, the town's fishing pier, and several shops and restaurants; it is a 25-minute drive southwest from Disneyland. Details: The Seal Beach Inn and Gardens; 212 Fifth St.; Seal Beach, CA 90740; 213-493-2416.

R.M.S. QUEEN MARY: The ship that once ruled the waves now reigns over Long Beach harbor as a grande dame hotel. Operated by The Walt Disney Company, all 365 staterooms and 8 suites have been refurbished. Floral bedspread designs are replicas of the originals. Carpets carry the same color scheme and art deco motif, and built-in dressers have new forest-green granite tops. Many furnishings and fixtures from the ship's glory days have been preserved: peach glass on the mirrors, for instance (so that seasick passengers couldn't see how poorly they looked), and shower knobs marked for fresh or saltwater. The public areas feature Italian silver railings on the staircases, beautiful art deco furnishings, lovely wood-paneled hallways, and paintings by leading artists of the 1930s. There are a number of restaurants and specialty shops. First-rate entertainment and special events are featured aboard ship year-round. Double-occupancy rates range from about $95 to $140, depending on location and view. Cribs are free. Since staterooms are rather small for rollaways, suites (which cost from $185 to $650) or adjoining rooms provide the best family accommodations. "Passengers" get a 50 percent discount on admission to the *Spruce Goose* and the *Queen Mary* attractions (see *In All Directions*). Plans are currently underway to make the *Queen Mary* part of a new "Port Disney" development as extensive as Disneyland itself. Details: R.M.S. Queen Mary; Pier J, Box 8; Long Beach, CA 90801; 213-435-3511.

BED AND BREAKFAST

Bed-and-breakfast accommodations have become increasingly popular in the United States, and anyone who has stayed in one knows how convenient they can be. For they not only provide a comfortable room, but also prepare you to meet the day with at least a continental breakfast under your belt. Sometimes these private quarters are furnished with antiques, or boast fireplaces or fabulous sea views. Sometimes the accommodations are in restored farmhouses, elegant Victorian mansions, or contemporary architectural marvels; occasionally, you lodge in just a pleasant middle class home. Some offer private baths, or transportation to nearby sightseeing attractions; some don't. Some can accommodate a couple alone, while others are able to put up whole families, with one or more of the kids sleeping on cots or rollaways. The common denominator is lodging with a family—and that certain homey, personal atmosphere is not available even in the best hotels. Rates range from about $40 to over $100 or so for two, including breakfast, plus an extra $5 to $15 per child—in most cases, this must be paid in cash or traveler's checks.

Several bed-and-breakfast reservation services will match you up with a B&B in the area of your choice. These include:

- **American Family Inn/Bed & Breakfast San Francisco**; Box 349; San Francisco, CA 94101; 415-931-3083 (mainly in Northern California)
- **Bed & Breakfast California Style**; c/o Sue Wild; 2857 Via de la Guerra; Palos Verdes, CA 90274; 213-377-8950
- **Bed & Breakfast Exchange**; 1458 Lincoln Ave. Suite 3; Calistoga, CA 94515; 707-942-5900
- **Bed & Breakfast International**; 1181-B Solano Ave.; Albany, CA 94706; 415-525-4569
- **Bed & Breakfast of Southern California**; 1943 Sunny Crest Dr.; Suite 304; Fullerton, CA 92635; 738-8361
- **California Houseguests International**; Box 643; Tarzana, CA 91357; 818-344-7878
- **American Historic Homes Bed & Breakfast**; Box 336; Dana Point, CA 92629; 496-6953
- **Bed and Breakfast of Los Angeles**; 32074 Waterside Lane; Westlake Village, CA 91361; 818-889-8870 or 805-494-9622

For further listings of B&Bs in the United States, consult *Bed & Breakfast U.S.A.* by Betty Rundback ($12.95; Penguin, U.S.A). The California Office of Tourism (Box 189; Sacramento, CA 95812-0189; 800-862-2543) has a free listing of a number of B&Bs all over the state. The Automobile Club of Southern California also offers free guidebooks to members.

Note: To get the most out of a guesthouse stay, contact the B&B service or the individual establishment as far in advance as possible, specifying the number of adults and children in your party, the date and time of arrival, the planned length of stay, and any special needs you may have.

CAMPING

Most of the recreational vehicle parks situated within a mile of Disneyland offer only vehicle camping, since the greater part of the area was developed before tenting was allowed within city limits. Nearly all establishments offer full hookups, convenience stores, and other camping facilities, but few offer much in the way of planned activities. However, the managements usually will arrange with local tour companies for sightseeing tours outside Disneyland during your stay. Here's a selection of some of the best in the area. Unless otherwise noted, the campgrounds mentioned accept major credit cards and offer full hookups, and reservations are suggested. *In season* refers to Christmas and Easter vacation periods and the summer months of June through August.

ANAHEIM JUNCTION: Located just a short walk from the Disneyland hotel, this 124-site campground is blessed with a handful of trees that provide dappled shade, and there's grass around the paved parking slots. Kids will enjoy the sandy play area, the rectangular pool (the latter refreshing for dips, but not really large enough for the serious lap swimmer), and the gameroom, which is equipped with about six electronic games. There is also a laundry room. Rates for two are about $25 in season and $21 the rest of the year, $2 per additional person over age two, and 50¢ for pets, which must be kept leashed when outside your vehicle. Note that no credit cards are accepted. Details: Anaheim Junction Campground; 1230 South West St.; Anaheim, CA 92802; 533-0641.

ANAHEIM KOA: In this campground, also situated within walking distance of the *Disneyland* hotel, there are leafy shade trees and shrubbery to separate the sites, all of which are paved. There are two pools (one a wading pool for kids, the other a semicircular adult pool) plus a spa, a recreation room that boasts almost two dozen games in all, including pinball and Pac-Man, and a 24-hour laundromat. The sandy playground has swings and heavy-duty climbing equipment. There's also a good bathhouse set-up. In addition to conventional women's and men's shower stalls, there are ten family-size showers large enough for a parent to bathe small fry. There are 221 RV sites in all, divided about evenly between back-in and pull-through spaces. Rates for two are about $33 in season and $27 the rest of the year, $4 per additional adult (over age 18), $3 for children over three. Free-standing tents (without stakes) are allowed. Pets must be leashed when outside vehicles. Note that the campground is also well equipped for the handicapped, with huge roll-in showers with grab bars, and no curbs. Details: Anaheim KOA; 1221 South West St.; Anaheim, CA 92802; 533-7720.

DISNEY'S VACATIONLAND CAMPGROUND: Just a short walk from the *Disneyland* hotel and a monorail ride into the park, this well-kept campground offers 385 paved, full-service RV slots, with bushes between them to buffer sounds and afford some privacy, plus 60 tent spaces on a grassy area at the back of the park near a group of picnic tables and built-in barbecues. Amenities include a good-size pool (but with steps across one end that make it difficult for lap swimmers) and separate carpeted recreation rooms for adults and teenagers. The adult lounge has couches, chairs, and tables that would be convenient for

cards and board games, plus a pool table. The children's game area has pinball, plus just about every electronic game imaginable. There's also a play area with a slide and merry-go-round. The laundry room is equipped with 22 washers and 11 dryers. Rates are $24.95 to $29.95 in season, $21.95 to $26.95 off-season, for two persons, $2.50 per extra person, plus $1 per day per pet. Details: Disney's Vacationland Campground; 1343 South West St.; Anaheim, CA 92802; 533-7270 or 778-6600, ext. 1256.

ORANGELAND: This 212-site campground is located on eight acres of an orange grove with an abundance of trees for shade and plenty of grass around the sites. It's only three miles from Disneyland and half a mile from Anaheim Stadium. Facilities here include a pool, Jacuzzi, laundromat, gameroom, and a grocery store. Rates for two are about $24, $2 for each additional person, and $1 for pets. Reservations are recommended. Details: Orangeland; 1600 West Struck; Orange, CA 92667; 633-0414.

TRAVELERS WORLD: Occupying some acreage roughly three-quarters of a mile from Disneyland, this 300-site park is large and open, and has some shade trees. All the sites are paved. Tents are permitted, and there's a coin-operated wash rack for cars and RVs and a small gameroom (with three electronic games and four pinball machines). Rates for two are about $21 in season and $17.50 the rest of the year for back-in units. Pull-throughs are $2 extra. It costs $2 to $2.50, depending on the season, per additional person age three and over (or for a pet). Details: Travelers World RV Park; 333 West Ball Rd.; Anaheim, CA 92805; 991-0100.

THE MAGIC KINGDOM

Every day is a holiday at Disneyland. Children giggle and grin, and parents not only enjoy their offsprings' glee, but are hard pressed to contain their own enjoyment. No one seems immune to the magic of Sleeping Beauty Castle, rising majestically at one end of Main Street, and even the most cynical hearts instinctively respond to the sound of the marching bands that play here every day of the year. Even visitors who have toured this wonderland dozens of times still react with uncamouflaged delight.

What may be the most extraordinary fact of all is that this enjoyment has remained constant for 37 years. Attractions have come and gone, whole new "lands" have been added, and young musicians who began performing here during the 1950s have now grown to middle age. But a visitor who originally came here as a first-grader returns with his own children to find the Disneyland of his memory unchanged in spirit and appeal. The "magical little park," for which Walt Disney borrowed on his life insurance, is still one of America's greatest success stories. Except for its siblings in Florida and Tokyo—and now outside Paris—it has no equal.

Be aware, however, that part of Disneyland's charm is its abundance, and it's all too easy to miss the best of the Magic Kingdom unless you prepare for your visit. This chapter should help you make the decisions that can keep you on track, so read it carefully before embarking on your own Disneyland adventure, and keep it with you during your visit.

Every land here has a theme, maintained from the hosts' and hostesses' costumes to the merchandise in the shops, the food in the restaurants, and even the design of the trash bins. These delightful details will help make your visit even more enjoyable.

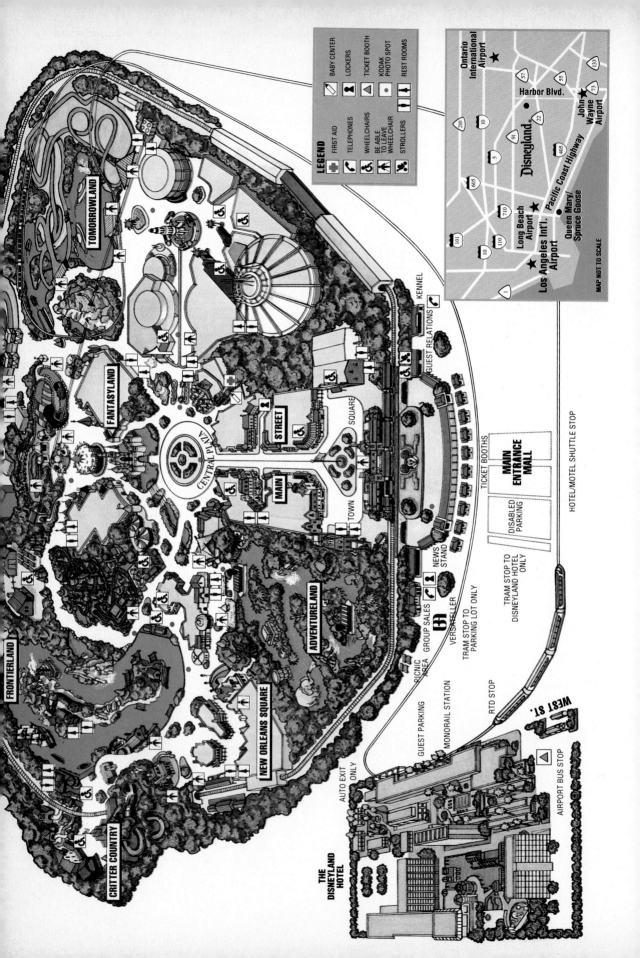

LEGEND

	First Aid		Baby Center
	Telephones		Lockers
	Wheelchairs		Ticket Booth
	Be Able to Leave Wheelchair		Kodak Photo Spot
	Strollers		Rest Rooms

MAP NOT TO SCALE

Ontario International Airport

Harbor Blvd.

Disneyland

John Wayne Airport

Long Beach Airport

Los Angeles Int'l. Airport

Queen Mary/Spruce Goose

Pacific Coast Highway

TOMORROWLAND

FANTASYLAND

FRONTIERLAND

CRITTER COUNTRY

NEW ORLEANS SQUARE

ADVENTURELAND

CENTRAL PLAZA

MAIN STREET

TOWN SQUARE

GUEST RELATIONS

KENNEL

NEWS STAND

VERSATELLER

GROUP SALES

PICNIC AREA

TRAM STOP TO PARKING LOT ONLY

TRAM STOP TO DISNEYLAND HOTEL ONLY

TICKET BOOTHS

MAIN ENTRANCE MALL

DISABLED PARKING

HOTEL/MOTEL SHUTTLE STOP

GUEST PARKING

MONORAIL STATION

RTD STOP

AUTO EXIT ONLY

WEST ST.

THE DISNEYLAND HOTEL

AIRPORT BUS STOP

GETTING IN AND AROUND

Many Anaheim hotels and motels are within walking distance of Disneyland, or at most a short drive away. Many provide shuttle-bus service. If a bus is available, you're well advised to take it to avoid the bother of parking and retrieving your car in the enormous Disneyland parking lot.

If your lodging place offers no shuttle service and you're too far away to walk, driving becomes the most convenient alternative. Here are directions from nearby points. Driving times are given for optimal conditions; rain or rush-hour traffic may double (at least) the duration of the trip.

FROM POINTS NORTH

From downtown Los Angeles: Santa Monica Freeway (I-10) east, then Santa Ana Freeway (I-5) south to the Harbor Boulevard exit. The trip should take 45 minutes to an hour.

From Santa Monica: Santa Monica Freeway (I-10) east, then Santa Ana Freeway (I-5) south to Harbor Boulevard exit. About an hour.

From Beverly Hills: Santa Monica Freeway (I-10) east, then Santa Ana Freeway (I-5) south to Harbor Boulevard exit. About an hour.

From Century City: Santa Monica Freeway (I-10) east, then Santa Ana Freeway (I-5) south to Harbor Boulevard exit. About an hour.

From Los Angeles Airport: San Diego Freeway (I-405) south to Garden Grove Freeway (Rte. 22) east. Take Harbor Boulevard exit and go north about 2 miles to Disneyland. About an hour.

From the San Fernando Valley: San Diego Freeway (I-405) south to Santa Monica Freeway (I-10) east, Santa Ana Freeway (I-5) south to Harbor Boulevard exit. About 90 minutes.

From Long Beach: Long Beach Freeway (Rte. 7) north, then Rte. 91 east, then Santa Ana Freeway (I-5) south. Alternative: Long Beach Freeway (Rte. 7) north to San Diego Freeway (I-405) south, then Garden Grove Freeway (Rte. 22) east to Harbor Boulevard exit and north about two miles to Disneyland. About 45 to 50 minutes.

FROM POINTS SOUTH

From Newport Beach: Newport Freeway (Rte. 55) north, then Santa Ana Freeway (I-5) north to Harbor Boulevard exit. Turn left and you're a block away. About 30 to 35 minutes.

From San Diego: Santa Ana Freeway (I-5) north. Exit at Harbor Boulevard. Turn left and you're a block away. About two hours.

PARKING: Disneyland has a sizable parking lot—about 110 acres, or enough space to accommodate approximately 15,000 cars. The lot is divided into sections, each of which is named for a Disney character. When passing through the Auto Toll Plaza (where visitors pay the $4 parking fee), you'll receive a small leaflet that includes a map of the parking lot. *Before leaving your car, carefully mark its location on the map.* Then be sure to take the folder along. If you plan to visit on July 4, on Saturdays in August, or on any day during the third week of that month or the last week in December—and we strongly advise you to try to arrange your visit for some time other than these very busy periods—plan to arrive as close as possible to the time Disneyland opens. Although the parking lot is large enough to make finding your car difficult, it's not always big enough to accommodate everyone who hopes to park in there. On the busiest days, it usually fills up before 2 P.M. Trams run throughout the day to and from the park's main entrance.

If the parking lot is full: Those who are unfortunate enough to encounter an SRO situation may park in the lot at the nearby Convention Center and then walk across the street (at the crosswalk) to the edge of the Disneyland property, where they will be picked up by a Disneyland tram (free). Cost of parking in the Convention Center lot is $5 per day. A more expensive alternative is to park in the large lot at the *Disneyland* hotel and take either a Disneyland tram (free) or the monorail (ticket required) from there into the park. The trams run from about half an hour before Disneyland opens until about half an hour after it closes. The monorail runs during park hours.

Note that during such busy periods Harbor Boulevard and the freeway leading up to the exit are both often backed up with traffic. So it's a good idea to take the Katella Avenue exit from the Santa Ana Freeway (I-5), even though it's a little farther from Disneyland and may mean a slight detour for those arriving from the north. This alternative route does allow easy access to Disneyland's Katella Avenue entrance, which is utilized on peak days.

Parking for recreational vehicles: Ample space is available in the Donald Duck section, close to the small picnic area.

Lost cars: Contact security. If you can remember approximately when you arrived, parking lot personnel can usually provide a general location of the car to an officer, who will then comb the aisles on a small scooter.

TIPS ON TIMES AND TICKETS

HOURS: Disneyland is open daily. Weekday hours are usually from 10 A.M. to 6 P.M., with extended hours during July and August. Saturday and Sunday hours vary: 9 A.M. to midnight, 8 P.M. to midnight, or 8 A.M. to 1 A.M. depending on the month.

For the exact opening and closing hours that will be in effect during your stay contact Disneyland Guest Relations; Box 3232; Anaheim, CA 92803 (714-999-4565).

When to arrive: Especially during the busy summer and Christmas holiday seasons, it's very wise to arrive first thing in the morning so you can get to all the popular attractions before the queues build up outside. In fact, if you get there too late, the parking lot may be closed. This happens frequently—on such dates as July 4, during the third week in August, and the last week in December. For more details, read our "Special Tips."

ALL ABOUT TICKETS: When you present yourself at the main gate ticket booths, you buy an admission ticket called a Passport. This one-price ticket includes general admission to the park and unlimited use of all attractions except the arcade.

Where to buy tickets: Disneyland Passports are available at the main gate ticket booths and at the monorail station at the *Disneyland* hotel.

Tickets by mail: Passports and tickets for special events are available by mail at no extra charge. Just send your check or money order for the appropriate amount with a request that specifies what kind of tickets you need and how many. Allow 15 *working* days for processing. Send your check and ticket request to Disneyland Admissions Office; 1313 Harbor Blvd.; Anaheim, CA 92803.

Ticketmaster: Tickets for some special events at Disneyland are sold at Ticketmaster outlets in Southern California.

How to pay for tickets: Cash, traveler's checks, personal checks, American Express, Visa, and MasterCard are all accepted as payment for Disneyland admission media. Personal checks must be imprinted with your name and address. You must also present a driver's license and a major credit card—American Express, Carte Blanche, Diners Club, MasterCard, or Visa (department store and oil-company credit cards are *not* accepted for check identification purposes).

NON-HOLIDAY HOURS

The following are Disneyland's normal operating hours during non-holiday periods. At these times, you will note, schedules vary. Though the seasonal hours are usually as listed below, it's always wise to phone ahead (999-4565) for verification since changes in operating hours frequently occur.

	WEEKDAYS Monday to Thursday	Friday	WEEKENDS Saturday	Sunday
January	10 A.M. to 6 P.M.	10 A.M. to 6 P.M.	9 A.M. to midnight	9 A.M. to midnight
February	10 A.M. to 6 P.M.	10 A.M. to 6 P.M.	9 A.M. to midnight	9 A.M. to midnight
March	10 A.M. to 6 P.M.	9 A.M. to midnight	9 A.M. to midnight	9 A.M. to midnight
April	9 A.M. to 7 P.M.	9 A.M. to midnight	8 A.M. to midnight	9 A.M. to midnight
May	9 A.M. to 7 P.M.	9 A.M. to midnight	8 A.M. to midnight	9 A.M. to midnight
First 3 weeks of June	9 A.M. to midnight	9 A.M. to midnight	8 A.M. to midnight	8 A.M. to midnight
Balance of June	8 A.M. to 1 A.M.	8 A.M. to 1 A.M.	8 A.M. to 1 A.M.	8 A.M. to 1 A.M.
July	8 A.M. to 1 A.M.	8 A.M. to 1 A.M.	8 A.M. to 1 A.M.	8 A.M. to 1 A.M.
First 3 weeks of August	8 A.M. to 1 A.M.	8 A.M. to 1 A.M.	8 A.M. to 1 A.M.	8 A.M. to 1 A.M.
Balance of August	9 A.M. to midnight	9 A.M. to midnight	8 A.M. to 1 A.M.	8 A.M. to 1 A.M.
First week of September	9 A.M. to midnight	9 A.M. to midnight	8 A.M. to 1 A.M.	8 A.M. to 1 A.M.
Balance of September	10 A.M. to 6 P.M.	10 A.M. to 6 P.M.	9 A.M. to midnight	9 A.M. to midnight
October	10 A.M. to 6 P.M.	10 A.M. to 6 P.M.	9 A.M. to midnight	9 A.M. to midnight
November	10 A.M. to 6 P.M.	10 A.M. to 6 P.M.	9 A.M. to midnight	9 A.M. to midnight
December	10 A.M. to 6 P.M.	10 A.M. to 6 P.M.	9 A.M. to midnight	9 A.M. to midnight

HOLIDAY HOURS

During certain holiday periods, opening and closing hours are expanded as follows:

New Year's Day   9 A.M. to midnight

Martin Luther King, Jr. Birthday weekend
January 18 & 19   9 A.M. to midnight
January 20   9 A.M. to 7 P.M.

President's weekend
February 15 & 16   8 A.M. to midnight
February 17   9 A.M. to 10 P.M.

Easter season
April 11 through April 18   8 A.M. to midnight
April 19 (Easter Sunday)   8 A.M. to midnight
April 20 through April 25   8 A.M. to midnight
April 26   9 A.M. to midnight

Memorial Day weekend
May 23 & 24   8 A.M. to midnight
May 25   9 A.M. to 10 P.M.

Independence Day
July 4   8 A.M. to 2 A.M.

Labor Day weekend
September 5 & 6   8 A.M. to 1 A.M.
September 7   9 A.M. to midnight

Columbus Day
October 12   9 A.M. to 10 P.M.

Thanksgiving week
November 23, 24, & 25   10 A.M. to 6 P.M.
November 26 (Thanksgiving Day)   9 A.M. to midnight
November 27 and 28   8 A.M. to midnight
November 29   9 A.M. to midnight

Christmas season
December 19 & 20   9 A.M. to midnight
December 21, 22, & 23   9 A.M. to 10 P.M.
December 24   8 A.M. to 7 P.M.
December 25 through 30   8 A.M. to midnight
December 31   8 A.M. to 3 A.M.

GUIDED TOURS: Disneyland's three-hour guided walking tour is a great way for a first-timer to get to know the park with a minimum of fuss and bother. Your guide can answer questions along the way, and visits to (and rides on) several major attractions are included on the itinerary. Tour tickets are available at the main gate ticket booths where you purchase your admission Passport, or at City Hall once you have entered the park. Note that tours are offered only in the morning. Be aware, too, that a guided tour does *not* relieve tour participants of the need to wait in line at attractions.

MONEY MATTERS: Cash and traveler's checks are accepted at all food and merchandise locations throughout Disneyland. American Express, MasterCard, and Visa can be used to pay for charges at all the shops, cafeterias, fast-food eateries, snack bars, and waitress-service establishments. Only cash is accepted at ice cream and popcorn wagons and at burrito carts. As payment for merchandise and meals, personal checks are also accepted (under the conditions outlined in "How to pay for tickets," above).

Guests may also want to purchase Disney Dollars, available in $1, $5, and $10 denominations. Disney Dollars are accepted at all Magic Kingdom restaurants, shops, and food stands, as well as at the *Disneyland* hotel, and can be redeemed for real currency at any time. Many visitors, however, take at least one home as an inexpensive souvenir. When purchasing tickets or Passports at Disneyland, guests can request Disney Dollars as change.

TICKETS IN BRIEF

	Adults	Children (ages 3 to 11)
Passports	$27.50	$22.50
Guided Tours$ (without Passport)	9.50	$7.50
Annual Passports	$180	$145

These prices were in effect as we went to press, but are subject to change.

LAY OF THE LANDS

Disneyland's layout is so simple that getting around is very easy. However, the numerous nooks and crannies, bends and curves, and small alleyways can be confusing until you're sure of your way. The many entrances to each shop or restaurant, and the often angular and irregular placement and architecture of many of the buildings, don't always help orientation. To get the most out of your experience in the Magic Kingdom, it's essential to understand the organization *before* arriving.

The following paragraph offers a basic description of what's where. But a major expansion during the next ten years will significantly change the size and breadth of Disneyland. New attractions planned for the so-called "Disney Decade" include Mickey's Starland and a completely redesigned Tomorrowland.

For now, there are seven sections, or "lands," in the Magic Kingdom—Main Street, U.S.A.; Adventureland; Frontierland; New Orleans Square; Critter Country; Fantasyland; and Tomorrowland. The area just inside the main gate is known as Town Square; that in front of Sleeping Beauty Castle is known as the Central Plaza, or, more aptly, the Hub. From it, avenues extend into the various lands like spokes of a wheel. The first bridge to your left as you face the Castle takes you to Adventureland; the next, to Frontierland and New Orleans Square. To your right, the first walkway leads to Tomorrowland, and the next—known as Matterhorn Way—goes directly into Fantasyland. If you cross the Castle's moat and walk through the archway, you'll also end up in Fantasyland. Critter Country occupies its own cul-de-sac extending from New Orleans Square. In addition, connecting the spokes of the wheel to each other are a number of avenues around the perimeter. The Big Thunder Trail connects Frontierland and Fantasyland. Another meandering walkway links Tomorrowland and Fantasyland. The Disneyland Railroad circles the outer edge of the park, just inside the berm that insulates Disneyland from the rest of the world.

A glance at the park maps in this book and inside the front cover of the Disneyland Souvenir Guide (available at no charge at City Hall in Town Square and at Carefree Corner on Main Street) will help clarify Disneyland's layout.

A note on north, south, east, and west: When you stand at the Magic Kingdom entrance and face Sleeping Beauty Castle, you're looking north. Main Street is straight ahead, with Fantasyland beyond the Castle. Adventureland, Frontierland, New Orleans Square, and Critter Country are all to the west. Tomorrowland lies to the east.

MAIN STREET, U.S.A.

This pretty thoroughfare represents Main Street at the turn of the century—you know, life in "the good old days." Instead of the traffic, blasting horns, and garish commercial buildings found on so many American small-town Main Streets nowadays, Disneyland's version offers the gentle clip-clop of horse hooves on pavement, the melodic ringing of streetcar bells, and nostalgic old tunes like "Bicycle Built for Two" and "Old Gray Mare." There are the sounds of brass bands, barbershop quartets, and ragtime piano. An old-fashioned steam train huffs into a handsome brick depot as elaborately embellished with frills and furbelows as a Victorian wedding gown. And an array of picturesque buildings with mansard roofs, dormer windows, and wrought-iron accents lines the street. The gaslights flicker once more at sundown in the ornate lampposts lining the walkways, and the storefronts, painted in all the pastels a sophisticated palette might offer, couldn't be more inviting. The buildings are not scaled to ⅝ size as is commonly supposed. The first floor is ⅞ scale, the second story is ⅝, and the third is half-size. The dimensions of the whole are small enough that the place seems intimate and comforting, and the proportions appear correct. (The same technique, a set designer's device known as forced perspective, is also used to make the Matterhorn and Sleeping Beauty Castle seem taller than they actually are.)

Although there are only a few specific attractions along Main Street, and they're not as compelling as some of those in the other lands, there's hardly a guest who passes through the entrance tunnels who doesn't find something of interest in at least one of the shops. Few can manage to stroll the entire avenue without lingering over some treasure.

Maintenance and housekeeping are superb, both inside and out. White-suited custodians whisk stray candy wrappers into dustpans at remarkable speed, and shovel up droppings from the horse-drawn streetcar just as quickly. The pavement here, like that in the rest of the park, is washed down with high-pressure hoses every night (a 5½-hour job). There also are Disneyland staffers whose job it is to scrape up every bit of squished gum. The sole job of one crew is to change the tiny white lights that edge every roofline, while another spends its time painting woodwork. Another keeps the brass door handles gleaming, and another keeps the window sills dusted. Still another crew—three workers in all—washes windows. The horse-shaped hitching posts, which one youngster once mistook for funny-looking parking meters, are touched up daily and get a complete sanding, wash-down, and new coat of paint about once a month. Even professional painters never fail to marvel at the quality of the work they see at Disneyland.

The landscaping also is outstanding, since this section of the park boasts more flowering annuals than any other. First there's the showy mouse face at the entrance, which just happens to be one of the most-photographed spots in the park. *Zoysia tenuifolia* (variety emerald) gives the carpet effect around the park perimeter. Pansies, petunias, and snapdragons brighten the scenery elsewhere. In

winter, some 6,000 poinsettias splash the townscape with scarlet, while in spring the Central Plaza blossoms with tulips and Easter lilies. Veteran Disneyland visitors may note the absence of the big trees that once shaded the streets: These Chinese elms had grown so large and leggy over the years that they dwarfed the Castle and the shops along the avenue. After great debate they were replaced in late 1981 with West Coast live oaks, the same type found along Main Street in Walt Disney World's Magic Kingdom in Florida.

The trees in the Central Plaza have been kept for the shade they provide—particularly great on a summer afternoon. The other interesting-looking trees there, and in Town Square, are Brazilian peppers—evergreens from South America that can take on a variety of moods depending on how they're pruned. Their gnarled-looking companions include olive trees nearly 70 years old; their blossoms are treated with a special spray to curtail the production of their potentially slippery, messy fruit.

While strolling down the street, be sure to see the window displays in the Emporium—elaborate, unusually animated, and usually related to the latest Disney movie release. Also note the names emblazoned on the second-floor windows. This was Walt Disney's way of acknowledging the contributions of the men from whom he had learned and with whom he had worked. Elias Disney, whose name can be seen above the door to the Emporium, was Walt's father. Wally Boag, identified nearby, played Pecos Bill and the traveling salesman in Frontierland's Golden Horseshoe Revue (now the Golden Horseshoe Jamboree) for more than two decades until his retirement in 1982. Above the New Century Jewelry Shop, there's the name of Gunther Lessing. He was the head of the Walt Disney Company's legal department for many years and was noted for having been Pancho Villa's lawyer. Bruce Bushman, whose name can be seen nearby, helped design the Mr. Toad cars and worked closely on the King Arthur Carrousel, among other attractions. Ken Anderson, an art director for the film *Snow White*, was a key figure in the design of the Haunted Mansion, Storybook Land, and the original Fantasyland. In the earliest stages of the park's development, he was kept on Walt's personal payroll solely to sketch ideas. Edward T. Meck, who was editor-in-chief of *Disneyland News*, was an early Disneyland publicity director. Emile Kuri, honored above the Market House, was another longtime art and set designer. He was responsible for designing Below Decks at Frontierland's *Columbia* and was Walt's own interior decorator. The names around the Carefree Corner are those of Herbert Ryman, who drew the first overall plan for the park, and of art directors John Hench and Peter Ellenshaw.

Now, some advice: Before you head toward Sleeping Beauty Castle, stop at the information desk at Carefree Corner and find out when and where you'll be able to catch up with the singers and musicians who perform all over the park. Schedule your time and direction to intersect with them wherever possible. Do your shopping in the

morning or early afternoon, rather than at the end of the day when stores are so mobbed you can't really enjoy looking at the merchandise. You can store your purchases in the lockers located at the Lost and Found (halfway down Main Street, behind Market House, next to the *Cone Shop*), and just outside the main entrance (to the right when leaving the park). Have your hand stamped on the way out, hold onto your Passport and you'll be able to re-enter freely on the same day.

The following Main Street attractions are listed in the order in which you'll encounter them while walking from the Main Entrance to the Central Plaza and Sleeping Beauty Castle.

DISNEYLAND RAILROAD: The four narrow-gauge steam trains circle the park through Adventureland, New Orleans Square, Critter Country, Frontierland, Fantasyland, and Tomorrowland. Walt Disney so loved trains that he actually built a ⅛-scale model, the Carolwood Pacific, in the backyard of his Carolwood Drive estate in Holmby Hills. Not only did he relocate power lines in the process, but he surrounded his track with a berm (covered with special shrubbery) so he wouldn't disturb his neighbors.

It was only natural that Disney's park should include at least one railroad. The only question was how big it should be—this was easily calculated after it was determined that the cars needed six-foot doors. The four locomotives now serving the line are enough alike that it's easy to think they're identical. But according to the engineers, each has its own personality, its own sound, and its own feel. And each has its own history. Both the *C. K. Holliday* and the *E. P. Ripley*—the original pair, named for the founder of the venerable Santa Fe Railroad and an early president—were designed and assembled at Walt Disney Studios, using parts from outside contractors. Both are classed as 2-2-0 locomotives—that is, they have 2 wheels on each side, 2 drivers, and no tender or trailing truck. The *C. K.* has a diamond stack, the kind of smokestack found in the mid-19th century on the first transcontinental locomotives. The *E. P.*, modeled on more recent engines, has a capstack.

In 1958 a third engine, the *Fred G. Gurley*, was added. Named for the man who was chairman of the Santa Fe Railroad board at the time, the locomotive was built by the Baldwin Locomotive Works in 1894, and once hauled sugarcane from 3 plantations over the Lafourete Raceland and Longport Railway to shipping docks in New Orleans. After its purchase, it was completely rebuilt using parts from the original locomotive. It is a 1-2-2—that is, on each side it has 1 wheel in front, 2 drivers, and 2 wheels under the tender.

The fourth of the quartet—purchased in 1959 and named for Ernest S. Marsh, the Santa Fe's president at that time—was originally built in 1925, also by the Baldwin Works, and had been used at a lumber mill in New England. All of these iron horses are powered by oil-fueled steam boilers and have to stop several times a day to take on water. The engineers and the firemen have to keep constant watch on the gauges, keep the fires up, and watch the water levels. All the cars the locomotives pull are open-air. The original passenger train has been stored away for the last few years, since the small-windowed cars—reproductions of those used around 1890—offered only a limited view of the Grand Canyon Diorama and the Primeval World attractions. What remains of this train today is the *Lilly Belle*, the erstwhile observation car, which has been transformed into a sumptuous VIP caboose complete with live palms, silk roses, brass fixtures, stained-glass skylights, elaborate woodwork, and chairs and a settee upholstered in burgundy velvet.

The Grand Canyon Diorama and Primeval World: Taking his guests through jungles (in Adventureland), a gracious city (New Orleans Square), Northwestern-type pine woods (in Critter Country), a deciduous forest that resembles those in the Midwest (Frontierland), the Neverland that is Fantasyland, and the sleek world of Tomorrowland wasn't enough for Walt Disney, so he added the Grand Canyon, a $435,000 diorama that depicts this natural wonder as it appears from its South Rim. Measuring 306 feet in length and 34 feet in height, and done on a special seamless, handwoven canvas, the whole project took about 4,800 hours to complete and required 300 gallons of paint. Deer, a mountain lion, a golden eagle, wild turkeys, skunks, porcupines, desert mountain sheep (all showing off the fine art of taxidermy), quaking aspens, and piñon and ponderosa pines (also real and treated with preservatives), plus a snowfall, a storm, a sunset, and a rainbow make up the scenery. The music is the "On the Trail" section of Ferde Grofé's *Grand Canyon Suite*.

The Primeval World diorama, opened in 1966 after an interim stop at the Ford Pavilion at the New York World's Fair, consists of a series of misty swamps, deserts, rain forests, and erupting volcanoes inspired by the 1940 film *Fantasia*. In this diorama, the Audio-Animatronics process brings to life some 46 prehistoric creatures: a pair of edaphosauruses (the fin-backed dinosaurs munching tropical vegetation and shellfish seen early in the trip); a brontosaurus (the creature breakfasting on water plants in a shallow lake nearby); pteranodons (the vulture-like creatures perching atop rugged cliffs not far away); triceratops (the horned dinosaurs watching their young hatch from eggs in the next scene); ornithomimuses (the "ostrich dinosaurs" gathered around a watering hole in the desert layout); a stegosaurus (an armored sort of dinosaur); and a tyrannosaurus (the fierce one that is 22 feet high, who is clawing and growling at the stegosaurus).

Where to board: Although the Disneyland Railroad makes stops in Frontierland, Fantasyland, and in Tomorrowland, lines are usually shortest at the Main Street station, a composite of the railroad depots that American travelers encountered at the turn of the century. The handcar on the spur track adjoining the station was a gift to Walt from the Kalamazoo Manufacturing Company of Kalamazoo, Michigan.

THE WALT DISNEY STORY FEATURING "GREAT MOMENTS WITH MR. LINCOLN": The theme of this attraction, housed in the Disneyland Opera House, is the life and accomplishments of Walt Disney. His formal and working offices are on display, along with considerable Mickey Mouse memorabilia and a number of letters from such notables as Joseph Kennedy, Mary Pickford, Dwight D. Eisenhower, and Richard Nixon.

The real star of the show, however, is the Audio-Animatronics version of our 16th president, which is the most technologically advanced figure of its kind. After a brief slide show depicting the Civil War, Mr. Lincoln stands up and discourses on liberty, the American spirit, the dangers facing the country, respect for law, faith in Divine Providence, and duty. All the while, he's nodding and gesturing, turning, and shifting his weight in a realistic fashion.

The Lincoln figure in the show was completely reprogrammed in December 1984, following a jointly funded, three-year research project at the University of Utah. The university, a leader in the development of artificial limbs, was consulted by the Disney organization in its ongoing interest in improving the realism of the movements of Audio-Animatronics figures. The result—the Compliance System—allows Lincoln to shift his body weight as naturally as a human and enables him to sense when he is near another object. Incidentally, the speech is composed of excerpts from talks that Lincoln actually delivered—in Baltimore at the Sanitary Fair (April 18, 1864); in Edwardsville, Illinois (September 11, 1858); in Springfield, Illinois, for the Young Men's Lyceum (January 27, 1838); in a eulogy honoring Henry Clay (July 6, 1852); and at New York City's Cooper Institute (February 27, 1860).

The Fifth Freedom Mural: Measuring 53 feet in width and 5½ feet in height, this oil painting in the exit hallway of the Walt Disney Story portrays likenesses and vignettes of the contributions of Alexander Graham Bell, Thomas Edison, iron-and-steel magnate Andrew Carnegie, Wilbur and Orville Wright, Henry Ford, Pulitzer Prize-winning novelist Pearl Buck, agricultural chemist and educator George Washington Carver, communications executive David Sarnoff, rocket propulsion pioneer Robert H. Goddard, Albert Einstein, and Walt Disney—all of whom rose to greatness through the free enterprise system, the "fifth freedom" to which the mural's name refers. The first 4 freedoms—freedom of speech, freedom of worship, freedom from want, and freedom from fear—were described in a 1941 speech by President Franklin D. Roosevelt. The fifth freedom was highlighted in one of Lincoln's own addresses: "I believe each individual is naturally entitled to do as he pleases with himself and the fruit of his labor so far as it in no wise interferes with any other man's rights." This quote is reproduced on a brass plaque on the pillar in the middle of the room.

MAIN STREET VEHICLES: Main Street, U.S.A., wouldn't be Main Street without its motorized fire wagon, its horseless carriages, and its horse-drawn streetcars—Disneyland's main thoroughfare bustles with them all day long. The motorized fire engine—which, like all the vehicles, was designed and built by the Disney organization—is modeled after those that might have been found on an American Main Street around the turn of the century, except that there are seats where the hose would have been carried. The bell, acquired after an extensive search, is authentic.

As for the streetcars, they are modeled after those in 19th-century photographs. Each carries 30 passengers. A double track halfway down its 1,800-foot-long route, and circular tracks at each end permit cars to pass each other. Most of the horses that pull them are Belgians, characterized by their white manes and tails and lightly feathered legs. They wear shoes coated with polyurethane to give them better traction (it also helps make a neat clip-clop sound as they travel from one end of Main Street to the other). The farrier comes

every week to trim their hooves and see to their shoes. The animals work four-hour shifts, four times a week.

MAIN STREET CINEMA: Ironically, one of the very best things about this prominent Main Street attraction is that most visitors rush right by it on their way to Tomorrowland's Star Tours and Space Mountain, Frontierland's Big Thunder Mountain Railroad, and the other well-known and

most popular thrill-a-minute shows and attractions. This traffic flow headed off to other diversions means that the movie house is never very crowded—even though it's blissfully dark and blessedly air conditioned—making it one of the perfect places to rest and regroup on a scalding summer afternoon in Southern California.

There's more here than cool air, however, since six short, silent film cartoon classics play continuously. Remember, these are the original animated cinema attractions that founded Mickey's monumental reputation—even though he wasn't even named Mickey at the start. Everything that contemporary folks think about when the name "Disney" is mentioned began with these short subjects. The specific historic cartoon films change from time to time. At present the sextet of cinematic showings includes *Plane Crazy*, *Mickey's Polo Team*, *The Moose Hunt*, *Traffic Trouble*, and *Dog Napper*, in addition to the father of them all, *Steamboat Willie*, the early talkie that introduced a spindly-legged little mouse. The scene in which this Disney-drawn, musically inclined mouse plays "Turkey in the Straw" on a pig's udder drew one of the film's biggest laughs at its November, 1928, release. For film historians and modern moviegoers alike, this is a must.

PENNY ARCADE: Even that Cadillac among arcades—Tomorrowland's blipping, bleeping, and squeaking Starcade—is no match for this turn-of-the-century version with its blinking chaser lights. Among the quainter of the antique amusements found here are the World Soccer mechanical football game, the recently restored Kentucky Derby, and the Electric Shock (circa 1920), which delivers a reduced version of the jolt with which the brave were zapped before Disney engineers modified the mechanisms. The Uncle Sam strength test used to bear the picture of a scantily clad female, but the arcade wizards took care of that one, too. The funniest is the one with the Egyptian theme, to the left as you face the large band organ at the arcade's entrance, and the best surprises are the vibrating machines—a Massage-o-Matic chair, often found in old penny arcades and along boardwalks, and the early 1940s Vibrant Foot-Ease, which sets the body to tingling from feet to eyeballs when a dime is deposited.

In general, the machines closest to the street cost a penny and date from 1900 to 1920, while those in the rear of the room to the left date from 1920 to the present. Occupying center stage in the street area of the arcade are the Mutascopes and the Cail-o-Scopes. The former, first introduced around 1900, require a penny and feature hand-cranked moving pictures such as *Miracle Rider*, in which Tom Mix is shot off his horse by a truck driver; the *Absent-Minded Janitor*, which depicts a balletic Charlie Chaplin, an artist, and a pretty dancing model; *Outlaws' Getaway*, featuring a gun battle and an ambush; *In the Bag*, an exercise in animation that conveys some impression of just how sophisticated the Main Street Cinema's *Steamboat Willie* really was; *Bounced on the Bean*, featuring Chaplin's Tramp as a

baker; *The New Sheriff*, a vignette featuring the lawman, the lawman's daughter, and the handsome bandito; more Chaplin, in *The Dough Fight*; *Stage Coach*, about an attempted abduction; still more Chaplin, in *Dizzy Racket*; and *Galloping Fury*, perhaps the best of all, in which the cowboy with the white hat gets the girl and gallops off into the sunset. The Cail-o-Scopes, which appeared about a decade after the Mutascopes, give a slightly three-dimensional picture that moves mechanically. All of them offer a few minutes' pleasant diversion, but some are really good. For example, there's the *Painless Dentist*, featuring a hammer, saw, pliers—and a very sorry young boy; *Big Beauty Buster*, starring Bull Montana, tells of a ruffian and a weakling boxer who is caught hiding a hammer in his glove; *Forbidden Sweets*, has a terrific sequence in which father catches son pigging out on a stolen pie and smashes it in his face; and *A Wee Bit O' Scotch*, in which a Playmate of yesteryear takes a nip.

While you're looking, you can be feeding dimes to the arcade's big music boxes. There are two. The Wurlitzer Orchestrion Style L, introduced around 1921 and probably used to entertain guests in a restaurant or speakeasy until the juke box came along in the 1930s, combines a piano with 38 violin pipes (21 of them first violins, plus 17 violas) and an equal number of flute pipes, orchestra bells, a bass drum, a snare drum, and a triangle. Purchased by Walt Disney in 1953, it occupied a place on the *Mark Twain* dock until 1973, when it was restored and moved to the Penny Arcade. The larger Welte Style 4 Concert Orchestrion, which has called the Penny Arcade home since 1955, was built around 1905 in the German city of Freiburg. Its more than 300 pipes, plus a triangle, bass drum, and cymbals, are activated by an electric motor developed around the turn of the century. Change for all these diversions is available in a booth at the rear of the arcade.

ADVENTURELAND

For someone who grew up in Marceline, Missouri, more than 85 years ago, the very idea of the Amazon and the South Seas must have seemed terribly exotic. So it's not surprising that when Walt Disney was planning his new park, he designated one segment—Adventureland—to telescope all the far-off and mysterious destinations of the armchair traveler's world into one compact area.

No single piece of architecture here comes directly from Polynesia, Southeast Asia, or the Caribbean, but every structure has a few characteristics of each of these areas, and travelers in Adventureland get a definite feeling of being in a place that's nowhere in particular, but is unquestionably exotic and undeniably foreign. The shops overflow with wares imported from the far corners of the globe, and the snack foods have a tropical flavor—pineapple spears, pineapple juice, and jungle juleps.

The landscaping is remarkable, even in this bastion of the landscape architect's art. Clustered around the base of the Swiss Family Treehouse are such diverse plant varieties as elephant ear, tree fern, the attractive pygmy date fern, and the centipede plant, which is native to the Solomon Islands. A New Zealand tree fern keeps company with bamboo from China, and white Brazilian rhubarbs—whose leaves sometimes measure as much as six feet across—consort with araliads from Mexico. *Philodendron evansii*, commonly known as split-leaf philodendron, was named for one of the brothers who did the park's original landscaping. The plants in the rest of Adventureland come in similar exotic varieties, and the botanically minded should have a field day trying to identify them all.

Attractions here are described as visitors encounter them when walking from east to west.

ENCHANTED TIKI ROOM: Introduced in 1963, this was the first of the Audio-Animatronics attractions and the precursor of more elaborate renditions (such as "Great Moments with Mr. Lincoln"). This 17-minute show functions in a vaguely Polynesian complex at the entrance to Adventureland, next door to the Tahitian Terrace, and is vintage Disney. Yet it's as fresh as ever, with its four emcees (José, Michael, Pierre, and Fritz), its sextet of pastel-plumed, long-eyelashed parrots (Collette, Fifi, Gigi, Josephine, Mimi, and Susette), and its chorus of 54 orchids, four carved wooden tiki poles, 12 tiki drummers, 24 singing masks, 64 bird-of-paradise flowers, 7 birds of paradise, 8 macaws, 12 toucans, 9 fork-tailed birds, 6 cockatoos, and several others. The 225 performers all sing and whistle and drum up a tropical storm with such animation that it's hard to resist a smile. The voice of Michael belongs to Fulton Burley, the former Irish tenor/proprietor at Frontierland's Golden Horseshoe. José is played by Wally Boag, another

Golden Horseshoe star, whose name careful observers have probably noted on the Main Street window above the *Carnation Ice Cream Parlor*. The music includes a special arrangement of the "Barcarole" from Jacques Offenbach's opera *Tales of Hoffmann*; "In the Tiki, Tiki, Tiki Room," the show's theme song; "The Hawaiian War Chant"; "Let's All Sing"; and "Aloha to You." Presented by Dole Pineapple.

JUNGLE CRUISE: The spiel delivered by the skipper on this eight-minute adventure trip is not always quite as lively as it could be. After all, the average boatman does have to repeat the same jokes over and over again during his working day. But every once in a while, when your navigator turns out to be one of the handful of natural comics who do the job, the presentation can be genuinely funny. Incidentally, no less than former presidential press secretary Ron Ziegler once held his audiences captive in just such a way. As jungle cruises go, this one is as much like the real thing as Main Street, U.S.A., is like Marceline, Missouri—long on loveliness and very short on the visual distractions and minor annoyances that constitute most of the rest of human experience. There are no mosquitoes, no Montezuma's Revenge. And the Bengal tiger and the trio of king cobras at the ancient Cambodian ruins, the great apes, the gorillas, crocodiles, alligators, elephants, hippos, and lions in the water and along the shores represent no threat—though, according to maintenance crews, they're almost as much trouble as real ones.

Trivia buffs should note that Bob Mattey, who helped develop the creatures, also worked on the man-eating plants of many Tarzan movies, the giant squid from *20,000 Leagues Under the Sea*, and the mechanical shark in *Jaws*.

The large-leafed upright tree in the Cambodian ruins section of the attraction is a *Ficus religiosa*, an example of the tree under which the Buddha received enlightenment in India many centuries ago. Another specimen is located just outside the women's restroom in Adventureland.

Be sure to look for the hefty Canary Island date palm to the right as you approach the loading dock in the queue area. One of the few trees that Walt found on the property when it first came into his hands, it was planted in 1896 and had acquired so much sentimental value to the family that owned the land that they requested that it be preserved. Transplanted from its former location—which would have been just about in the center of the parking lot's Donald Duck section—it stands here today.

SWISS FAMILY TREEHOUSE: The Disney studios' 1960 film version of the 1813 Johann David Wyss classic novel, *The Swiss Family Robinson*, provided the inspiration for what must be one of the two best treehouses on earth (the other being this same attraction at Walt Disney World in Florida). It's well fitted out with real antiques (muskets, an 18th-century barometer, a ship's wheel and gimbal lights, and a sewing basket), and with an organ, beds, tables, and bookshelves built by Disney artisans. It even has running water in all the rooms—thanks to a waterwheel at the base of the tree, a rushing brook, and a series of bamboo buckets on pulleys capable of bringing up about 200 gallons an hour. "Everything we need right at our fingertips," was how John Mills, who played the father in the film, described the prototype for this arboreal home, which he and two of his three sons had built after the wreck of the *Titus* on its way to America. It's such an ingenious construction that it's not hard to understand why, several

adventures later when they got the chance to leave the island, all the family members except one son decided to stay on.

Unofficially christened *Disneyodendron semperflorens grandis* (that is, "large ever-blooming Disney tree"), the tree itself is another intriguing bit of Disney artifice. The 62 roots, which reach 42 feet into the ground, are made of concrete; the limbs, which extend 80 feet across, are of steel; and the more than 300,000 leaves, shaped like those of a banyan tree and hand-grafted onto 1,000 manzanita branches ranging in length from two to six feet, are pure plastic. The whole assemblage weighs some 150 tons (6 tons of it steel); used 110 cubic yards of concrete; and towers 70 feet in the air, high above the rest of Adventureland. Fluttering at the top—visible from almost everywhere in the park—is the Swiss national flag.

NEW ORLEANS SQUARE

Though New Orleans Square did not figure in the Disneyland layout until 1966, it's certainly among the park's most evocative areas. This would be true even if it were home only to the superb Haunted Mansion and Pirates of the Caribbean. But there's also its picturesque site on the shores of the Rivers of America, not to mention the architecture—a pastiche of wrought iron, pastel stucco, French doors, polished brass, shutters, and gleaming glass. Not to be missed are the pleasant open-air dining spots; the lovely *Blue Bayou* restaurant overlooking the romantic swamp section of the Pirates of the Caribbean; the assortment of shops, some of the best in the park; and the good music—performed by the Side Street Strutters, who play lively jazz and Dixieland, and the Royal Street Bachelors, who strum and tootle in the traditional New Orleans style. As you sit here on a summer evening and snack on fritters and hot chocolate, preconceptions of Disneyland-as-amusement-park tend to vanish altogether. Just as Main Street makes Disneyland a great place for shopping, New Orleans Square shows it off as a fine spot to spend a few relaxing hours, quite apart from the rides and attractions.

Those New Orleans Square attractions described below are listed as you encounter them when strolling from east to west.

PIRATES OF THE CARIBBEAN: The last attraction that Walt Disney worked on extensively himself, this boat trip through a series of sets portraying a pirate raid on a Caribbean village offers one of Disneyland's best adventures. But unlike the Walt Disney World version, which remains strangely uncrowded during the afternoons, the California incarnation attracts so many guests throughout the day that waits sometimes exceed an hour when the park is busy. If you're visiting during a peak period, stop here right after opening (or just before closing). The experience is well worth early rising. Beginning with a short cruise through a bayou where will-o'-the-wisps glow just above the grasses and fireflies twinkle nearby while stars spangle the twilight-blue sky overhead, the attention to detail nearly boggles the mind. There are flowerpots that explode and mend themselves—and a cast of 64 human figures and 55 animals: drunken pigs whose legs actually twitch in their soporific contentment, chickens so realistic that even a farmer might at first mistake them for the real thing, and a piccolo-playing pirate whose fingers move and cheeks puff as he toots out his little ditty. The keen-eyed will note the hairs on the leg of one swashbuckler perched atop a bridge overhead. The attraction's theme song, "Yo-Ho, Yo-Ho—a Pirate's Life for Me," manages to transform what is actually a picture of some fairly savage buccaneering into a great good time for all. A must—again and again.

HAUNTED MANSION: On a British radio interview, Walt Disney once explained how sorry he felt for those homeless ghosts whose hauntable mansions had fallen to the wrecker's ball. Feeling that they sorely needed a home, he offered this Haunted Mansion. It's unquestionably one of the park's very best attractions. From its stately portico to the exit corridor, special effect is piled upon special effect to create a mood that is eerie, but not quite terrifying. Judicious applications of paint and expert lighting heighten the shadows that play ghoulishly on the walls outside, and maintenance crews forswear the dusting and vacuuming that keep the other attractions looking so spiffy. The jumble of trunks and chairs and dress forms and other assorted knickknacks in the attic are always appropriately dirty. (Additional dust is purchased from a West Coast firm by the five-pound bagful, and is distributed by a device that looks something like a grass seeder. Extra cobwebs, which come in liquid form, are strung under the supervision of set-design experts who have more than once had occasion to rebuke the custodial workers for being too conscientious about their cleaning.) The eerie music and the slightly spooky tones of the Ghost Host often set very small children to whimpering as soon as their parents carry them through the door, and some members of the crews who work in the mansion at night find their nerves so taut they start at sudden noises. Nonetheless, any adult who expects to get the fright of his life may be in for a bit of a disappointment. What makes the attraction so special is the attention to, and abundance of, details—so many that it's next to impossible to take them all in during the first, or even the second, time around. In the Portrait Chamber (the room full of fearsome-looking gargoyles that adjoins the chandeliered and lace curtain-adorned foyer), it's fun to speculate on whether the ceiling moves up or the room goes down; it's one way here and the opposite way at the mansion's Walt Disney World counterpart. Once in your Doom Buggy, look for the raven that appears again and again as you go through the house, the bats' eyes on the wallpaper, the TOMB SWEET TOMB plaque, and the rattling suit of armor in the Corridor of Doors. Then there are the dead plants and flowers and broken glass in the Conservatory, where a hand reaches out of a half-open casket, the terrified cemetery watchman (and his mangy mutt) in the Graveyard, the ghostly teapot that pours ghostly tea, the ectoplasmic king and queen on the teeter-totter, the bicycle-riding spirits, the transparent musicians, and the headless knight and his supernatural Brunhilde. Nice stuff all.

The mansion was constructed in 1963, based on studies of houses around Baltimore; the attraction inside opened in 1969 and cost $7 million. "Grim Grinning Ghosts," composed especially for the Haunted Mansion, is the name of the music. The voice of the Ghost Host belongs to veteran radio actor Paul Frees.

With Big Thunder Mountain punctuating the skyline to the north and the Rivers of America lapping at its shore, rural Frontierland telescopes the lands that the pioneers knew as they pushed westward. It highlights such rough wilderness outposts as Forts Pitt and Defiance, shows off life on the Mississippi as Tom Sawyer might have known it, confronts the dangers of hostile Indians, and marvels at the dense forests that early Americans took for granted. Hosts and hostesses wear denims, long skirts, and other period togs; security hosts dress like the cavalrymen in the old *Rin Tin Tin* television series. Shops, restaurants, and attractions are walled in with unpainted barn siding, stone, or adobe. The rattly wooden sidewalks that have been a part of almost every American's image of life in the West are outside. The sights here are just about as pleasant as they come at Disneyland. And that's especially true in the afternoon, when the riverboat *Mark Twain*—looking a bit like an oversize wedding cake with its elaborate wooden lacework trim—pulls majestically away from its dock for a cruise along the clay-bottomed Rivers of America.

Be sure to note the landscaping. Near the *Mark Twain* dock, the bougainvillea "tree" is actually the skeleton of an Australian tea tree (*Leptospermum laevigatum*) entwined with the branches of a nearby real bougainvillea. In front of *River Belle Terrace* there's an immense old rubber tree. A gift of a major oil company, it had a good-size fuel-carrying pipe embedded in its root system. When it was transplanted, the oil company had to shut down its operations temporarily and lay a new pipe section around the roots so the Disney gardeners could cut the old pipe and move the tree—which to this day grows around that section of pipe.

The following Frontierland attractions are discussed in the order in which visitors come upon them while moving westward from the Central Plaza gateway toward Big Thunder Mountain.

DAVY CROCKETT PIONEER MERCANTILE: Primarily a merchandising location, this area near the entrance to Frontierland also boasts an eight-gun electronic shooting arcade on the left wall as you enter, near the leather bags. Adults intent on the attractive wares for sale here sometimes miss it altogether, but kids seldom fail to notice it.

FRONTIERLAND SHOOTIN' ARCADE: Following its 1985 renovation, the spanking-new shooting gallery is now completely electronic. The 18 rifles fire infrared beams which, if they strike the red reactive targets, trigger humorous results. The arcade is set in an 1850s town in the Southwest Territory. Gun positions overlook Boothill, a town complete with bank, jail, hotel, and stables. Hit the jail target and the cell door opens, freeing the prisoner; a strike at the "Boothill" sign causes it to read FOR SALE; zero in on the mine entrance and an ore cart races out one side and back in the other. The toughest target is the moving shovel which, when struck, causes a skeleton to pop out of a grave. Note that Disneyland Passports do *not* include use of the arcade. Cost: 50¢ for 20 shots.

GOLDEN HORSESHOE JAMBOREE: A half-hour show at the *Golden Horseshoe Saloon* stars Miss Lily Langtree; three vivacious and savvy young women in search of stardom; Sam, the saloon's owner, bartender, and chief cook and bottle washer; and his three cowboys. Miss Lily is in love with Sam, but won't admit it; and Sam is wild about Lily. She belts out a few fine songs, and her troupe of three shines brightest in the can-can number. There's a dance competition between Sam's boys and Lily's girls, and some amusing audience-participation sequences, including one in which Sam calls upon two assistants to do sound effects for a rendition of "Old MacDonald Had a Farm." Walt Disney had his own private box, the one just to the left of the stage. The hall itself, said to have been inspired by a *Golden Horseshoe Saloon* that once flourished in New York City, is lovely, with its polished floors, a long brass railing, chandeliers, and western paintings.

There are usually five shows daily, but performance times change throughout the year, so check on show times when you arrive at the park. Also, there are usually twice-weekly evening performances during the busy summer season. Reservations are required, and they must be made in person on the day of the performance. Since they are accepted on a first-come, first-served basis only, it's important to present yourself at the hall to claim one shortly after park opening. If you don't have a reservation, you can queue up for cancellations by arriving at the door at least 45 minutes before show time. Cold sandwiches and soft drinks are served here, making it a good spot for lunch.

BIG THUNDER MOUNTAIN RAILROAD: As roller coasters go, this one is relatively tame. It's short on the kind of steep climbs and precipitous drops that put hearts in throats and make stomachs protest, but long on tight curves that provoke squeals of glee and delighted laughs. The big deal on this ride is not the speed, however, or the thrills, but the scenery along the way—a pitch-black bat cave, giant stalactites and stalagmites, a waterfall, a canyon inhabited by coyotes, a natural-arch bridge that affords fine views over the Big

Thunder landscape, mine walls ready to cave in, and the quaint mining town.

The show is almost the equal of New Orleans Square's Pirates of the Caribbean, though you might think it's even better because it starts in the queue area. There, in the aforementioned community—which boasts two hotels, a newspaper, and a dance hall, in addition to its saloon and general store—life goes on usually in full view. If you listen closely, you'll hear a local barmaid flirting with a miner to the accompaniment of such songs as "Red River Valley" and "Listen to the Mockingbird." As you proceed toward the loading area, the walls on either side are made of about a hundred tons of real gold ore from Rosamond, California—brownish-colored stone that sold for around $80 a ton when the attraction was built, and purplish rocks that cost $120 a ton. The Silver Queen Mine (in the same former mining center) also yielded a real, ten-foot-tall stamp mill designated BIG THUNDER MINE 1880—rare because most are about twice the size. At the time it was spotted by the Disney scouts, it was owned by 4 partners, each of whom had to be contacted before the sale could go through. In the loading area, there's a single-bore compressor engine that really works, from Tonopah, Nevada. Elsewhere around the attraction, there's a scattering of corrugated tin, most of it found on the roofs of mining shacks in the Southwest. The steam engine that sits just below the town was used in the 1978 Disney feature film, *Hot Lead, Cold Feet*, which starred Don Knotts, Jim Dale, Karen Valentine, Darren McGavin, and Jack Elam. The Pat Burke identified on one of the packing crates helped scour the swap meets, abandoned mines, and even museums in Colorado, Minnesota, Nevada, and Wyoming, where the thousands of dollars worth of authentic mining equipment in the queue area (and the attraction itself) was located. In addition to the stamp mill and the compressor, there's also a 1,200-pound cogwheel once used to break down the ores; an ore car that once hauled gold in Nevada (seen here at the commencement of the earthquake scene); a 400-pound ore bucket; a drill press powered by hand; and a huge winch motor from Tonopah, Nevada (that's the machine that looks as if it's hauling the train up the second lift.

As for the mountain itself, it is entirely Disney-made, composed of steel and cement by the ton and of paint by the thousands of gallons—3,000 to 4,000 gallons, to be more exact. It was built by a crew of diversely skilled rock makers, who layered cement and paint, threw stones on the product, kicked dirt at it, and banged on it with sticks and picks to realize the designs of art director Tony Baxter, the former Tomorrowland-attractions host who is also responsible for much of Fantasyland's new look. Inspired by Utah's Bryce Canyon and named in reference to an old Indian legend about a certain sacred mountain in Wyoming that would thunder whenever white men took out its gold, the mountain required seven years of planning, two of them spent on actual construction, and cost some $16 million—almost as much as all of Disneyland in 1955. The painting of the 9½ acres of rock surface was done under the supervision of Bob Jolly, whose other credits include sets for the films *The King and I*, *South Pacific*, *The Diary of Anne Frank*, and *The Greatest Story Ever Told*.

Incidentally, while the ride itself is similar in many respects to the one offered at Walt Disney World's Big Thunder Mountain Railroad, there are several small differences both inside and out. In Walt Disney World's Magic Kingdom, for instance, you won't find the wonderfully scenic queue area that prefaces the ride here. But the Florida mountain is much larger, rising to a height of 197 feet, in keeping with the larger scale of that park. Also, instead of the handsome little mining town that greets passengers at the end of Disneyland's trip, WDW's Big Thunder Mountain Railroad riders have a flooded mining town full of real-looking chickens, donkeys, a rainmaker, and a sinking saloon, midway through the trip.

A sign warns that pregnant women and guests who suffer from heart conditions, motion sickness, weak backs, and other limitations are not permitted to ride. Children must be at least three years old and at least 40 inches tall to board. Children under seven must be accompanied by an adult.

About your timing: Since this is a very popular ride, try to visit first thing in the morning, during a parade, or just before park closing, when the lines are shorter. For the best of both worlds, ride twice—once by day, when you can see the scenery much better, and again after dark, when there's the added pleasure of hurtling through the cool night.

BIG THUNDER RANCH: A re-creation of a late 1880s working horse ranch wouldn't be complete without a ranch house, farrier shop, pasture area, and petting barnyard. Skilled craftsmen make harnesses and shoe horses right in front of guests. The pasture area showcases the award-winning Disney draft horses. This spot offers one of the most unusual souvenirs available anywhere, through the "Adopt-A-Burro" program. There is also a banjo player, a fiddler, or a storyteller on hand to entertain.

MARK TWAIN STEAMBOAT: One of the original Disneyland attractions and the first paddle wheeler built in the United States in half a century, this

150-ton, 105-foot-long, ⅝-scale vessel, with its nine-ton paddle wheel, circumnavigates Tom Sawyer Island. It passes by *River Belle Terrace*, the Royal Street Veranda, the docks for the Mike Fink Keel Boats and the Tom Sawyer Island Rafts, and piney Critter Country, and takes in a waterfall and an abandoned railroad track (which old Disneyland hands will remember as part of the Mine Train Thru Nature's Wonderland attraction, lately superseded by Big Thunder Mountain), plus moose, elk, Indians, the burning cabin of a moonshiner, and lovely dense woods full of the alders, cottonwoods, maples, and willows that might have been found along the Missouri frontier more than a century ago. Wild European iris and southern rose mallows, some with blooms eight inches across, line the shores, and ducks can be seen preening themselves and chasing each other through the water along the way.

All in all, the ride is more pleasant than thrilling—but it does provide a respite from the crowds on a busy day—especially when there are musical performers aboard. And if you manage to get one of the few chairs in the bow, the *Mark Twain* also offers a golden opportunity to put your feet up.

The ducks are real; the other animals come to Disneyland thanks in part to the efforts of Bob Mattey, who also helped design the creatures that haunt the jungle rivers in Adventureland. The flag that flies atop the stern of the *Mark Twain* has 34 stars and 13 stripes—a design that dates from the mid-19th century.

The hull of the paddle wheeler was built at Todd Shipyards in San Pedro, the superstructure at Walt Disney Studios. Constructed in sections and then dismantled, it was shipped over the freeways in pieces and then reassembled at Disneyland.

Flags on the *Mark Twain* dock: It's always fun to pick out the eight flags that fly above this Frontierland landing. The John Cabot Flag, the first flown over the American mainland as the *Constant* brought settlers to Jamestown in 1607 and the *Mayflower* transported the Pilgrims to Plymouth 13 years later, bears the red cross of St. George (an *X*) on a white field. The King's Colors Flag, the one that flew over the Colonies for more than a century, superimposes England's red cross of St. George on Scotland's white cross of St. Andrew (a plus sign) on a blue background. The Continental Flag, carried at the Battle of Bunker Hill, is red with a green pine tree on a white field in the upper corner. The Pine Tree Flag, carried by the American navy when it amounted to a mere six ships, bears a green pine tree and the words AN APPEAL TO HEAVEN in black on a white field. The Grand Union Flag, which General Washington raised at Cambridge in 1776, has 13 stripes and, in the upper corner, the red cross of St. George and the white cross of St. Andrew on a blue field. The Betsy Ross Flag, adopted by the Continental Congress in 1777, has the same 13 red and white stripes, but in the upper corner, representing the new constellation of states rising in the sky, a circle of 13 stars shines on a blue field. The Star-Spangled Banner, the flag that inspired the words of the national anthem, has 15 stars and 15

stripes. And, finally, there's Old Glory with its 13 red and white stripes and 24 stars. Adopted in 1818, it was named in 1831 by a young Salem, Massachusetts, sea captain. Labels identifying the flags can be found on the flagpoles.

SAILING SHIP *COLUMBIA*: Though operating only on very busy days, this full-scale replica of the ten-gun, three-masted "Gem of the Ocean," the first American craft to circumnavigate the globe, is an imposing sight towering majestically over the treetops at Fowler's Harbor, opposite the Haunted Mansion, where she is usually moored. The original ship, a 212-ton merchant vessel registered as the *Columbia Rediviva*, was constructed in Plymouth, Massachusetts, in 1787, at a cost of $50,000. Her maiden voyage, which began on September 30, 1787, took her around Cape Horn and into Nootka Sound, just off the coast of what is now Vancouver, British Columbia. On this trip, her first captain, later dismissed, cheated the ship's owners, tried to shortchange Nootka Indians from Oregon to Alaska in the fur trade, and, before sailing for China, mounted armed raiding parties to slip ashore at night and steal Indian furs to trade later for china, teak chests, spices, and tea. During her second voyage, made under the command of Captain Robert Gray, the Columbia River was discovered and became the vessel's namesake; her owners' names are still attached to many small harbors and coves along the river's shores. English and Russian ships, which had been trading furs in the Northwest for several years before this, had thought that the river's mouth was only a cove and never attempted to cross the sandbar that blocked the mouth. So when the *Columbia* sailed into the river, natives turned out by the hundreds to gaze at her in wonder, as Gray reported in his log. Under other captains, the *Columbia* made other fur-trading trips before she eventually disappeared "somewhere in the Orient" without a trace. (Some legends say that a crew member took her over and made her a pirate ship.) The only picture of the ship is a steel engraving in the Massachusetts Historical Society's *Voyages of the Columbia*, and it was this document, supplemented by research in the Library of Congress and in ports along the Massachusetts coast, that inspired the designs for Disneyland's ship. Some of it was built in a dry dock adjoining the Rivers of America, and completed in a yard representative of an 18th-century New England shipyard, using, in part, antique tools of the period. Measuring 110 feet from stem to stern, 83 feet 6 inches along the deck, and 27 feet 3 inches across the beam, with an 84-foot mainmast, she was the first ship of her kind to be built in more than a century and had cost about $300,000 by the time of her dedication on June 14, 1958. She has a steel hull, a deck planked with Douglas fir, and stays, shrouds, and ratlines made of steel-wire rope wrapped with Manila. During an eight-week renovation in 1984, the ship was completely rerigged and redecked. The work crew was the very same one that had built the *Columbia* 29 years before. Since most of the work was done during Disneyland's operating hours, crew members wore sailor costumes so as not to upset the overall feeling at Frontierland.

Below Decks: This maritime museum (opened in 1964), on view whenever the *Columbia* is operating, illustrates the way sailors lived on the original vessel during its later voyages, as reported in the ship's log and in letters between the owners and the captain. Emile Kuri, once chief art director for Walt Disney Studios and Walt Disney's personal interior decorator, was in charge of set decoration. (This attraction operates only during busy periods.)

TOM SAWYER ISLAND: Disneyland is home to what must be two of the three best treehouses on earth—the Swiss Family Treehouse in Adventureland and Tom and Huck's Treehouse, atop Indian Hill on Tom Sawyer Island, the landfall that the *Mark Twain*, the *Columbia*, the *Gullywhumper*, the *Bertha Mae*, and Davy Crockett's Explorer Canoes circle as they ply the Rivers of America. Once the highest point in Disneyland, this is the archetypal treehouse, right down to the spyglasses and peepholes that let visitors see out over the treetops to the *Mark Twain* dock across the river. The treehouse is only one of the wonders on this island planted with sweet gums and southern red cedars, Carolina cherry, sycamores, live oak, honeysuckle, and blackberry bushes. There's the Suspension Bridge, which heaves and bounces wildly enough to make a weak stomach churn, and the Barrel Bridge, where it's nearly impossible to maintain a stride more decorous than a lurch. (The more energetic have occasionally been known to fall in.) Near the Suspension Bridge, there's a small hill studded with log steps up which kids like to scramble. And then there's Castle Rock Ridge, a fantastic group of boulders that includes the mightily spinning Merry-Go-Round Rock; the aptly named Teeter-Totter Rock; and inside the Ridge, the spacious Pirate's Den and the smaller Castle Dungeon, full of niches and cul-de-sacs just the right size for a six-year-old, but so narrow and low-ceilinged in places that grown-ups who don't bend double or turn sideways risk getting stuck, just like Pooh Bear. Even cooler, darker, and spookier than either of these, though, is the labyrinthine Injun Joe's Cave, one of the very best spots on the island. At the landfall's southernmost extremity, not far from its entrance, there's the perpetually creaking Old Mill. Then, at the island's opposite end, there's Fort Wilderness, where there are air rifles (free), which make lots of noise but emit no bullets, and statues of a buckskin-clad Davy Crockett and George Russel that look for all the world like Fess Parker and Buddy Ebsen, who acted the parts of those historical figures on the old *Disneyland* show. In this scene they're conferring with Andy Jackson, who was played by Basil Ruysdael on the same show. The flag that flutters above the fort is the same 15-star, 15-stripe model that inspired Francis Scott Key at Fort McHenry in 1814.

There are small signs pointing to all of these landmarks on the island. Even though the footpaths are decidedly well trodden, the time spent on Tom Sawyer Island always seems like an adventure and may well offer some of the happiest moments at Disneyland.

Be sure to see all the wonderful details: leather thongs that bind the split rails together to fence the landing for the rafts to Tom Sawyer Island; the wooden packing cases on the landings that punctuate the pathway along the east side of the island; and the trash bins, here designed to look like oversize logs. The names on the graves near Fort Wilderness are, for the most part, fictitious.

On the island, there are two sets of rest rooms—one set in Fort Wilderness, the other on the southeast corner near Injun Joe's Cave, opposite the mainland's *Mark Twain* dock. Snacks are available at the *Fort Wilderness Canteen*, in the Fort, and at the *Fishing Pier Snack Stand* near the second set of restrooms (open during holiday periods and in summer only). Note that the island closes at dusk.

MIKE FINK KEEL BOATS: Mike Fink, who lived from around 1770 until about 1823, was noted as a marksman and a fighter—and for telling such tall tales about his own life that he eventually became a sort of Paul Bunyan of flatboat life on America's rivers. One yarn, for instance, recounts the time that Fink, as part of a ceremony of friendship then common among keel boatmen, shot an apple off a companion's head and, when the man fell, was himself shot by the fellow's brother, who had been watching. This was very much to the later consternation of Fink's friend, who had only fainted in fright. The ride in the *Bertha Mae*—named for Davy Crockett's keel boat in Walt Disney's November 1955 television production of *Davy Crockett's Keel Boat Race*—and the *Gullywhumper*—named for Crockett's opponent's vessel—is not so colorful. But floating along the Rivers of America in these squat, oddly shaped craft does provide a close-up look at the river scenery not available from the larger, grander *Mark Twain* and *Columbia*. You probably wouldn't want to travel aboard all four on a single day, but a short cruise on one of the keel boats is an excellent choice. Incidentally, the best view is from the pair of seats on the bow and from those on the roof. This attraction operates only during Disneyland's busier periods, and closes at dusk.

CRITTER COUNTRY

Regular visitors to Disneyland will notice transformations, both large and small, in the park's northwestern territory. In 1972, this land debuted as Bear Country, the backwoods home of the perennially popular Country Bear Playhouse. During 1989, the bears were joined by foxes, frogs, geese, rabbits, crocodiles, and a fair number of the other critters who make up the Audio-Animatronics cast of Splash Mountain. To make these new neighbors feel welcome, the bears (and a handful of Disney Imagineers) have rechristened the area Critter Country.

A quick walk through the new premises will make it readily apparent how quickly the newcomers have settled in. Observant guests will spot scaled-down houses, lairs, and nests tucked into hillsides and along the river. Some of the neighborhood shops have new proprietors—the former Wilderness Outpost is now Crocodile Mercantile and the Indian Trading Post has become The Briar Patch. (Actually, the old Trading Post was one of the last remnants of 1950s Frontierland, way back when this section of the park was an Indian Village, complete with teepees and a ceremonial dance circle.)

Critter Country is still one of the most pleasant corners of Disneyland, bordering lush shady forests full of Aleppo, Canary Island, Monterey, and Italian stone pines, coast redwood, locusts, white birch, and evergreen elms.

Attractions are described according to their east-to-west locations.

SPLASH MOUNTAIN: Disneyland's mountain range of thrill rides—Matterhorn Mountain, Space Mountain, and Big Thunder Mountain—has a new peak, Splash Mountain.

Unlike the preceding attractions, however, in which passengers ride roller-coaster style cars down tubular steel tracks, Splash Mountain, as its name implies, takes visitors on a waterborne journey through backwoods swamps and bayous, down waterfalls and, finally, over the top of a steep spillway, hurtling them from the peak of the mountain to a briar-filled pond five stories below.

Splash Mountain is based on the animated sequences in Walt Disney's 1946 film, *Song of the South*. The principal characters from the movie—Brer Rabbit, Brer Fox, and Brer Bear—appear in the attraction through Audio-Animatronics technology. In fact, Splash Mountain's stars and supporting cast of 103 performers constitute the

largest group of Audio-Animatronics characters ever assembled in a single Disneyland attraction.

Comparisons to the Pirates of the Caribbean are particularly apt, as Splash Mountain was consciously designed as a "how-do-we-top-this" response to the long-running popularity of the pirate adventure. The Disney Imagineers used such time-proven elements as a watery drop into a fantasy world, humorous characters, and a scrupulously detailed show in an entirely new way.

Splash Mountain's designers not only borrowed the attraction's characters and color-saturated settings from *Song of the South*, they also included quite a bit of the film's Academy Award-winning music. As a matter of fact, the song in the attraction's finale, "Zip-A-Dee-Doo-Dah," has become something of a Disney anthem over the years.

Splash Mountain breaks new ground in a number of ways. In addition to setting a record for total animated characters, it also boasts one of the world's tallest and sharpest flume drops (52½ feet at a 45-degree angle), and at a top speed of 40 miles per hour, it is the fastest ride ever operated at Disneyland.

One other new twist makes Splash Mountain unique in the annals of flumedom: After hurtling down Chickapin Hill, the seven-passenger log boats hit the pond below with a giant splash—and then promptly sink underwater (or seem to) with only a trace of bubbles left in their wake.

A point for Disney Trivia buffs: The voice of Brer Bear is performed by Nick Stewart, the same actor who spoke the part of Brer Bear in *Song of the South* when it was released in 1946.

DAVY CROCKETT'S EXPLORER CANOES: Of all the boats that circle the Rivers of America, these 35-foot fiberglass crafts—replacements for the wooden originals made by Maine's Old Town Canoe Company—may offer the most fun, at least for the stalwart. They're real canoes, and they're not on tracks. Though the helmsman and the sternsman are always strong enough to do the work, the guests' contributions also matter when it comes to completing the 2,400-foot trip.

Note that the attraction operates only during busier periods, and that it closes at dusk.

COUNTRY BEAR PLAYHOUSE: A handful of blasé travelers do manage to sit through this country-and-western vacation hoedown without cracking a smile, but they're few and far between, because this is surely another one of the park's best attractions. Ostensibly dreamed up by one Ursus H. Bear at the end of an especially good winter's nap, it is presented, with remarkably believable results, by an assortment of nearly 20 Audio-Animatronics bruins—among them Henry, the sporty, seven-foot-tall master of ceremonies; the big-bodied pianist, Gomer; the Five Bear Rugs (Zeke on banjo, Zeb on fiddle, Ted on white lightnin' jug, Fred on mouth harp, and Tennessee picking the guitarlike one-string "phang"); and the ample Trixie, lamenting her lost love after being jilted at an ant-plagued picnic. Dressed in a yellow slicker, rain bonnet, and red galoshes, Teddi Barra

floats down from the ceiling crooning "Singing in the Rain." Bubbles, Bunny, and Beulah, in sweet harmony, sing "Wish They All Could Be California Bears." The cast is completed by Wendell, the "over-*bear*-ing *bear*-itone"; Liver Lips McGrowl; and last but not least, the show-stopping Big Al, one of the few Audio-Animatronics figures in the park with a following great enough to create a demand for his image on postcards and stuffed animals.

The same cast members show up in several other parts of the park, and it's interesting—but usually next to impossible—to see whether you can recognize them from one persona to the next.

When Christmastime rolls around, the Country Bear Playhouse gets into the holiday spirit with special costumes, music, and scenery. A real treat.

TEDDI BARRA'S SWINGIN' ARCADE: This entertainment center, named for one of the big stars of the Country Bear Playhouse, is no ordinary arcade. Marksmen test their accuracy on empty honey pots, and Big Al, also from Country Bear Playhouse, challenges golfers. The basketball game features the stars of Walt Disney's 1946 film, *Song of the South*. There are 17 machines in all.

FANTASYLAND

SLEEPING BEAUTY CASTLE: Rising above the treetops at the end of Main Street, it seems like something you've just imagined, especially on warm summer nights, when fireworks explode about the battlements like Tinker Bell's pixie dust. Closer inspection, however, shows the building to be real enough. A composite of various medieval European castles, primarily in the French and Bavarian styles, Sleeping Beauty Castle is constructed of concrete with towers that rise to a height of some 77 feet above the moat. And the whole thing looks even larger because of the use of forced perspective. In a real castle, blocks of stone near the top appear smaller than those at the bottom simply because they really are farther away. By artificially decreasing the dimensions of Sleeping Beauty Castle's uppermost blocks, the structure is made to appear much taller. The drawbridge functions just like a real one, too. It was lowered when the park first opened, in 1955. Inside the castle, a rather sweet series of dioramas, not unlike the Emporium shop windows, tells the story of the beautiful Princess Aurora; three bright-eyed fairies named Flora, Fauna, and Merryweather; the magnificently evil Queen Maleficent; a finger pierced by a spindle; a long sleep; handsome Prince Philip; true love's first kiss; and one of the best loved of fairytaledom's happily-ever-afters—all to the tuneful accompaniment of Tchaikovsky's music for the *Sleeping Beauty* ballet. The swans that inhabit the moat surrounding the castle are as real as most people think; they were obtained in exchange for 300 homing pigeons in a "trade" with Walt Disney World. The vegetation around the water's edge is juniper—planted there because it's one of the few green plants that the big birds will not eat. The two graceful trees to the right of the drawbridge (on the way into Fantasyland) are not weeping willow, as you might first guess, but willow leaf pittosporum (*Pittosporum phillyraeoides*), which bear hundreds

Walt Disney called this a timeless land of enchantment, and his successors term it the happiest land of all. It is the sort of European village that provides the background for all the best fairy tales—on a day that the circus has come to town. The village lanes twist between houses done in half-timbers, brick, stone, and stucco, often embellished by brightly colored folk paintings. Weathered beams peek from below roofs of slate or shingles, and the rooflines lurch and lean this way and that as turrets and towers above poke at the heavens. The skyline, dominated by the peak of the Matterhorn, fairly bristles with chimneys and weather vanes in more shapes and styles than any single architect could possibly imagine. At the center of it all, as if brought to town by a traveling carnival, is the King Arthur Carrousel.

When Walt Disney originally created Snow White's Scary Adventures, Mr. Toad's Wild Ride, and Peter Pan's Flight, the black-light and glow-in-the-dark paints he used (which became so popular during the psychedelic 1960s) were great novelties. But in the last three decades the palette of available hues and the spectrum of special effects techniques have taken quantum leaps forward, and Fantasyland's major adventures have become the prime beneficiaries of these remarkable technological advances. Fiber optics, rear projection, holography, and other advanced special effects techniques (developed in the course of the construction of Epcot Center at Walt Disney World and Tokyo Disneyland) have been put to good use. As a result, Fantasyland is now a visual treat for all.

Children under age seven must be accompanied by an adult on all "dark" rides in Fantasyland. These include Peter Pan's Flight, Mr. Toad's Wild Ride, Alice in Wonderland, Matterhorn Bobsleds, Snow White's Scary Adventures, and Pinocchio's Daring Journey. Attractions are described here as you come upon them when moving roughly counterclockwise from Sleeping Beauty Castle.

of tiny yellow flowers in spring, and melaleuca (*Melaleuca nesophila*), bedecked with fragile lavender flowers for several weeks in early summer.

SNOW WHITE GROTTO: Tucked away off Matterhorn Way, at the eastern end of the moat around Sleeping Beauty Castle, this is one of those quiet corners of the park easily overlooked by visitors.

There's a wishing well (the coins go to charity); and then every so often Adriana Caselotti, the original voice of Snow White, can be heard singing the lovely Larry Morey/Frank Churchill melody "I'm Wishing," from the Oscar-winning 1937 film based on the Grimm Brothers' fairy tale. While she sings, jets of water rise and fall in the waterfall-fountain just on the other side of the walkway, and a quartet of small fish rise up from the bottom of the pool at the base of the cascade to swim around in little circles. You might well think that this grotto has been here since the very beginning of the park's history. Not true: The Seven Dwarfs and the Snow White figure, all of them sculpted from blocks of pure white marble, arrived at Walt Disney's studios one day in packing crates—an anonymous gift postmarked from Italy. Surmising that the carving may have been executed by a class of art students and based on some Seven Dwarfs hand soaps recently licensed at that time, Walt Disney made a place for them. John Hench, the art director whose name the keen-eyed may have noted on one of the windows above Main Street's shops, was not as delighted with the idea as Walt seemed to be, mainly because the Snow White figure was the same height as the dwarfs—an error no Disney carver would ever have made. By elevating her to the top of the fountain, however, designers made sure that Snow White's diminutive size would go almost unnoticed. Ironically, when plans were being laid for Tokyo Disneyland, the Japanese sponsors insisted that *their* Snow White Grotto be identical to this one.

PETER PAN'S FLIGHT: In Fantasyland's new scheme of things, this attraction (based on the play by the Scottish writer Sir James M. Barrie about the boy who wouldn't grow up, by way of Walt Disney's 1953 animated feature) is the most unabashedly beautiful one. The special effects

soar to celestial heights as the pirate ships carry travelers through the clouds and into a sky full of infinite numbers of tiny fiber-optic stars. The water ripples and gleams softly in the moonlight. The lava on the sides of the volcano glows with almost the intensity of the real thing. And then the ship seems to pass *through* a waterfall—and into an unloading area that is all the more jarring after the magic of the trip through Never Land.

Disneyland trivia lovers will be interested to learn that of the approximately 350 miles of fiber optics used throughout Fantasyland, the majority appears in this attraction, and the twinkling new London layout is an enlarged model of an authentic map of the city. (Only a few landmarks, however, such as Big Ben, are included.) About half of the attraction's sound track came directly from the Disney film. Longtime Disneyland visitors may recognize some of the cannons and the rigging on the pirate ship as those that once stood aboard the large-scale vessel that occupied a prominent place in Fantasyland years ago.

MR. TOAD'S WILD RIDE: Based on the October 1949 Disney film *The Adventures of Ichabod and Mr. Toad*—which itself was partly inspired by Kenneth Grahame's classic novel *The Wind in the Willows*—this zany attraction, housed in an English manor bristling with ornate chimneys that really smoke, takes guests on a wild ride with the eccentric but lovable Mr. Toad, who loves automobiles but is about as inept a driver as you would expect a toad to be. During his peregrinations he crashes through the fireplace in his library, scattering the embers; bursts through a wall full of windows; careens through the countryside; charges headlong into a warehouse full of TNT, which blows up; lurches through the streets of London and (still in his car) rams into, and out of, an evocative pub; goes to court and is soundly berated for his tomfoolery by a local judge; nearly collides head-on with a railroad train; and eventually, as if in expiation of his sins, ends up in a fiery inferno that features some of Fantasyland's best special effects. (The place even *feels* hot.) The whole journey takes place so quickly that passengers are apt to overlook some of the details that make the new settings so enchanting. Take the ornaments on the exterior of the building—vines interspersed with pictures of little toads. Or the Toad Hall shield emblazoned with the words *Toadi Acceleratio Semper Absurda*, which translates roughly as "speeding with Toad is always absurd." Or the titles of the books on the shelves in the library at the very start of the journey—*Anderson's Froggy Tales*, *Famous Paintings by Van Toad*, *Frogeon Psychology*, *Frogs I Have Loved*, etc. In Toad Hall, as you burst through the leaded glass window, the observant will note a tiny shadow of Mickey Mouse near the center, close to the sill. In Winky's Pub, the label on one of the liquor bottles reads: "Walt Disney's Distilled Spirits of London." Nearby, above the bar, guests who have already visited Critter Country will recognize the head of Melvin the Moose from the Country Bear Vacation Hoedown. The slip of paper tacked to the wall next to the dart board announces a marriage and a celebratory "wild party" (which really did take place when one of the principal sign painters tied the knot during the course of work on the show). The shadow of Sherlock Holmes (complete with pipe and cape) can be seen in the window on the second story. Then there are the lovely sets, where stars glitter like diamonds in a dark-blue moonlit sky, and lights twinkle in windows along dark city streets. The ride vehicles are all named after friends of Mr. Toad, and the music came straight from the film.

ALICE IN WONDERLAND: The spring of 1984 saw the premiere of this attraction—the final redesigned adventure for the newly reconstructed Fantasyland. New characters and scenes from the motion picture are brought to life for the first time in this tale of Alice's crazy chase after the White Rabbit. Traveling in oversize caterpillars, visitors fall down the rabbit hole—and embark upon a bizarre adventure in that strange world known as Wonderland. It is populated by Tweedledum and Tweedledee; a garden full of singing roses; the Cheshire Cat; the Queen of Hearts and her playing-card soldiers; the White Rabbit; and more. At the end of the ride, the explosion of the giant "unbirthday" cake provides a suitably exciting climax.

MAD TEA PARTY: The sequence in Walt Disney's 1951 production of Lewis Carroll's *Alice in Wonderland* in which the Mad Hatter hosts a tea party for his un-birthday is the theme for this attraction—a group of oversize pastel teacups that spin and whirl wildly on a spinning platform. (Be sure to let a reasonable interval pass after eating before you embark on this mad whirl.) A bright festive look, with colorful Japanese lanterns that hang above the tea table, is part of the redesign. Don't miss the shrubs outside that spell A–L–I–C–E.

MATTERHORN BOBSLEDS: Opened during the summer of the premiere of Walt Disney's 1959 *Third Man on the Mountain*, which dramatized an ascent of this mighty Swiss peak, this ride, like the more sophisticated Space Mountain and Big Thunder Mountain Railroad attractions, has to be counted among Disneyland's most thrilling rides.

The Matterhorn bobsleds were quite a novelty when they were dedicated in 1959 (by Richard Nixon, who was then Vice President) because of the block system dispatch, unique at that time, which allowed more than one car to be in action at once, and because of the cylinder-rail track and urethane wheels, which have since become quite commonplace on modern roller coasters. The real allure of the ride is that along with the speed goes a show. You take a long climb into the cold, black innards of the mountain and make a long, speeding, twisting, and turning descent through a cloud of fog and past giant icicles and ice crystals—the wind howling about you all the while—toward a brief encounter with the awesome Abominable Snowman (a sort of albino version of King Kong) and a splashdown in an alpine lake. The speed of the downhill flight away from the creature seems even greater than it really is, since much of the journey takes place inside tunnels.

Since the designers carefully studied photographs of the real peak when developing the designs, the mountain itself is a pretty good reproduction of the real one, which Walt saw for the first time in 1958 when traveling through Europe. It even faces in the proper direction. The mountain's hooked peak is a bit more bent than that of the original in Switzerland, and this Matterhorn is smaller, a hundredth the size of the real McCoy. Like the Sleeping Beauty Castle, it uses forced perspective to make the summit look even loftier than the approximately 147 feet it actually is. Even the trees and the shrubs get into the act. The ones at the timberline—that is, 65 to 75 feet from the base of the mountain—are far smaller than those at the bottom. In fact, these Atlas and deodar cedar, European white birch, and Chinese tallow trees are among the most interesting aspects of the attraction. Growing in cement pockets whose small size retards root growth and plant growth above ground, they're watered by a gardener who must walk the attraction's bobsled track to reach them.

As for the mountain itself, its framework consists of some 2,175 pieces of steel of varying lengths and widths. The contours were molded and shaped using a second skeleton of ⅜-inch steel wire topped with a layer of metal mesh and layers of plaster—two of them sprayed on and the third and final one applied with a trowel for maximum verisimilitude.

FANTASYLAND AUTOPIA: This sibling of the Tomorrowland Autopia boasts scenery a shade less interesting, but it's fun nevertheless. For the small fry for whom the miniature freeway ride is designed, the distinction is almost too fine to matter. You must be at least 52 inches tall to drive, or be accompanied by an adult. Open during holiday weekends and special seasonal periods only.

MOTORBOAT CRUISE: Though far from being the most exciting of Disneyland's offerings for most adults, visitors with children often call this a favorite attraction. The faces of the youngsters as they steer the small three-passenger craft through the channels underneath the freeways are the equal of any Disney-made show. The names on the boats are those of favorite Disney characters. Open weekends and special seasonal periods only.

IT'S A SMALL WORLD: The background music for this attraction—"It's a Small World," written by Richard M. and Robert B. Sherman (the Academy Award-winning composers of the music for *Mary Poppins*, among other Disney scores)—is almost maddeningly cheerful and singsong. Children love it, senior citizens love it, and the more sophisticated among the in-betweeners wish they could expunge it from their consciousness after disembarking from the boats that carry them through the attraction. It does seem to become more lovable as you know it better, however, much like the show itself. While not necessarily the most sophisticated, it certainly is splendid, from the gloriously towered-and-turreted white-and-gold facade to the troops of stylized Audio-Animatronics dolls, representing all the world's children, on view along the way.

In all, there are 297 children representing some 100 regions, plus 256 toys native to those areas—a real pageant. The facade, which is embellished with stylized representations of the Eiffel Tower, the Leaning Tower of Pisa, Big Ben, the Taj Mahal, and other world landmarks, is equally splendid—and the fantastic mechanized clock outside, whose loud ticktock can be heard from most parts of Fantasyland, is just frosting on the cake. The parade of toys and jesters and the whirring of gears and springs that marks every quarter hour alone warrant a trip to the attraction's spacious plaza on the edge of Fantasyland. Just as fascinating are the topiary figures—an assemblage of some 20 living olive, podocarpus, eugenia, and dodonea plants grown over chicken-wire frames and pruned into the shapes of giraffes, a llama, unicorns, elephants, seals, lions, and other animals to form a balletic troupe almost as whimsical as the attraction itself.

STORYBOOK LAND CANAL BOATS: This cruise past miniature scenes from classic Disney animated films is not one of Disneyland's major attractions (like Pirates of the Caribbean or Big Thunder Mountain Railroad), yet few who take the trip deny that the journey is one of the loveliest on the property. It's so chock-full of delightful details and wonderful little scenes that even the tour guides' often infuriatingly mechanical recitations can't spoil it. Even after several trips, there are still new sights to see. For the church near the beginning of the trip, Walt insisted on having imported stained glass. "The day we start cutting the detail," he declared, "is the day we won't have a Disneyland." And so it goes, from the Old English Village of Alice in Wonderland (where the White Rabbit boasts his very own mailbox) to the London park that Peter Pan, Tinker Bell, and Wendy, John, and Michael Darling flew over on their way to Never Land. Miniatures of Toad Hall, with Ratty's house nearby, the Seven Dwarfs' mine, and Cinderella's Dream Castle are among the other sights en route. Ken Anderson, one of the art directors intimately involved with the project, tells of his anguish when he learned that union laborers (and not skilled craftsmen from the Disney Studios) would be building the mountain at the base of the delicately pink castle there. The clock at the top of the castle reads midnight, and the turrets are covered in gold leaf. Anderson himself applied the first coat and, not being experienced in the technique, initially watched a good deal of the precious tissue-paper-like substance blow away. The houses in Geppetto's Village, near the end of the cruise, have doors that really open. Because funds were short when the attraction was being developed (just after Disneyland opened), expensive Japanese bonsai trees were out of the question. But at Van Dam State Park, one scout turned up a handful of stunted, suitably small-scale redwoods growing in some scrabbly limestone soil on a cliffside. A bit more hunting unearthed a few more of these dwarf trees nearby on a piece of private property whose owners were willing to sell.

DUMBO, THE FLYING ELEPHANT: When former President Harry Truman came to Disneyland in 1957, he and his wife visited almost every attraction in the park except this one—"a Republican symbol," he proclaimed. A more plausible explanation is that it has always been something of a kiddie ride, an experience especially loved by youngsters in the two-through-seven age group (and their parents, who happily go along to watch their kids' smiles). The ride is now a showpiece of the area, and this mechanical marvel, full of filigreed metalwork and cogs and gears and pulleys galore, can hold even the most blasé grown-up's attention. The pipes that spew water out of the base are plated with real gold—not only for the

plus a real caboose. Children seem to love this ride. The tree next to the Casey Jr. railroad station is a Chinese weeping elm.

SKYWAY TO TOMORROWLAND: Walt Disney well understood the joys of people-watching, and this attraction offers one of the best examples of how Disney put that knowledge into practice. Traveling to Tomorrowland through the friendly skies of Disneyland, 60 feet up, allows a peek at the people below riding in the Teacups, eating ice cream, and otherwise going about the business of having a terrific time in Fantasyland. You are also able to see the submarines gliding through the aquamarine waters of the lagoon, and as you pass through the center of the Matterhorn, you'll see the bobsleds hurtling downhill past a growling Abominable Snowman. The touchdown in Tomorrowland, so sleek and futuristic in its way, always comes as a bit of culture shock after Fantasyland's enchanted environment. The Skyway was the first of its kind to be installed in the United States. There are 44 gondolas, each large enough to accommodate four passengers.

SNOW WHITE'S SCARY ADVENTURES: Even this attraction's facade, with its sober evergreen plantings, its somber brown shingled roof, and its stone-gray castellated towers, suggests that the adventure within includes many of the same frightening moments found in the Oscar-winning 1937 film of the Grimm Brothers' fairy tale on which it was based. Look above the castle door and you might see the evil Queen pulling apart red velvet curtains and peeking out through her small-paned Gothic window. Ornamental stone ravens perch on carved stone skulls atop a stone tower, and the base of the twisted pillars supporting the half-timbered section of this foreboding structure is composed of hearts pierced through with a sword. Inside, the visitor's route snakes through the Queen's cobweb-draped dungeon, inhabited by ghostly voices. With all this preparation, you might well expect an attraction even more scarifying than the Haunted Mansion. It isn't, though the tale of Snow White as it unfolds in the course of this brief ride (in small cars named after the Seven Dwarfs) includes several fairly menacing scenes. There's one in which the Queen changes into a scraggly haired, wart-nosed old hag right before your eyes, for instance, and another in which this wicked green-eyed crone turns and offers a poisoned apple to you. The cars travel through another skeleton-scattered dungeon, pass the workshop where the Queen labors over a steaming caldron of poisoned apples, and venture into the Frightening Forest, where mists swirl around floating logs that look like crocodiles, and smoke-wreathed, moss-draped trees point talon-like branches at unwary travelers as if to snatch them away from the relative safety of the small vehicles. The visit to the jewel mines, where the Seven Dwarfs labor during the daytime, is more beautiful than scary, full of masses of glow-in-the-dark topaz, emeralds, rubies, and sapphires. Happily, it all ends in true storybook fashion: As the evil

show value of their gleaming brightness, but also for ease of maintenance. The music is supplied by a vintage band organ housed in a small, ornate structure nearby, which is completely climate-controlled to preserve the delicate instrument's leather parts and safeguard it from dust. The baroque wooden casing is a new Disney design. The topiary elephants, similar to those in front of It's A Small World, were moved here from Walt Disney World in Orlando, Florida. Dumbo was the flying elephant character in the 1941 film about a baby elephant who discovers, after drinking from a bucketful of champagne, that his inordinately large ears, which have previously been such a source of embarrassment, can actually help him to fly. Timothy Mouse, who becomes his friend's manager after the flying elephant is hired as a star (by the same circus folk who once scoffed at him), stands in command at the center of the attraction.

CASEY JR. CIRCUS TRAIN: One of the key sequences in Walt Disney's 1941 film *Dumbo*, in which the engine named Casey Jr. pulls a circus train up a steep hill, is the inspiration for this attraction—a train trip that circles Storybook Land. The fact is, the Canal Boats are better for viewing the landscaping and the details there, but it's hard to resist the charm of a ride inside one of those wild-animal-cage cars—the kind that always show up in circus films. Each train has two of them—

Queen attempts to roll a stone down the side of a mountain to crush the dwarfs below, she tumbles over the edge of a cliff and dies, leaving Snow White, her handsome prince, and the Seven Dwarfs to live happily ever after, as portrayed in the mural near the exit. Curious visitors will be gratified to know that the bizarre calligraphy in the Queen's recipe book in the caldron scene reads "Poison Apple Antidote." In the "magic mirror, on the wall" scene, the floor on which the Queen stands is actually painted wood (the fact that it looks exactly like stone even when examined very closely is a tribute to the skill of the painters who worked here). Most important of all, which dwarf is which? In the cottage scene at the beginning of the ride, it's Grumpy playing the organ, Sleepy on fiddle, Bashful on the guitar, Happy on the accordion (a Regoletta-brand instrument made in Italy), Doc on the mandolin, and Dopey, who has climbed up on the shoulders of Sneezy. (In this same scene, be sure to note the small totem-pole-like columns of chipmunks and mice that stand like candleholders atop the organ.) The music comes from rare recordings used to create the film's original sound track.

PINOCCHIO'S DARING JOURNEY: This addition to the roster of Fantasyland attractions, based on Walt Disney's 1940 animated feature, is a sort of small morality play, with Jiminy Cricket, conscience personified, as host and guide. Pinocchio, the creation of the toy maker Geppetto, goes to Pleasure Island, a land of popcorn and candy-cane Ferris wheels where a happy green worm lives in a fire-engine-red candy apple, to find the right way to live. But almost imperceptibly, vehicles move to the seamy world of Tobacco Road. Here the Mona Lisa wears a mustache, the candy is broken or half-eaten, and the brightly colored Pleasure Island hues are supplanted by drab, dirty shades of brown and gray. This is the home of the Rough House and its perpetual free-for-all, and the poolroom where little boys turn into donkeys

and the coachman sells them to the salt mines. Pinocchio escapes that fate, nearly misses being gobbled up by Monstro the whale, and ends up back at home in the care of Geppetto—to live happily ever after.

It's worth noting that the poolroom scene in which Lampwick turns into a donkey is the first in which Disney designers have used holograms at Disneyland. The tableau at the end, in which the dazzling Blue Fairy turns into a cloud of sparkles right before your eyes—and then disappears, leaving only a pile of pixie dust on the floor—is accomplished partly by means of fiber optics. The tree out in front, an *Acer oblongun* found in a Claremont, California, nursery, is a sort of aberrant maple tree that Disney landscape gardeners attest is unique in the world. Atop the turreted ride building, be sure to note the attractive weather vanes. These represent Monstro the whale, a school of fish, and a stork, a bird that is supposed to bring good luck in the part of eastern Europe that provided the inspiration for the onion-shaped dome that tops one of the ride building's turrets.

KING ARTHUR CARROUSEL: One of the landmarks in the park, the carousel has been moved back a few feet to allow guests to see its graceful and colorful entirety as they stroll toward the Sleeping Beauty Castle passageway into Fantasyland. One of the few attractions in the park that is an original rather than a Disney adaptation, the carousel boasts 18 rows of 4 elaborately carved horses each—72 in all, no 2 alike (plus 13 spares). According to Bruce Bushman, one of the early park planners (whose name adorns a window on Main Street), the main unit of the carrousel, an 1875 Dentzel model, was purchased in Canada, but at the time it wasn't a carrousel at all—it had a whole menagerie of giraffes, lions, and other creatures, plus some sleighs, in addition to its handful of horses, and not everything moved. But Walt wanted all the animals to move, and he wanted them all to be horses, so he sent his scouts out to search for the prancing steeds that grace the big turntable today. Neglected for most of the first half of the century, they're now as pampered as the live Belgian horses on Main Street, cared for by an expert painter whose responsibility it is to keep them looking as sleek and shiny as they must have been when they were carved in Germany over a century ago. At the rate of about 40 painting hours per horse, it takes about two years to get to them all—and then the cycle starts again—always using the original color scheme. The same care goes into keeping the 182 brass poles on the carrousel turntable shiny. The man in charge of the job spends six hours at it every night.

Incidentally, the shields on the lances that support the big overhead canopy are those of the Knights of the Round Table, and because there were more shields needed than authentic designs, the crests of the various families involved in the park in the early days are included as well. Atop the carrousel's main face, be sure to note the nine hand-painted panels bearing scenes from the film *Sleeping Beauty*.

TOMORROWLAND

Walt Disney cherished great hope for the future. "Tomorrow," he said in 1955, offers "new frontiers in science, adventure, and ideals: the atomic age . . . the challenge of outer space . . . and the hope for a peaceful and unified world." To this vision he dedicated Tomorrowland, "a vista into a world of wondrous ideas signifying man's achievements, a step into the future, with predictions of constructive things to come." Certainly, in terms of today's big-budget sci-fi films, Tomorrowland doesn't look much like the contemporary fantasy view of the years to come. Instead it represents a more accessible tomorrow, one that is truly within our grasp. So while there are attractions focused on space travel and journeys to Mars, there are others that offer more realistic options for tomorrow's transportation.

Tomorrowland entertainment is not futuristic but contemporary: groups perform rock music at Tomorrowland Terrace. There's also the Starcade nearby, full of the hottest video games around. Movement is everywhere: The Rocket Jets whirl and bob high above the small cars of the People-Mover, the Skyway gondolas parade through the air, and submarines circle through the Disneyland sea while miniature motorcars *vroom* and sputter along the scaled-down highways of the Tomorrowland Autopia and sleek monorails glide from their station toward the *Disneyland* hotel. Meanwhile, just to remind everyone where it all began, the traditional trains of the Disneyland Railroad chug into the Tomorrowland depot, a bit of the past visiting the possible future. It could only happen in Disneyland.

Be sure to take note of Tomorrowland's landscaping. The overall scheme was not easy to develop, and the designers decided to use familiar materials available in contemporary landscape design. Many trees and bushes have been pruned into geometric shapes; note the poodle-cut ligustrums around the train station. Other plants were picked for their slightly exotic natural configurations. But there's warmth in Tomorrowland, too: The flower beds at the entrance are the setting for the park's greatest show of annuals—more than 5,000 plants

for each season. The results of these efforts make for a comfortable, inviting sort of place.

The following attractions are described as you come upon them when moving counterclockwise from the entrance to Tomorrowland.

STAR TOURS: The most spectacular attraction at Disneyland was inspired by George Lucas's *Star Wars* film trilogy. It offers guests the chance to board StarSpeeders, which are actually the same type of flight simulators that are regularly employed by the military and commercial airlines in the training of pilots. Synchronizing a stunning film with the virtually limitless motion of the simulator allows guests to truly feel what they see. (Note that when instructed to put on your seatbelt, do so. This is a very rough ride.)

Visitors enter an area where the famed Star Wars characters R2D2 and C3PO are working for a galactic travel agency. They spend their time in a bustling hangar area servicing the Star Tours fleet of spacecraft. Riders board the 40-passenger craft for what is intended to be a leisurely trip to the Moon of Endor, but which quickly develops into a harrowing flight into deep space, including

encounters with giant ice crystals and laser blasting fighters. The flight is out of control from the start, as the rookie pilot proves that Murphy's Law applies in the entire universe.

The sensations are extraordinary and the technology quite advanced. Astute passengers will note that the voice of the spacecraft's captain belongs to Pee Wee Herman.

Signs outside Star Tours warn that passengers must be free of back problems, heart conditions, motion sickness, and other physical limitations to ride. Pregnant women and children under three are not permitted to board. Children under seven must be accompanied by an adult. The least bumpy seats are near the center of the compartment.

STARCADE: This two-level games arcade (adjoining Space Mountain) is by all accounts the best in Orange County—if not in all of California. There are about 200 games—though which are on hand at any given time may vary. There are always a few for traditionalists and a couple that were custom-made for Disneyland to allow more than one player to participate at a time. Most of the rest are whatever happens to be hottest at the time—and there's someone on the Disney staff to keep an eye on the games field to make sure that no state-of-the-art machine is omitted. All the machines take from 25¢ to $1. There are $1 and $5 change machines, as well as cashiers, right on the premises.

SPACE MOUNTAIN: Without a doubt one of the best attractions in the park, and certainly one of the most popular, Space Mountain must also rank among the best roller coasters in existence. Its greatness derives not so much from the fact that it will leave your stomach behind as from the fact that most of the trip shoots through pitch blackness with stars whizzing by on all sides. It's an experience so splendid and magical that it can be enjoyed many times without any disappointment. It's not a rocket journey, really: The 12-passenger "rockets" are similar to those boarded by many a roller-coaster buff, with two-abreast seating, and the ride's route is traveled at the relatively moderate speed of about 30 miles per hour. But between the stars and the Cosmic Vapor Curtain and the Solar Energizer and the glowing nebula, the attraction boasts such beauty that it's not hard to understand why Southern Californians queued up for as long as two hours to experience it when it first opened. (Though the situation isn't nearly so bad nowadays, it still behooves a queue-hater to make a beeline for the mountain immediately upon arriving in the park.)

Such a marvel doesn't develop overnight. Walt Disney had the idea for the attraction early in the park's history—long before the technology to operate it had been developed. The original sketch for the many-spired white cone, not all that different from the present structure, was drawn in 1964 by John Hench (whose name appears on the Main Street window above Carefree Corner). Subsequently, workers representing about 150 different crafts and specialties put almost a million man-hours into the design and construction of this bit

of manmade mountain magic. It took nearly two years to construct, and the whole thing is sunk 15 feet into the ground—so as not to dwarf Sleeping Beauty Castle or the Matterhorn.

Pregnant women, children who are under three or less than 40 inches tall, and other guests who suffer from weak backs, heart conditions, motion sickness, and other physical limitations are not permitted to ride. Children under seven must be accompanied by an adult. Those who don't normally enjoy roller coasters should be sure to ride the PeopleMover instead, since it offers a look at the scenic wonders inside the mountain. Those who decide they might want a still closer look should line up with the brave at the base of the Speedramp. Note that if you get cold feet once inside the mountain, there are three "chicken exits" in the queue area en route to the loading dock—one just past the entrance to the building, another farther along by the turnstiles, and the last right at the loading area. Parents can wait with their youngsters until this final coward's exit and rendezvous at the end, after the ride is over.

MISSION TO MARS: Many times over the years Disneyland planners have been reminded of the difficulties of attempting to portray a future that persists in becoming the present. This attraction

represents one of them: It was originally called Flight to the Moon. The vibrating and heaving of the seats and the terrific roars and hisses that play over the big sound system are fine, but there is also something of the sensation of being inside a giant washing machine. Kids are inevitably delighted.

SKYWAY TO FANTASYLAND: The trip is pleasant enough: four-passenger cars suspended from a 2,400-foot-long moving cable ride 60 feet above the ground across the Submarine Lagoon and through a tunnel in the Matterhorn, where you get an idea of the thrills available there. For other details, see the description in the "Fantasyland" section of this chapter.

CAPTAIN EO: This 3-D musical fantasy stars Michael Jackson as the captain of a spaceship. His band of characters include Hooter, Fuzzball, and The Geek. Their mission: to transform the dismal planet ruled by the Evil Queen (played by Academy Award winner Angelica Huston) into a happy place through the magic of music and dance. Jackson wrote and performs two original songs: "We Are Here to Change the World" and "Another Part of Me." The theater has been redesigned and outfitted with state-of-the-art audio and video equipment, as well as apparatus to provide a dazzling group of special effects.

DISNEYLAND RAILROAD: The old-fashioned trains that circle the park can be boarded in Tomorrowland, as well as in the Frontierland station (in New Orleans Square), in Fantasyland, at Videopolis, and on Main Street. Though the latter usually boasts the fastest-moving queue, those who want to ride only long enough to view the Primeval World and Grand Canyon dioramas that constitute the scenery between the Tomorrowland and Main Street stations may want to board here.

TOMORROWLAND AUTOPIA: Anyone who contends with the Southern California freeways every day may find it difficult to get excited about queuing

up to steer these small, streamlined sports cars around an equally pint-size highway. But youngsters absolutely adore the trip and can spend hours driving these Mark VII-model, ten-foot-long, 1,100-pound vehicles along the twisting roadways here. To someone used to steering nothing more powerful than a bicycle, the top speed—seven miles an hour—comes as a big thrill. Engines are one cylinder, four cycle, air cooled, and made of cast iron, generating seven horsepower each. As for the difference between this attraction and its Fantasyland counterpart, it's mainly one of scenery. Many adults find the trip here marginally more interesting because there seem to be more overpasses and bridges en route. You must be at least 52 inches tall to drive.

SUBMARINE VOYAGE: The scenery along the way here is attractive enough to keep you wide-eyed from the plunge at the start of the journey through the sojourn in the Graveyard of Lost Ships, the trip under the North Pole, to Atlantis, and on to your rendezvous with a sea serpent. Most of the sights en route approximate those associated with the sea now and down through the ages: Giant clams, weighing 500 pounds or more, really do inhabit coral environments of the East Indies and Australia. There actually was a submarine trip under the North Pole—made in 1958 by the U.S.S. *Nautilus*. Giant squids can be found in waters deeper than 600 feet; they do grow to lengths of 50 feet and more. Mermaids have figured in the folklore of the sea for centuries, and Atlantis was described in Ignatius Donnely's *Atlantis, the Antediluvian World* in 1882, while marine monsters have appeared regularly in world literature since the earliest years of Chinese history. The lagoon holds about 6 million gallons of water, and is said to be 25 times as clean as drinking water, since any bit of grease or dirt would distort viewing of the underwater "show."

DISNEYLAND MONORAIL SYSTEM: America's first daily operating monorail system might have been a novelty in 1959, when it was introduced. But even though it was replaced with four new Mark V, five-car, 137-foot-long trains a decade

later, the attraction still doesn't provoke wows of excitement today. The 2.5-mile-long "highway in the sky" does, however, add immeasurably to Tomorrowland's aura of urban futurism, and it does provide speedy transport for 2½ miles through the edge of Tomorrowland and off the property to the *Disneyland* hotel. Straddling its concrete beamway, the train has rubber tires to move it along, plus braking wheels atop the beam and guiding and stabilizing wheels on either side—for a total of 10 load-carrying wheels, 40 stabilizing wheels, and 4 steering wheels. Four 100-horse-power traction motors, operating on 600 volts of direct current, supply the power for each train.

PEOPLEMOVER: Disneyland's PeopleMover offers guests a preview of Tomorrowland's various attractions. The most intriguing view is the look at Space Mountain—just long enough to entice those who plan to go and to help the indecisive make up their minds. But the PeopleMover's 38 motorless cars, which are powered by electric motors in the track itself, also take in the Super Speed Tunnel,

an attraction in its own right, presenting several scenes from Disney's movie *Tron*.

ROCKET JETS: This is a thrill ride, pure and simple—though it does add considerable visual interest to Tomorrowland as viewed from the Central Plaza. A good choice for anyone who loved Space Mountain, but doesn't want to get in line all over again.

WORLD PREMIERE CIRCLEVISION: Motion pictures created for Disney's Epcot Center in Florida provided a testing ground for this type of film technique. Here *American Journeys* literally surrounds the viewer with breathtaking scenery—Rocky Mountain meadows, the Mississippi River, and New York City's Park Avenue—while telling a visual story of America's heritage. *American Journeys* alternates with *Wonders of China*, another Epcot Center creation that surrounds viewers with spectacular footage from that country. The Disney group was, in fact, the first Western crew to film some sites in China.

SHOPS IN THE MAGIC KINGDOM

Until you really get to know Disneyland, you might not expect that anyone would visit just to go shopping. But among Southern Californians, Disneyland is a favorite spot in which to consume conspicuously. Employees find Christmas and birthday presents here, and it's not unusual for local residents to make a special trip to the park to purchase an item they may have noticed during a previous visit.

It's not hard to see why Disneyland is such a popular shopping site. Although Mickey Mouse key chains, T-shirts, and hats, and other such trinkets may all be found here in abundance, there are also many other enticing treasures.

Antiques and silver-plated tea sets, eggbeaters and cookbooks, mock pirate hats and muskets, 14-karat-gold charms, and filigreed costume jewelry round out the available goods. Shops stock merchandise to complement the themes of the various lands. And so, in Adventureland, there are imports from all over the world—hand-carved elephant statues from India, for example, silk blouses from China, and seashells from the South Seas. In Critter Country, look for plush toys and dolls and other items in the handmade styles of early American pioneers. In New Orleans Square, buy perfume and antiques, silver and specialty cookware. In Frontierland, leather belts and hats, Mexican trinkets, and rugged country clothing are the main fare. In Fantasyland, there are sweets aplenty, toys, and European handicrafts. In Tomorrowland, Disney character merchandise is the big deal, but so are futuristic-looking lamps and clocks. Nearly every store offers a broad selection, from the inexpensive to the quite costly.

Consequently, there's no need to spend a fortune to acquire mementos. Budget watchers should be aware of the vast temptation to buy on impulse and plan expenditures carefully in advance.

MAIN STREET

NEWSSTAND: Located outside the main gate, this is a good spot to pick up a last-minute souvenir on your way out—but be prepared for crowds.

SOUVENIR STANDS: Located on both sides of the Disneyland Railroad depot in Town Square, these kiosks sell film and Disney-related books, postcards, stuffed animals, key chains, children's sunglasses, and the like. The selection is not as wide as elsewhere, but that can be an advantage if you have a good idea of what you want.

WEST SIDE OF THE STREET

EMPORIUM: The wares in this sprawling establishment at the Town Square end of Main Street are by no means as old-fashioned as the mansard-roofed, tin-ceilinged, velvet-curtained setting might suggest. Sunglasses and designer handbags, china figurines and music boxes, T-shirts and sweatshirts, folding umbrellas and nylon totes, and character hats make up the bulk of the stock. There's a little bit of everything, and the variety and the selections are likely to please. China figurines come in all kinds of variations: Mickey Mouse appears as cowboy, adventurer, pirate, sorcerer, cyclist, policeman, doctor, baseball player, tennis player, jogger, and golfer; even Donald and Minnie are seen in an assortment of roles. Goofy, Pluto, Daisy, Lady, Tramp, the Dalmatians, Alice, the Cheshire Cat, the White Rabbit, the Mad Hatter, Dumbo, Peter Pan, Tinker Bell, Mary Poppins, and other familiar Disney figures also crowd the shelves. There are more than three

dozen cash registers, and at the end of the operating day they're all mobbed. As you're queuing up to pay for your purchases, it's easy to understand why the store accounts for better than 25 percent of all Disneyland merchandising sales annually. For maximum enjoyment, by the way, visit the Emporium in the morning, when Disneylanders have the most time to show off their wares. Also, be sure to note the detailed window displays, usually related to the latest Walt Disney Company film release.

STORYBOOK STORE: Children's books are the stock in trade in this section of the Emporium building. Coloring books and children's classics—in the standard versions, as well as the Disney editions—are all available: *Heidi*, *Black Beauty*, *Treasure Island*, *Charlotte's Web*, and *Tom Sawyer* are among the most popular offerings. Golden Books, compact discs, plush toys, and games are in stock. Presented by Western Publishing Company.

NEW CENTURY TIME PIECES AND JEWELRY SHOP: Timepieces in all shapes and sizes are displayed in polished wood cases at this store across from the *Carnation Ice Cream Parlor*. Some are decorated with the faces of Disney characters. There are Mickey Mouse alarm clocks and Donald Duck clocks, plus Mickey Mouse watches. And

there are clocks for the kitchen and the living room, clocks with and without chimes, clocks for travel, and clocks meant to roost on a bedside table. The pins, earrings, necklaces, pendants, and rings available here are more delicate and more feminine looking than those available in other Disneyland shops. Among the choice offerings are 14-karat-gold charms representing Tinker Bell, Donald Duck, and Minnie Mouse.

CANDY PALACE: An old-fashioned pageant in pink and white, this shop is alluring at any time of day, but never more than when the candy makers are at work in a glass-walled kitchen confecting candy canes, nuttles, chocolate-covered strawberries, fudge, and other temptations for a sweet tooth. Their aromatic scents perfume the air on this part of Main Street (greatly abetted by a strong fan). The sweets produced are for sale on the premises, along with a bounty of chocolates, peanut brittle, almond rocky road, caramel pecan rolls, divinity, hard candies, licorice, and more.

EAST SIDE OF THE STREET

MAD HATTER SHOP: Located near the *Town Square Café*, this hat shop sells bowlers, top hats, and frilly bonnets that beg for an Easter parade, Mickey Mouse ears in black and various colors, and a good assortment of other toppers to protect tender skin from the sun.

MAGIC SHOP: When film star Betty Hutton came to Disneyland some years ago, she tired of being hounded for her autograph, so she bought herself a pair of long false eyelashes, a pirate's hat, and a special sword that looked as if it pierced her head. People kept on stopping her, but not because they recognized her—they just wanted to know where she had bought her crazy hat. The array of possible disguises for sale in this boutique, the surviving member of a pair of magic shops that graced Disneyland for years, is wonderful indeed. With adequate funds and the aid of some realistic-looking latex masks, you can transform yourself into Frankenstein's monster or a gorilla, a grandfather or a ghoul, a skeleton or Darth Vader. Smaller budgets may only allow for a pair of bloodshot eyes, or a box of clown makeup. But because this

is a magic shop, there are also plenty of tricks and books about tricks. Store personnel will occasionally demonstrate the magic tricks they sell.

PATENTED PASTIMES: Located next to the Magic Shop, hobbyists will love the train sets, models, and arts and crafts kits. Even the most avid baseball or football fan will find that special collectible in this newest Main Street shop.

MARKET HOUSE: This Disney version of an old-fashioned general store sells apples, nuts, preserves, malted milk balls, candy sticks, spice drops, rock candy, and other staples of daily life in years gone by. But this is one case in which the setting really outshines the merchandise. At the entrance, for instance, there are a half dozen captain's chairs surrounding a real antique potbellied stove and an honest-to-goodness checkerboard where the competitive among the footsore actually do strike up games. Scattered around the warm,

paneled premises are a few old-fashioned telephones. You can listen in on a typical turn-of-the-century conversation in which a mother expounds to her daughter on fried-onion poultices as a cure for the common cold, newfangled union suits, hauling water and cutting wood, eligible bachelors, the use of sliced cucumbers to perk up a complexion, and the exorbitant price of steak—all of 11¢ a pound! In the southeast corner of the store, there's a small room with seasonal merchandise, and a line of cooking utensils emblazoned with Mickey Mouse's image. And on the east wall of the store there is a handful of quaint old photographs and antique tools.

DISNEYANA SHOP: One of Disneyland's least obvious pleasures is offered by the wicked witch who occupies a glass-walled cage in the center of this shop. She has a bulbous nose, huge round yellow eyes, and a black mouth, and she looks so altogether frightening that little children cling to

their parents, especially when, every so often, she moves. Her chains clank, and she begs you to let her out, promising to show you how to fly and to turn water into gasoline if you do—and then threatening you if you don't. She was originally part of a display in the windows of Walt Disney World's Emporium. At the last minute, a crew of imagineers decided to animate her and added the audio only hours before shipping her to California. So successful is this creation that occasionally it is difficult to concentrate on the shop's wares, which include original "cels," short for celluloids, from Disney animated classics (priced from around $250 for a single image unframed to about $6,000 for a set of four in a good case); interestingly enough, similar items used to sell for only a few dollars each in Fantasyland. Mickey and Minnie Christmas figurines and plates, Mickey Mouse telephones, and similar items round out the selection.

DISNEY CLOTHIERS, LTD.: Disney-character merchandise has always been popular, as evidenced by the number of T-shirts, Mickey Mouse ears, wristwatches, and sweatshirts sold each year. This shop caters to fashion-conscious shoppers with a love for Disney gear. There is a vast

array of men's, women's, and children's clothing and accessories, all of which incorporate Disney characters in some way. There are men's golf shirts with a small Mickey Mouse embroidered on the pocket, women's oversize nightshirts with Mickey or Minnie Mouse, and satin-look jackets with Mickey (as the Sorcerer's Apprentice in *Fantasia*) embossed on the back. Hats, ties, exercise clothing, handbags, and belts round out the adult selection. Children's items include socks, suspenders, tops, pants, and bathing suits.

KODAK CAMERA CENTER: If your film gets stuck or you can't get it loaded in the first place, or if you encounter other minor mechanical problems, the Disneylanders who work here will try to help you out. If not, they either can rent you a Kodak 35mm or instant camera, or sell you a new one from the gleaming cases full of popular models from Kodak, Canon, Olympus, Pentax, and other well-known makers. The selection of film is the best in the park. Presented by Kodak.

CRYSTAL ARTS: Gleaming glasses and pitchers, mugs and trays, and other mementos can be engraved and monogrammed while you wait, or you can purchase them unornamented. There is a similar shop in New Orleans Square. Presented by Arribas Brothers.

SILHOUETTE STUDIO: Working at the rate of about 60 seconds per portrait, Disneyland's silhouette artists are a wonder to watch. They have endless patience, terrific senses of humor, and wonderful showmanship that makes queuing for a turn almost as much fun as receiving the final product. Horses, cats, dogs, and loved ones (scissored according to a careful description) have all

been portrayed over the years. The art form itself, made almost obsolete by the invention of the camera, was developed in the mid-18th century by a French finance minister, Étienne de Silhouette.

CHINA CLOSET: This bastion of breakable things offers the usual assortment of Disney character figurines, but they make up only a very small percentage of the merchandise. Teacups and teapots come in dozens of colors and styles. Canisters and soap dishes, jars and lamps, and sugar bowls and creamers in colored glass fill the shelves, along with accent pieces from Royal Doulton, statuettes from the Spanish company Lladro, and intriguing Norman Rockwell plates and Fitz & Floyd giftware. Blessedly, the aisles are wide enough so that there's little danger of knocking anything over.

CAREFREE CORNER: A wide selection of greeting cards, plus ribbons and wrapping paper, party supplies, pens, postcards, and postage stamps. A large assortment of stuffed animals also is available.

NEW ORLEANS SQUARE

Shops are described as you encounter them when moving from east to west through the park.

ONE OF A KIND SHOP: It would be nice to be able to relate that this popular and eminently browsable corner of New Orleans Square still sold props from Disney movies, as it once did. Nowadays, antiques and some reproductions are the stock in trade, but the selection is just as intriguing as ever. The recent manufactures are mainly replicas of ephemera of a century ago. Among the antiques might be weather vanes and old-fashioned sleds, coal stoves, dolls, washbasins and hatstands, chandeliers and inlaid boxes, paintings and bed frames, glass grapes and paperweights, chamber pots, and china cups. There's a little bit of everything to see here, and the aura of chaos makes the place fun. A must.

PIECES OF EIGHT: Wares with a pirate theme are purveyed at this shop near the exit from the Pirates of the Caribbean attraction. A dime can get you a "noggin o' seamanly advice" from a scuzzy-looking redheaded, green-eyed Audio-Animatronics character named Fortune Red, who occupies a glass box atop the steps. For intermediate sums, there are pirate rings, ship's lanterns, mirrors framed in portholes, stocking caps, and fake knives in plastic and rubber.

CRISTAL D'ORLEANS: The marble floor and doorsteps make a beautiful setting for the transparent trinkets and glasses glittering atop mirrors in this small Royal Street boutique adjoining Laffite's Silver Shop. Glasses and chandeliers, decanters and ashtrays, pitchers and paperweights are typical treasures here. Presented by Arribas Brothers.

MASCARADES D'ARLEQUIN: The glitter and excitement of Mardi Gras is re-created in this charming little shop adjacent to Le Gourmet. Dazzling displays of harlequin dolls, masks, and jewelry draw customers inside.

LE GOURMET: Anyone who ever liked to putter around in the kitchen will relish this attractive store chockablock with interesting cookware. The selection of cookie cutters is purely and simply fabulous: They come, for instance, not in one Mickey Mouse shape but three—a head and two full body shapes. Soup tureens, butter dishes, dippers and Delftware, scrub brushes and rolling pins, linen towels and napkin rings, cheese slicers, soufflé dishes, wooden bowls in a regular menagerie of shapes, pretty chandeliers for the kitchen, copper pots that will last a lifetime, tea kettles and corkscrews, and even artichoke cookers—all are on display, some in pretty antique chests, which are also for sale. There's also an excellent selection of first class cookbooks.

MLLE. ANTOINETTE'S PARFUMERIE: If prizes were to be given for the most beautiful of Disneyland's shops, this tiny, fragrant corner of New Orleans Square would get the blue ribbon. Doorsteps are lovely marble mosaics, cabinets have doors made of glass, and lighting is from an antique chandelier that Walt Disney himself brought from Louisiana just for this purpose. The floor is decoratively tiled and the woodwork a soothing pink overglazed with silver leaf. In addition, there are eight reverse-painted mirrored panels around the shop, shining marvels—believed to be the largest of their type ever created—exemplifying a Chinese art that was popular in Europe from the 14th century to the beginning of the 19th. Painting the butterflies, bluebirds, garlands, and bouquets meant executing the detail work first, then the background—just the opposite of the technique used when putting oils on canvas—then silvering the entire piece. The effect is unabashedly pretty, perfect for displaying the shop's wares—potpourri, scented soaps, atomizers, and perfumes and toilet waters in some 33 different brands, some 54 different fragrances—from Chanel, Guerlain, Ralph Lauren, Gloria Vanderbilt, Myrurgia, Givenchy, Paco Rabanne, Yves Saint Laurent, Patou, Balenciaga, Rochas, Nina Ricci, Worth, Lanvin, Dior, and others. Perfumes also can be blended to order using a half dozen different basic oils, small paddle-shaped blotters, graduated cylinders, and long, glass funnels. The formula you choose is recorded with thousands of others in a large black notebook, and refills can be ordered by mail.

On your way out, take a look at the bronze plaque adorning the wall above the drinking fountain outside. It was discovered by members of the prop department while on a buying trip to New Orleans. The fountain, not part of the original plan, was added just to show it off to best advantage.

DISNEY GALLERY: Located above the entrance to the Pirates of the Caribbean, in several rooms originally designed as an apartment for Walt Disney, this gallery displays original drawings and designs for Disneyland. Changing exhibits will feature the works of Disney Imagineers, long stored in vast archives. Selected pieces of artwork have been reproduced in limited editions and are available for purchase.

MARCHE AUX FLEURS, SACS ET MODES: This "flower, handbag, and fashion market," as its French name translates, specializes in hats. The handsome old-fashioned oak shelves and counters are piled and stacked with them—bowlers and top hats, gangster hats and tweed caps, not to mention a bounty of ladies' bonnets beribboned and befeathered by Disneyland's own hat decorator, who will decorate still others on request. These are not the frilly, net-draped bonnets of Town Square's Mad Hatter Shop, but are instead chapeaus well suited to Easter Sundays, and even if you don't buy they're fun to try on. Barrettes, film, and cigarettes are also available.

CANDY CART: Sweets have always been an important part of New Orleans life, and New Orleans Square has its own purveyor of confections—licorice, hard candies, gumdrops, and such—stationed prominently outside *Café Orleans*, near the entrance to Royal Street.

FRONTIERLAND

Shops are described in the order in which they are encountered moving from east to west through the land. There are a few new shops here.

WESTWARD HO TRADING COMPANY: Authentic turquoise Indian jewelry, as well as fancy belt buckles and carved wooden frames. A unique copper train and stage coach are on display. Also, there are many items with a Southwestern feeling, from jewelry to nativity scenes. Guests can choose from chili pepper earrings and necklaces to a carved lamp whose base is a coyote howling at the moon.

FRONTIERLAND CANDY SHOP: A variety of mouth-watering treats, from delicious, old-fashioned saltwater taffy to tempting candy bars.

SILVER SPURS SUPPLIES: Southwestern-style jewelry, wall hangings, collectibles, and all you need to round out a western-wear outfit can be found at this Frontierland shop.

BUFFALO HAT CO.: Once you've acquired the cowboy duds, this is the place to top it off with a wide variety of western-style hats.

BONANZA OUTFITTERS: Mosey in and try on the wildest western apparel this side of the Mississippi. Custom-designed jackets, western shirts, and fancy pants are just a few of the duds that can be found in this recent Frontierland addition.

DAVY CROCKETT PIONEER MERCANTILE: Located to the left as you enter Frontierland from the Central Plaza, this log-walled, wooden-sidewalked structure offers leather goods and souvenir items. On the way out look above the door and note the framed reproduction of a letter Davy Crockett wrote to his son and daughter from St. Augustine, Texas, in 1836. You can find ornate

belts, bags, billfolds, hair ornaments, watchbands, hats, visors, vests, and moccasins all made of leather. It all smells delightful. Also available here are heart-shaped cutting boards, quilts, calico bonnets, stick horses and rocking horses, toy chests imported from England, 1830s reproduction coloring books, cloth dolls, hand-carved toys, and country-kitchen items.

FRONTIERLAND MENAGERIE: A large selection of Disney character merchandise with a western theme can be found in this shop. This is also a great place to personalize your new western hat by having your name embroidered on it.

CRITTER COUNTRY

Shops are described in the order in which you come upon them while strolling toward Critter Country.

THE BRIAR PATCH: Located right at the base of the Splash Mountain briar patch, this little dwelling specializes in rabbits and other characters from "Song of the South." There are collectible rabbits and bears—some stuffed, others handcarved or painted porcelain with hats, carrots, and ribbons. Winnie the Pooh has his own corner of the shop with honey, books, and apparel. There are also miniature rabbits and bears that adorn rings, necklaces, and earrings.

The grass on the roof is real, seeded with a variety known as creeping red fescue. The grass is hand mowed around the carrots, which grow right through the roof and can be seen from inside the shop.

CROCODILE MERCANTILE: This lace-curtained, log-walled, woodsy-looking emporium is the Disneyland source for the handspun and the homemade. Buyers comb the Appalachian countryside and other rural quarters for many of the wares: carvings, tote bags that would be perfect for carrying diapers, throw pillows, tea towels and potholders, spices, bear pencils, country-themed decorative items for the home, along with a whole assortment of poppets, including some in pigtails and sailor outfits. Among the more unusual items on display are the pins and cufflinks and other jewelry made of Black Hills gold, which, because of the copper and zinc mixed into the metal, has sections tinged with green and pink. Toy rifles, Big Al dolls and mugs and cookie jars, and Splash Mountain T-shirts, sweatshirts, and key chains are also available. The store is a good place to buy film, too.

ADVENTURELAND

Shops are described in the order in which they are encountered while strolling from east to west through the land.

ADVENTURELAND BAZAAR: Except for the fact that bargaining is impossible, this small marketplace is well named. There are goods from most of the exotic corners of the world. From India, assorted brass-crafted jewelry and leather accessories. Africa sends wooden zebras and giraffes and other carvings. From the Orient come pretty little boxes, porcelain figurines, ornate tea sets and jade jewelry, carvings and cloisonné, satin change purses, and hand-embroidered and appliquéd tea towels, lacquered trays, and more. Then there are the American-made products designed for life in tropical climes—bathing togs, sunsuits, and shirts in bright colors. While browsing through the shop, don't miss the handsome Japanese silk wedding gown hanging high against one wall; it sells for about $1,600.

SOUTH SEA TRADERS: This is the place for men's and women's resort and leisure wear. Adjacent to the Adventureland Bazaar, the store features a colorful selection of men's swimming trunks

and women's one- and two-piece bathing suits, walking shorts, and Hawaiian-style shirts. There are also sandals, jewelry, and hats, plus suntan lotion.

TROPICAL IMPORTS: Opposite the Adventureland Bazaar, an island of its own near the entrance to the Jungle Cruise, this emporium is nearly irresistible to young boys. The reason: Rubber snakes and iguanas are part of the stock in trade. The squeamish will, of course, be more interested in the seashells, ashtrays, and other souvenir items. There is also a large selection of stuffed "jungle" animals, including a five-foot-tall gorilla. Film is available here as well.

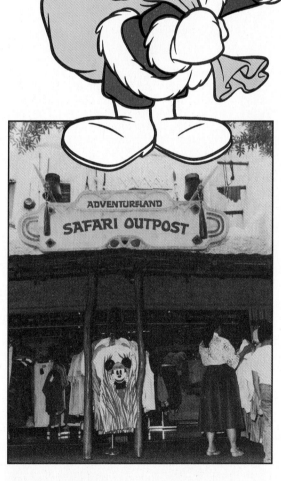

SAFARI OUTPOST: Leather jackets, khaki shorts and knapsacks, and wooden bracelets, necklaces, and earrings are the stock in trade here.

FANTASYLAND

Shops are listed in the order in which a visitor would encounter them while moving in a clockwise fashion through Fantasyland.

CASTLE CHRISTMAS SHOPPE: If anything can make thoughts turn to the yule season in the heart of Southern California in July, it will be this slate-floored, beam-ceilinged establishment, which took over the space formerly occupied by Castle Arts in Sleeping Beauty Castle. Decked out in red and green, with Christmas music playing year-round, this holiday boutique offers all manner of Christmas souvenirs, Mouse-themed and otherwise, that should prove well-nigh irresistible to even budget-conscious guests—trinkets like Santa Clauses and wooden soldiers, bells and drums and Christmas sleighs, plus trifles in velvet, clothespins, dough, and china to decorate next year's tree or mantelpiece.

TINKER BELL TOY SHOPPE: This wonderland installed at the western end of Sleeping Beauty Castle is Disneyland's main stop for serious toy

a trinket or two and avoid the brouhaha of Main Street's Emporium or Tomorrowland's Star Trader. Children's sunglasses, postcards, decals, change purses, pens and pencils, key chains, and the like—some of them bearing likenesses of the Disney characters—are typical wares.

SMALL WORLD GIFTS: Souvenirs predominate at this stand, near It's a Small World, but there are also plush characters, T-shirts, sweatshirts, and custom-made Mickey Mouse name tags..

shopping. Youngsters who have some vacation money burning a hole in their pockets will go for the inexpensive souvenirs. Fond grandparents will relish the children's clothing—red-and-white polka-dotted Minnie dresses and pale blue pinafored Alice in Wonderland dresses for little girls, and pint-size jogging suits and overalls for little boys. Books, tapes, paint-by-number sets, games, and the like complete the offerings. The selection of dolls is particularly good: There are violet-eyed Pierrots with china heads, all very expensive; dolls representing Heidi, Hansel, Gretel, Mother Goose, and other fairy-tale figures. Be sure to take a look at the miniature cars near the north entrance. The same section of the store also sells toy soldiers, Matchbox cars, wonderfully detailed miniature motorcycles, and such. Longtime Disneyland fans may recognize the 2 cannons sitting atop the poop deck at the far end of the store as the weapons from the pirate ship that occupied a prominent place in Fantasyland before the renovation.

GEPPETTO'S ARTS AND CRAFTS: This establishment, now located alongside Pinocchio's Daring Journey, is a treasure trove of handcrafted wares from all over Europe—and from a few other corners of the world. There are all kinds of thimbles, for example, some carved and others covered with the tiniest petit-point embroidery. Cuckoo clocks fill a whole wall. Some have figurines that circle around the clockface. There are music boxes, too. From England come Toby mugs, from Austria there are cowbells, and from Germany there are character dolls and "smokers," carved wooden figurines with a receptacle for an incense pellet and an outlet in the mouth for the smoke to escape. A pair of unique chess sets rounds out the selection, including an $8,000 handmade Alice in Wonderland chess set from England. A must.

SOUVENIR STAND: Near the Matterhorn and It's A Small World plaza, this is a good spot to pick up

THE MAD HATTER: This was always a great place for hats—and it still is. There are traditional black bowlers, and fedoras in several colors, Mouse ears, cowboy hats and feathered Tyrolean hats, gangster hats, and such. But since the debut of the Fantasyland, this establishment has taken on a atmosphere inside and out, and it now looks something like the dwelling that the famous rabbit from *Alice in Wonderland* inhabited. (The small door and window on the Mad Tea Party side are meant to be the entrance of the White Rabbit's house.) The thatching atop the whole structure is, by the way, nonflammable plastic; Disneylanders are still giggling about the spectacle of the crew of brawny construction workers clambering over the rooftop wielding a half dozen hair dryers—which provided the heat to mold the "straws" into the curved edge of the roof. The tree next to the side facing the King Arthur Carrousel is a cork oak (*Quercus suber*), whose bark provides the material for bulletin boards and the like.

BRIAR ROSE COTTAGE: This gift shop, tucked away in a quiet corner of the castle courtyard, carries Disney character ceramic figurines and other collectibles. It's a must for thimble, spoon, and plate collectors. The Capodimonte sculptures, elaborately detailed, handpainted porcelain artworks, inspired by Disney's classic animation, are the work of Italian sculptor Enzo Arzenton. While these are among the most pricey Disney character items sold in the park (Cinderella and her pumpkin coach command a hefty $3,000), they are still fun to look at.

TOMORROWLAND

Shops here are listed counterclockwise from Tomorrowland's Central Plaza entrance.

STAR TRADER: One of the best places in the park for Disney-themed items, it offers T-shirts and sweatshirts galore, pens and rulers, tennis balls and shoehorns, back scratchers, books, magazines, soaps, lollipops, key chains, jogging jackets, pewter charms, and more—all emblazoned with the names and likenesses of one or more of the Disney characters. Stuffed animals are here by the hundreds, including oversize Baloos, Plutos, and Dumbos for $250 to $350 each, which can be ordered when not in stock, and can usually be delivered. In addition, because this is Tomorrowland, there's naturally a good selection of space-age items.

CASTLE CANDY SHOPPE: Somehow a day in Disneyland without candy is like a day in Southern California without sunshine. Despite management's solicitous attention to health-food fans who want to be able to order salads at the fast-food restaurants, Disneyland is simply full of sweets. The Castle Candy Shoppe is just one of nearly a score of spots designed to satisfy the most insatiable sweet tooth. Here, lemon drops and Boston baked beans, rock-candy swizzle sticks, and red hots and lollipops, sour balls and spice drops, fudge, and other treats are dispensed for eating on the spot or for judicious munching along the way. Those who eschew sweets are not forgotten: Peanuts, mixed nuts, and Spanish cashews also are available.

PREMIERE SHOP: Located next to World Premiere CircleVision, this shop specializes in California souvenir merchandise, jewelry, and unique gift items including, floating phones, robots, pastel-colored flashlights, and sunglasses. There are also hats, visors, and sweatshirts.

HATMOSPHERE: Located at the base of the Tomorrowland terminus of the Skyway, this shop stocks hats in all styles—hats made of tweed, felt, and terry cloth, hats with bills and hats with ears, as well as pirate hats, sailor hats, and hats in a dozen other styles. Names can be embroidered on most for free.

SOUVENIR STAND: Located in Alpine Gardens, this spot offers a relatively limited selection, but there's no competing with the crowds for a turn at the cash register. This stand also embroiders names on selected hats.

ENTERTAINMENT

One of the wonders of Disneyland is that even after you've visited all the attractions, browsed in all the shops, and eaten in all the restaurants, there's still plenty to keep visitors coming back again and again. A nearly endless array of performers and performances is continuously available—from Dixieland to big-name bands. Together with Walt Disney World, Disneyland books more entertainment than any other organization in the world. No two years provide quite the same mix of shows, but here are some of the current offerings.

PERFORMERS AND LIVE SHOWS

One of the best things about Disneyland is the array of musicians who stroll, march, croon, and pluck their way through the Magic Kingdom every day. There are so many groups who perform so frequently that you don't have to try very hard to find them. During busy periods, and for special events and private parties, the groups listed below are joined by a number of others. And most days, high school, college, or youth marching bands parade through the park or perform in Town Square as well. In the following descriptions, the term *busy seasons* refers to the summer months plus Christmas, Easter, Thanksgiving, and other holiday periods. *Daily* means just that, but occasionally performers do get days off, so they might not be working every day during your visit.

MAIN STREET

DISNEYLAND BAND: Disneyland's own signature group is as versatile as can be. They'll be performing in Town Square on your way into the park in the morning, but if you miss them then, catch them later during the late afternoon Retreat Ceremony at the flagpole, or at any number of other locations. Their repertoire is mainly turn-of-the-century band music, but they can play just about anything.

SAX QUINTET: Dressed in firemen's costumes—flame-red shirts, black trousers supported by suspenders, and shiny black shoes—members of this group toot away on soprano, alto, tenor, baritone, and bass saxes. They originally came in as extras for a big party in the park, but were so popular they were invited to stay on. Main Street is their primary playing ground; you might see them in the Central Plaza, at the fire station, or at Carefree Corner. They also have been known to play along Matterhorn Way. Group members are currently working on building the world's smallest sax, as well as the world's largest. Their repertoire includes everything from the *William Tell Overture* to Glenn Miller tunes, plus an occasional country-and-western favorite. Weekends and holidays.

DAPPER DANS: Whether strolling along Main Street, or cruising along on their bicycle built for four, the lilting harmonies of Disneyland's only a cappella barbershop quartet are not to be missed.

COKE CORNER PIANIST: Someone is almost always on hand to tickle the ivories on the snow-white upright at this centrally located soda-and-hot dogs restaurant. Daily.

RETREAT CEREMONY: Every day at dusk, the Disneyland Band and a color guard march into Town Square, haul down the American flag, and release a flock of snowy homing pigeons with blue-and-red streamers on their tails. It's a ceremony reminiscent of one that took place during Disneyland's opening, when hundreds of the white birds were released.

ADVENTURELAND

SOUTH SEA PARADISE REVUE: Polynesian dancers perform in a hip-twitching dinner show presented at the *Tahitian Terrace* about once every hour, beginning in late afternoon, during summer, Christmas, Easter, and Thanksgiving periods. For the earliest show, you can arrive as late as 15 minutes beforehand and still claim a seat. For others, it's best to arrive up to an hour in advance. The food that is served here is among the park's best.

NEW ORLEANS SQUARE

SIDE STREET STRUTTERS: A six-member Dixieland jazz group performs weekends and holiday periods at the French Market.

ROYAL STREET BACHELORS: A banjo, an upright string bass, and a clarinet are the instruments for this Dixieland group. The style is early traditional New Orleans Dixieland, a flat four-beat sound influenced by the old funeral marches that were once commonly heard in the Storyville section of the Crescent City. The Bachelors can be seen in the French Market. Daily.

FRONTIERLAND

IMAGINATION: A brand-new nighttime spectacular combines Disney characters, a Disney score, and lasers, fireworks, and water. The show is staged on the Rivers of America between Frontierland and Tom Sawyer Island. Mickey Mouse stars as the Sorcerer's Apprentice using his magical powers to create an array of fantastic displays.

BIG THUNDER MOUNTAIN BREAKDOWN BOYS: Formerly known as the Main Street Maniacs, this group is great by any name. A must. Daily.

BIG THUNDER RANCH: A fiddler is on hand to entertain guests. Daily.

GOLDEN HORSESHOE JAMBOREE: This lively, funny musical show is usually staged five times daily, with performance times changing throughout the year. Check on times upon arrival. The routine is one of the funniest around and makes it well worth your while to reserve a place as soon as possible after your arrival in the park. For further description see "Frontierland." For information about the food served, see our land-by-land restaurant guide. Reservations are required. Daily.

CRITTER COUNTRY

BUFORD T. BARLEY: This entertaining storyteller can be found wandering near the queue for Splash Mountain, spinning some of the most outrageous tales ever heard. On weekdays, Farley the Fiddler strolls the area, delighting guests with a blend of country and bluegrass fiddling.

FANTASYLAND

VIDEOPOLIS: The former teen dance club has been transformed into a performance theater featuring stage shows and holiday entertainment.

TOMORROWLAND

VOYAGER, DISCOVERY, and GALAXY: Soft rock and Top 40 tunes are the staples of these contemporary groups, holding forth from the stage at Tomorrowland Terrace. Daily.

TRANSTAR: A futuristic, three-member electronic band performs intergalactic versions of Top-40 tunes. Performances are held near the *Space Place* restaurant in front of Mission to Mars.

FIREWORKS

Even the rare diehards who put fireworks displays in a class with other people's home movies find few bones to pick with Fantasy in the Sky, the spectacular fireworks show presented nightly in summer, on selected nights in May, on New Year's Eve, and on other special occasions. At about 9:30 P.M. each evening during these times, Tinker Bell waves her magic wand to start the spectacular fireworks, which are accompanied by a medley of Disney tunes and traditional patriotic favorites. More than 250 rockets are used each evening for this extravaganza. The shells that were once detonated over the course of about 15 minutes are now fired in about a third of that time—a rate of one shell every couple of seconds, right in time to the music on the PA system, thanks to new computerization. The rockets, Roman candles, saxons, shells, and stars that make up the show come from all around the world. The ones from England look as if they have been poured from a pitcher, with a particularly concentrated area of color at the center. Japanese and Chinese shells are those with the symmetrical star bursts. Heretofore, Fantasy in the Sky shows have been roughly similar at Disneyland and Walt Disney World.

DANCING

Between the parades, the fireworks, the fireflies twinkling in the trees of the Central Plaza, and a certain air of subdued excitement, there's scarcely a more romantic place in the world than Disneyland on a summer evening. An unsung pleasure that completes the effect is going dancing. You can do it to big band sounds in Carnation Plaza Gardens and to contemporary music on the dance floor at Tomorrowland Terrace. On your way into the park, be sure to inquire about what is going on.

PARADES

No Main Street is really complete without a parade, and Disneyland has always had plenty of them. The usual route is between Town Square (from the *Town Square Café*) and It's a Small World. The direction varies somewhat from time to time, as does the route, so it's wise to inquire at City Hall on your way into the park.

On summer evenings, Disneyland features the Main Street Electrical Parade, a splendiferous spectacle of lights—500,000 in all—that are arranged on floats to depict various scenes from classic Walt Disney motion pictures. At Christmas, a unit features toy soldiers out of a scene from *Babes in Toyland*, with Santa Claus himself bringing up the rear.

Where to watch: Of all the spots along the route, the single best vantage point is the center of the platform of the Disneyland Railroad's Main Street depot. The second-best viewing point is from the curb on either side of Main Street. There's more space here, as there is on either side of the plaza leading to It's a Small World, whose white-and-gold facade provides a fine only-in-Disneyland backdrop. The Plaza Terrace, outside the *Plaza Inn*, and the patio at the *Town Square Café* also are pleasant, though the seating is more limited. In any case, it's important to arrive about an hour beforehand to claim your piece of curb. If you hate crowds, Main Street isn't for you, and any other location in the park will do better. Better still, time your visit to catch the later parade on nights when there is more than one.

WHERE TO SEE THE CHARACTERS

It's Disneyland policy that there will always be plenty of Disney characters (as many as 50) roaming visibly through the park. Sometimes you'll find them keeping company with one of the musical groups during a performance.

For pictures, your best bets are in Town Square, near Carefree Corner on Main Street, and at the *Plaza Inn* nearby; at the Snow White Grotto; and around Fantasyland, especially near Sleeping Beauty Castle. Like real people everywhere, they don't like being pushed, and you will get their attention most easily by being friendly and patient.

HOLIDAY CELEBRATIONS AND SPECIAL EVENTS

Except for Christmas, New Year's Eve, and Easter, Disneyland does not celebrate specific holidays in a major way. Yet there are plenty of special events all year-round. Some of these simply offer a bit more in the way of live entertainment during regular park operating hours. For others, the park is only open to those who purchase special admission tickets. The number of tickets available is restricted so visitors will enjoy a higher-quality experience, and the level of live talent on hand tends to be higher.

Since Disneyland's plans do change, it is a wise idea to call the park's Guest Relations Office (714-999-4565) for up-to-date information on any specific event in which you may be interested.

For more detailed information about seasonal goings-on in the park, see our discussion of when to visit in *Getting Ready to Go*.

NEW YEAR'S EVE: This big, end-of-the-year bash is one of the best of Disneyland's annual affairs. Hats and noisemakers are handed out at the main gate, top-name talent entertains, and fireworks go off at midnight over Sleeping Beauty Castle and other areas.

EASTER: Always a popular time to visit, the park remains open late during these weeks (April 11 through 26).

SUMMER PREVIEW WEEKENDS: During the spring, the Main Street Electrical parade makes its yearly debut, running every weekend until the summer season begins.

SUMMER SEASON: Scheduled for June 22 through September 8, this is Disneyland's busiest season, and with good reason. The park is open daily from 8 A.M. to 1 A.M. The Main Street Electrical Parade is featured twice nightly, and Fantasy in the Sky fireworks are presented every night at 9:30 P.M. The greatest names in big band music are scheduled to perform nightly at Main Street's Plaza Gardens stage, and every attraction in the park will be operating (as opposed to the off-season, when refurbishments often take place).

FOURTH OF JULY: One of the busiest days of the year—and one to avoid if you don't like crowds—this holiday also features a bigger-than-usual fireworks display.

THANKSGIVING WEEKEND: Extended hours, musical entertainment, and the first installment of the Very Merry Christmas Parade (on Thanksgiving day) are the highlights.

CHRISTMAS: If there's a single time of year when Disneyland looks its prettiest, it may well be at Yuletide. Main Street is decked to the nines with traditional piney red-and-greenery, including hundreds of poinsettias and a huge white fir (trucked in from the northern part of the state) flecked with tiny Styrofoam beads, decorated with some 4,000 lights and ornaments, and surrounded by oversize Christmas packages. Carolers in costumes straight out of Dickens stroll along Main Street, and on two nights at the beginning of the holiday season there's a special ceremony that features a candlelight procession from Sleeping Beauty Castle to the train station, as well as Christmas music by a thousand-voice choir, backed by appropriate instruments, and a reading of the Christmas story by some well-known actor. (Jason Robards, Rock Hudson, Ed Asner, Jimmy Stewart, and Cary Grant have all done it in the past.) The "Hallelujah Chorus" from Handel's *Messiah* provides the rousing finale.

Also during the season, the Very Merry Christmas Parade, a Disney Yuletide favorite, is featured. Live music and hundreds of performers bring to life many Christmas traditions of the past. Christmas activities, including decorations, will begin this year on Thanksgiving.

Oddly enough, the week before Christmas is one of the best times of the year to visit the park. The crowds are relatively small and the entertainment usually abundant. In contrast, the day *after* Christmas is usually a madhouse: Disneylanders surmise that holiday togetherness makes Southern Californians fidgety and motivates them to come to the park in droves. Once they get there, the queues are enormous, and the seasonal chill in the air doesn't make the waiting pleasant. Anyone who plans to visit at this time of year should bring warm clothing.

SPECIAL TIPS

When purchasing tickets you will be given a guidebook (compliments of Kodak). Keep it as a handy reference.

- Study a map of Disneyland before you arrive so you understand the layout and have some idea of what you want to see and do.
- Check entertainment schedules, which are available at City Hall and Carefree Corner.
- Give yourself plenty of time to take it all in—and don't try to do too much in a single stretch.
- Avoid the park in summer, at Christmastime, and on weekends throughout the year. If you must visit on a weekend, try for Sunday rather than Saturday, and remember that Sunday night is one of the least crowded times in the park; ditto for Sunday morning. If you must visit in summer, try to arrive during the last two weeks of June, the last week in August, or the first week in September. If you're not really eager to see the fireworks, the first half of June also is fine. At the end of the year, try to travel during the week before Christmas, when the park is pleasant, beautifully decorated, and not too crowded—and avoid the following week, when it is usually mobbed. Year-round, Tuesdays, Wednesdays, and Thursdays are the least crowded days to visit. For the most satisfying experience in Disneyland, study our suggestions about when to go in *Getting Ready to Go* before you make your travel plans.
- Break up your day in the park. Arrive early, see the major attractions until things seem to be getting congested, return to your hotel for a swim and a nap, and then return to the park in the evening. Remember to have your hand stamped and keep your Passport to re-enter later in the day.
- Reserve your place at the Golden Horseshoe Jamboree immediately after arriving in the park. It's a good choice for a light lunch because you'll avoid waiting in line, and it's a fine hideout from the midday crowds at later showings.
- Have your lunch before 11 A.M. or after 2 P.M., and your dinner before 5 P.M. or after 8 P.M., to avoid lines. Note that the *Town Square Café*, the *Hungry Bear* restaurant in Critter Country, and the *Space Place* in Tomorrowland usually slow down before other eating spots on busy days.
- Avoid the Space Mountain and Star Tours attractions immediately after meals. Weak stomachs—and many that are usually strong—have been known to revolt.
- At mealtime, look at all the lines before stepping into the nearest (and usually longest) one.
- Wear your most comfortable shoes. Blisters are the most common malady reported to Central First Aid. (Note that no bare feet are permitted inside the park.)
- Roller-coaster haters should view the inside of Space Mountain from the PeopleMover and think twice before skipping the rocket ride. It's simply

too pretty to miss. Non-riding parents should note, however, that they can queue with their offspring until they reach the loading area, where they will find the last of three "chicken exits."

- At busy times and on busy days, use the Big Thunder Trail to get between the east and west sides of the park.
- Remember that lines for riding the Disneyland Railroad move most quickly at the Main Street station.
- Ride the major attractions—Pirates of the Caribbean, Space Mountain, Star Tours, Big Thunder Mountain Railroad, the Jungle Cruise, the Haunted Mansion, the Matterhorn, and Splash Mountain—early in the day or during parades. In the busy afternoon hours, go to the smaller attractions where the lines are comparatively shorter—the *Mark Twain* Steamboat and Mission to Mars are good choices. This is also a fine time for shopping, for enjoying musical performances, and for the Golden Horseshoe Jamboree.
- Avoid shopping at times when everybody else does—that is, in late afternoon and at the end of the park's operating hours. Shops are a good place to escape the midday heat.

WHAT TO DO WHEN IT'S BUSY

At busy times on busy days, visit the following less-crowded attractions:

Main Street: Disneyland Railroad, the Walt Disney Story featuring "Great Moments with Mr. Lincoln," the Main Street Cinema, the Penny Arcade

Adventureland: Enchanted Tiki Room, Swiss Family Treehouse

Critter Country: Country Bear Playhouse

Frontierland: *Mark Twain*, *Columbia*, Mike Fink Keel Boats

Fantasyland: It's a Small World, Sleeping Beauty Castle, Motor Boat Cruise

Tomorrowland: Starcade, Mission to Mars, PeopleMover

Go shopping; store your purchases in lockers on Main Street.

Enjoy one of the musical groups, or if you've made arrangements in advance, watch the Golden Horseshoe Jamboree.

Have your picture taken in costume at the Kodak Camera Center on Main Street.

Rent or borrow a camera there and take your own pictures around the park.

Leave the premises and return later in the day.

THE MAGIC KINGDOM'S BEST ATTRACTIONS

Everybody has his favorites, but here are a number that receive the highest ratings:

Adventureland: Jungle Cruise

Critter Country: Country Bear Playhouse, Splash Mountain

New Orleans Square: Haunted Mansion, Pirates of the Caribbean

Frontierland: Big Thunder Mountain Railroad

Fantasyland: It's a Small World, Pinocchio's Daring Journey, Snow White's Scary Adventures, Peter Pan's Flight, Mr. Toad's Wild Ride

Tomorrowland: Space Mountain, American Journeys, Star Tours, Captain EO

WHERE TO FIND THE RESTROOMS

Disneylanders tell the story of how, as opening day neared with park construction behind schedule, Walt had to choose between finishing the drinking fountains or the restrooms. Restrooms rated a high priority then—and still do. There are plenty of them. They are large and almost uniformly spotless—and relatively easy to find.

MAIN STREET
- In Town Square behind the Bank of America, just through the entrance tunnel to your right as you walk through the main gate
- Adjacent to Disneyland City Hall
- Just south of the *Main Street Ice Cream Parlor*, behind that restaurant's outdoor eating area
- In the *Plaza Inn* restaurant
- In the Central Plaza, behind the seating area in *Carnation Plaza Gardens*

ADVENTURELAND
- Adjoining the Adventureland Bazaar
- In the *Tahitian Terrace* restaurant

FRONTIERLAND
- On Tom Sawyer Island: one inside Fort Wilderness, the other at the entrance of Injun Joe's Cave
- At Big Thunder Ranch behind *Big Thunder Barbecue*

NEW ORLEANS SQUARE
- Between the *Mint Julep Bar* and the Marché aux Fleurs, Sacs et Modes
- Inside the *Blue Bayou* restaurant

CRITTER COUNTRY
- Below the *Hungry Bear* restaurant

FANTASYLAND
- Just off Matterhorn Way
- Across from the Skyway to Tomorrowland entrance

TOMORROWLAND
- At the exit to Space Mountain
- Below the entrance to the Skyway to Fantasyland
- On the Tomorrowland side of the *Plaza Inn*

SUGGESTED DISNEYLAND ITINERARIES

When you visit for the first time, it's hard to know just what to do first. The following programs should help put you on the right track. Use them as a guide, and add other stops as your fancy dictates within our framework. Most people visit about 10 attractions per day, but it's easy to do more during the quieter season. Note that the suggestions here are designed for an energetic family with children ages 10 and up. Families with younger children will want to add more attractions in Fantasyland. Also be sure to stop at City Hall or Carefree Corner on Main Street to find out about times and locations for shows and parades—many of which are well worth an effort to see.

	DURING BUSY SEASONS, WHEN THE PARK IS OPEN LATE	**THE REST OF THE YEAR**
ONE-DAY VISIT There's so much to see that it's impossible to do it all. But you can get the flavor of the Magic Kingdom if the visit is properly planned.	Arrive in the parking lot a half hour before park opening, and get oriented with a ride on the Disneyland Railroad (this attraction opens as early as ten minutes before official park opening). Window shop your way down Main Street. Circle the park, taking in Space Mountain and Star Tours in Tomorrowland, the Matterhorn and Pinocchio's Daring Journey in Fantasyland, and Splash Mountain in Critter Country. Visit some Main Street shops. Take a break: We suggest the lunch buffet at *Daisy's*, in the nearby *Hyatt*. Return to your hotel for a swim and a nap. Re-enter the park between 5 P.M. and 6 P.M. Dine at the *Tahitian Terrace* restaurant in Adventureland or at the *Blue Bayou* in New Orleans Square. At 8 P.M., take your place on Main Street for the parade. While adults are holding places, children can visit the Penny Arcade. Watch Fantasy in the Sky fireworks after the parade. Visit Big Thunder Mountain in Frontierland and the Haunted Mansion and Pirates of the Caribbean in New Orleans Square before park closing. **Note:** If there are no children in your party, or if they are older, it is better to reorder the evening's activities so that you visit Big Thunder Mountain, the Haunted Mansion, and Pirates of the Caribbean slightly before and during the early showing of the Main Street Electrical Parade, and to take in entertainment and snack on a fritter and hot chocolate at the *French Market* until the second showing of the parade.	Arrive in the parking lot just before park opening. Stroll down Main Street. Visit Space Mountain and Star Tours. Take the Disneyland Railroad to Frontierland. Go to the *Golden Horseshoe* to get reservations for an afternoon show. Visit Big Thunder Mountain in Frontierland, Pirates of the Caribbean and the Haunted Mansion in New Orleans Square, and Splash Mountain and the Country Bear Playhouse in Critter Country. Shop in New Orleans Square. Lunch at noon—no later— at the *Main Street Ice Cream Parlor*. Visit Main Street shops, and check purchases in lockers before going to the *Golden Horseshoe*. After the show, explore Fantasy—land and visit It's a Small World. Visit Tomorrowland attractions. Dine at the *Blue Bayou* in New Orleans Square, if time permits.
TWO-DAY VISIT Allows you to see more than the highlights.	**First day** Same as above. **Second day** Arrive 30 minutes before park opening. Breakfast at *Town Square Café*. At park opening, head for *Golden Horseshoe* to get reservations for an afternoon show. Visit Swiss Family Treehouse, Jungle Cruise, and Enchanted Tiki Room in Adventureland. Take in some Main Street shops; check purchases in lockers. Lunch at *Main Street Ice Cream Parlor* no later than noon. Visit shops in Adventureland. Watch Golden Horseshoe Jamboree. Ride the *Mark Twain* Steamboat or Davy Crockett's Explorer Canoes and go out to Tom Sawyer Island. Take in Fantasyland attractions you may have missed on the previous afternoon. On the way out, stop at the Main Street Cinema, the Penny Arcade, and "Great Moments with Mr. Lincoln." Return to the park later in the evening for entertainment at the *French Market* in New Orleans Square.	**First day** Same as above. **Second day** Arrive 30 minutes before park opening, for breakfast at the *Town Square Café*. Visit Jungle Cruise, Swiss Family Treehouse, and Enchanted Tiki Room in Adventureland. Lunch at *Blue Bayou* restaurant no later than noon. Ride the *Mark Twain* Steamboat or Davy Crockett's Explorer Canoes, and go out to Tom Sawyer Island. Take in Fantasyland attractions that are open when you visit, plus those in other lands you may have missed the previous afternoon. On the way out, if time remains, stop at the Main Street Cinema, take in "Great Moments with Mr. Lincoln," and visit the Penny Arcade (in that order).
THREE-DAY VISIT Allows for a really in-depth look.	**First and second days** Same as above. **Third day** Spend the day revisiting attractions that you particularly liked, exploring the shops, and taking in the live entertainment.	**First and second days** Same as above. **Third day** Follow program for the third day of a three-day visit as outlined at left.

GOOD MEALS, GREAT TIMES

Sit down for dinner at the *Blue Bayou* restaurant in Disneyland's New Orleans Square, and while you're enjoying the Louisiana fare, soak up the show all around you. It's part of the experience of dining at Disneyland, where there's always more to a meal than just food.

In Anaheim, which in the past has been noted more for its fast-food establishments than for haute cuisine, there nevertheless are some emerging authentic first class restaurants. There's some first-rate seafood, some tasty hot Mexican food, a little French nouvelle cuisine, and even a taste of buffalo meat—which is featured on one local menu. If you venture farther afield—into other areas of Orange County and Los Angeles, for example—it's hard to avoid dining in some of the best restaurants in the country. So while it is delightfully easy to find pleasant (and tasty) nourishment within and immediately around Disneyland, true gastronomic adventure may require a little traveling. Your own tastes and taste buds will determine whether you feel even the finest food is worth the effort.

This chapter is divided into two main sections, the first devoted to eating at Disneyland, the second to eating in Anaheim and environs, with additional information on nightlife and a list of special menus.

The Disneyland section is arranged by "land" and then according to type of restaurant—waitress-service, buffeteria (the Disney world for cafeteria), fast-food, and snack facilities. Off-property restaurants are classified by location—first those in the Anaheim hotels and elsewhere in Anaheim proper, then in the rest of Orange County, and then in Los Angeles. The last section is devoted specifically to mealtime opportunities that are worth a journey.

In the following restaurant descriptions, the letters that conclude each paragraph refer to the meals offered there: breakfast (B), lunch (L), dinner (D), or snacks (S). Most restaurants marked B (but not all in Disneyland) offer a full breakfast. All Disneyland menus were current as we went to press. (Unless otherwise noted, all phone numbers are in the 714 area code.)

First-time visitors to Disneyland expect to find little more than hamburgers and hot dogs, french fries, and fizzy soft drinks on the park's menus, so they're invariably surprised to find Disneyland's food so varied. White-toqued chefs whip up elaborately garnished omelettes at the *Town Square Café*, and red-and-white-gowned waitresses serve platters of pita bread sandwiches stuffed with chicken and avocado at the *Main Street Ice Cream Parlor*. Tacos, New Orleans-style fritters, massive fresh fruit salads topped with kiwi fruit in season, New York-cut steaks, and chicken dishes with exotic sauces are no less unexpected. And dieters who enter the park resigned to misery (or cheating) are delighted to find chef's salads and other low-calorie fare at fast-food establishments, and unsugared fruit juices and frozen fruit-juice bars for snacking and refreshment throughout the park.

With such a selection, mealtimes in the park become almost as enjoyable as the hours in between. The surroundings are perfect in every detail, and the colors, garnishes, and overall presentation of the food make everything look truly appealing. Somehow it scarcely matters that the food itself usually turns out to be standard, all-American cafeteria fare. Besides, when you're eating outside, on a terrace, basking in that fine, warm California sunshine and listening to the occasional marching band oompahing its way through the land, even everyday dishes seem special.

When hunger strikes between meals, there are dozens of choices—including ice cream and delicious frozen-juice bars from any number of wagons stationed strategically around the park, popcorn from distinctive bright red carts.

Cash, traveler's checks, or personal checks (imprinted with a guest's name and address,

drawn on a U.S. bank, and accompanied by proper identification—a valid driver's license and a major credit card such as American Express, Carte Blanche, Diners Club, MasterCard, or Visa) can be used as payment at all Disneyland sit-down and fast-food restaurants, as well as cafeterias. American Express, Visa, and MasterCard credit cards may also be used to pay for food at these facilities. Only cash is accepted at the ice cream, popcorn, and churro carts in the park.

In the following descriptions, note that an asterisk after the meal designation letter means that the meal is served only during Disneyland's busy season (see *Getting Ready to Go*).

MAIN STREET

TABLE SERVICE

TOWN SQUARE CAFE: Eggs and omelettes are the principal fare at this sunny establishment in Town Square, to the left of the Mad Hatter. While waiting in the small reception center that's papered in rosy pink floral stripes, watch the chef

whip up omelettes, such as the "Extraordinaire," which is served with ham, cheese, mushrooms, green onions, and salsa, or the "California," which comes with avocado slices, tomato, alfalfa sprouts, sour cream, and pine nuts. A Spanish omelette, made with tomato, chilis, Spanish sausage, green onions, and cheese, is also on the menu, as is the dish called "Fantasia," filled with seasonal fruits and a special yogurt sauce. All the omelettes are prepared with a reduced-cholesterol blend of eggs and egg whites. Whole eggs are available on request. These are served throughout the day. Then there are Belgian waffles in the shape of Mickey Mouse's head and ears, served with eggs or strawberries and whipped cream, steak and eggs, cereal, English or blueberry muffins, or bagels with cream cheese. At lunch and dinner, the fare includes salad selections, sandwiches and hamburgers; and fruit pies and strawberry-topped cheesecake for dessert. Youngsters can order special Mouseketeers' Treats (hot dogs or hamburgers). Meals are served indoors in a pretty, floral-carpeted room with pale turquoise curtains and attractive, white, wrought-iron chairs, or outdoors on a pleasant terrace full of bright-yellow umbrellas. After eating, be sure to take a look at the prints on the walls near the glass-fronted kitchen. They're reproductions of 19th-century images of English prize pullets: "Psyche," "Blossom," "Titania," and others. Open holidays, weekends, and summer season. B, L, D, S.

MAIN STREET ICE CREAM PARLOR: This bright red-and-white establishment is at its best in springtime, when the floral planters that surround its outdoor garden are ablaze with scarlet tulips. But it's an exceptionally pleasant place at any other time of year, too, and if you're in the mood for a California-style sandwich or salad, it's well worth a detour. At breakfast, Danish pastry, Mickey Mouse-shaped waffles, cereal, or eggs with bacon, sausage, or ham and fried potatoes are the offerings. For lunch and dinner, there are hamburgers, sandwiches filled with avocado, tomato, and alfalfa sprouts; chicken salad and sprouts; or avocado and turkey. The "Crossroads of America" sandwich, made with roast beef, avocado, and Jack cheese, grilled on sourdough bread, is quite tasty. The two main selections on the menu that are not a salad or a sandwich are lemon-herbed chicken breast (served with a baked potato and a fresh vegetable salad) and steak drizzled with cheddar cheese.

Since this is, after all, first and foremost an ice cream parlor, select from a variety of fancy sundaes made with Carnation ice cream and other ingredients listed on the menu. Don't overlook the "Golden West Freeze," which resembles a milkshake and is made with orange sherbet (an excellent variation, much favored by Disneylanders in the know, is made with half sherbet, half vanilla ice cream). Children's specialties are available. Note that Fantasia ice cream—made with burgundy cherry, pistachio, and banana—was developed by Carnation specially for Disneyland. On the hottest days, you may want to eat indoors, the better to admire the long, polished-wood fountain and the frosted crystal light fixtures. When you crave the sun, a seat on the terrace warrants the wait. Tables nearest Main Street are the most pleasant because of the overall view of the passing scene. Presented by the Carnation Company. B, L, D, S.

BUFFETERIAS

PLAZA INN: The split baked chicken served here was one of Roy Disney's favorite meals—and this was one of the restaurants that made Walt Disney proudest. Just one look inside tells why: Tufted velvet upholstery, gleaming mirrors, and a fine, ornate floral carpet elevate this cafeteria well above similar eateries. The draperies are a lovely shade of coral, and the silk-satin valances are trimmed with custom-made fringes, rosettes, and borders. The ceilings are stained glass, and the moldings are elaborate and immaculately painted. Sconces made of Parisian bronze and Baccarat crystal are mounted on the walls, and two dozen basket chandeliers, also of crystal and bronze, hang from the ceiling. There's even a 200-year-old French chandelier, found in an antiques shop, that's hung from the ceiling on a chain that allows the fixture to be raised and lowered for cleanings. (Plain old ammonia and water are used, and the process takes 3½ hours.) The four-shelf French cabinet, elaborately inlaid with fruit woods and trimmed in bronze ormolu, is just as old, and the ornaments that embellish it (and the rest of the establishment) are antique as well. Among the few decorative objects here that are not true antiques are the two ornate coffee urns behind the counter. The setting is so lovely that the food—prime ribs, spaghetti with meat sauce, stuffed baked chicken, and a daily fresh fish dish—pales a bit by comparison. There are seasonal variations in the menu also, and when the park opens before 10 A.M. (see hours of operation in the *Magic Kingdom* chapter), a character breakfast is held here. Children's portions are available. A birthday party held at Disneyland is a very special experience. Cakes decorated with the celebrant's name and appropriate appurtenances are served, upon advance arrangement (ten days' notice and payment one week before the event). B*, L, D, S.

PLAZA PAVILION: Facing the *Plaza Inn* across the Hub, this much less ornate establishment offers open-air dining during summer and holiday seasons. For lunch and dinner, the menu offers a variety of chicken dinners, including fried, lemon-herbed, and honeybaked, spaghetti with Italian sausage, vegetable lasagna, fresh soups, and several salads. Children can select chicken strips or a small portion of spaghetti. B*, L*, D*, S*.

FAST FOOD

COCA-COLA REFRESHMENT CORNER: Coke Corner, as this lively establishment at the northern end of Main Street (opposite Carefree Corner) is commonly called, is presided over by a talented ragtime pianist who tickles the ivories from park opening until the end of the day, while visitors nibble hot dogs, brownies, chips, soft drinks, milk, cookies, fruit, juice, hot chocolate, coffee, and, when the weather is cool, chili and beans. Even if this fare doesn't strike your fancy, stop in to see the handmade replica of an antique Coke advertising thermometer that hangs near the Coke Corner exit of the Penny Arcade. Presented by the Coca-Cola Company. L, D, S.

CARNATION PLAZA GARDENS: With its red-and-white striped awning and polished terrazzo dance floor, this is one of the most festive spots in the park. The small stage is the setting for character shows in the afternoons, and for band concerts (with dancing) on summer evenings— usually from about 7 P.M. until park closing. When the mirrored ball sends stars shooting all around, it's hard not to feel transported back a half century in time. Vanilla, strawberry, chocolate, chocolate chip, Fantasia, and orange sherbet sugar cones are available, along with hamburgers in adult and children's sizes. Presented by the Carnation Company. L, D, S.

SNACKS

MAIN STREET CONE SHOP: Tucked between the Disney Clothiers and Market House, this window service ice cream shop serves a limited selection of Carnation ice cream flavors, including vanilla, chocolate, strawberry, orange sherbet, and a flavor of the day. Ice cream sundaes (with two scoops of the flavor of your choice) are served in a waffle cone and covered with hot fudge, strawberry, or caramel toppings, plus real whipped cream and a cherry. A one-scoop junior sundae, a root beer float served in a souvenir mug, soft drinks, and coffee are also available. Tables with umbrellas provide a pleasant and shady resting spot. Presented by the Carnation Company. S.

MARKET HOUSE: This quaint turn-of-the-century market offers a generous selection of fancy cookies, tangy dill pickles plucked right from a barrel, dried fruit, and various candies. Hot coffee and ice-cold apple cider are also available. S.

BLUE RIBBON BAKERY: Fresh-baked cookies, muffins, and pastries are tempting treats at this snack spot. Lowfat and nonfat yogurt are also offered with a variety of toppings, including candy, nuts, cookies, fruit, and hot and cold syrups. S.

ADVENTURELAND

TABLE SERVICE

TAHITIAN TERRACE: Believed by many to be the site of the Magic Kingdom's best food, diners get plenty of atmosphere here and, at dinner, a fine, hip-wriggling Polynesian show. The coral tree onstage and overhead is a special Disney creation—it wouldn't do, after all, to have one that would shed its leaves on your plate. The tree trunk was built on location, the limbs made on a back lot, and the 14,175 leaves and bright flowers were then grafted on by hand. During the construction

process, Walt Disney saw the tree, decided it was "too low," and ordered it raised three feet, with cranes, to its present 35-foot height. To this backdrop, add a handful of sarong-clad, grass-skirted dancers who play with fire and sway their way through the dances of the South Pacific. It's a first-rate show. Note that the show is presented only during the summer season.

The food is a pleasant surprise. At dinner, there's steak marinated in teriyaki sauce; pork back ribs in a Polynesian barbecue sauce; shrimp with Tahitian sauce, flash fried in a wok; Australian lobster tails; grilled chicken; fresh fish of the day; pineapple upsidedown cake, and other exotic desserts. At lunch there is a charbroiled ½-pound hamburger with a choice of cheese, and fresh mushrooms, onions, or pineapple toppings. Showtimes are subject to change, so double check upon arriving at the park. (Seats for the first show are available up to 15 minutes before performance time; for all the others, it's a good idea to arrive an hour in advance because the later shows are more popular and seating is allocated on a first come, first served basis.) Lunchtime is also pleasant here because not too many people know that the restaurant is open at midday (albeit without a show). L*, D*.

FAST FOOD

BENGAL BARBECUE: Skewered beef and chicken and a daily special highlight the menu at Adventureland's newest establishment. Fresh fruit is served with a raspberry yogurt dip, and fresh vegetables are available with a dill dip. Specialty items include the "Adventure Quencher" (fruit slush) and the "Bengal Freeze" (sorbet). L, D, S.

SNACKS

TIKI JUICE BAR: Located at the entrance to the Enchanted Tiki Room, this stand sells fresh Hawaiian pineapple spears and pineapple juice. Hot coffee and soft-serve frozen pineapple dessert are also offered. Presented by Dole Pineapple. S.

CRITTER COUNTRY

FAST FOOD

HUNGRY BEAR: This is an immense place, yet when you sit on the ground-level veranda, with the Rivers of America lapping so close to your feet that you could cool your toes on a hot day, the activity of the rest of the park seems miles away. Ducks dive for occasional tidbits, canoeists in Davy Crockett's Explorer Canoes paddle by, the *Mark Twain* towers above you as it steams downstream, and the air rifles in Tom Sawyer Island's Fort Wilderness (just opposite) are tap-tap-tapping away. There's commotion all around, but you're strangely (and quite pleasantly) removed from it all. Better yet, during busy periods, the restaurant's

crowds begin to build up a little later in the day than they do at more centrally located establishments, and they also thin out a little earlier. The menu includes hamburgers, cheeseburgers, chicken breast sandwich, french fries, and barbecued beef and tuna sandwiches—plus smoked turkey salads, fresh fruit plates, garden vegetable salad, tuna salad, and an array of sweets (cookies, ice cream sandwiches, frozen bananas, and the like). Presented by Wonder Bread. L, D, S.

BRER BAR: If a hot dog or sandwich will do, make a meal stop at this lace-curtained, paisley-wallpapered establishment alongside Teddi Barra's Swingin' Arcade. But even if you prefer something more substantial elsewhere, stop in for a look at the polished-wood bar, which almost looks as though it's a mile long thanks to an ingenious arrangement of mirrors. Hot pretzels, chips, dill pickles, cookies, ice cream snacks, frozen bananas, yogurt cups, fresh whole fruit, and soft drinks are all available, as is apple cider, which is served hot or cold. There are small tables set up on the board sidewalk outdoors, by the waterfall at the exit to Country Bear Playhouse—an altogether lovely, sweet-smelling, fern-decked corner of the park. Be sure to look at the three figures above the bar—Melvin the Moose, Buff the Buffalo, and Max the Stag, the Audio-Animatronics heads that preside over the Country Bear Playhouse next door. L, D, S.

HARBOUR GALLEY: Critter Country's newest restaurant is tucked into the shanties that line the docking area for the *Columbia* and the *Mark Twain*. Specialties include bacon-wrapped scallops, spicy Cajun "popcorn" shrimp, clam chowder served in a bread bowl, and tasty curly fries. L, D.

NEW ORLEANS SQUARE

TABLE SERVICE

BLUE BAYOU: This popular dining spot offers food in a Louisiana bayou setting—including a fresh catch of the day, boneless chicken breast served with a Caribbean cream sauce, crab cakes, Caribbean shrimp scampi, the Royal Bayou Salad (avocado stuffed with bay shrimp, on a bed of lettuce, with assorted fruits and vegetables), and other dishes that are similar. Prime ribs and New York-cut choice sirloin steaks are also available, along with an assortment of desserts ranging from chocolate mousse with whipped cream and chocolate shavings to assorted flavors of cheesecake. A children's menu is also available.

But the lure here is as much the atmosphere as the menu. Occupying a terrace alongside the bayou inside the Pirates of the Caribbean building, the restaurant's lighting is designed so that it appears perpetually moonlit. Fireflies twinkle above the bayou grasses, and stars shine through Spanish moss draped languidly over the big old live oaks, against a sky that manages to be bright

fresh fish specials. There's Dixieland music played on stage periodically throughout the evening, when, in summer, the Royal Street Bachelors hold forth with such spirit that you could listen for toe-tapping hours and get your money's worth and more. If all you want is a snack, stop at the adjacent *Mint Julep Bar* and pick up a fritter (a large, hollow, spherical doughnut) and some hot chocolate and take it to one of the small round tables on the *French Market*'s terrace. L, D, S.

blue and dark at the same time. Careful listeners will hear bullfrogs calling and crickets chirping, and off in the distance an old settler rocks away on the porch of a tumbledown shack, apparently watching over the boats full of sightseers heading off into the bayou and their Disney adventure among the Pirates of the Caribbean. Busiest periods are from noon to 2 P.M. and again from 5 P.M. or 5:30 P.M. until as late as 10 P.M. L, D.

BUFFETERIAS

CAFE ORLEANS: Visitors can dine inside on small, round, oak-topped tables, or outside under blue-green umbrellas on a terrace that offers a splendid view of the gristmill on Tom Sawyer Island, and of the *Columbia*, the *Mark Twain*, and other craft plying Disneyland's main waterway. On the menu, there's the "Croissant Mardi Gras" (ham, turkey, swiss cheese, lettuce, and tomato); Cajun-spiced chicken; "Bayou Italien" (beef, ham, salami, tomato, onion, and bell peppers tossed in Italian dressing and served on a roll); the "Delta Club" (turkey, bacon, cheddar cheese, lettuce, and tomato tossed in a honey-mustard dressing, served on a roll); and "Neptune's Delight" (a croissant filled with a mixture of crabmeat and other seafood). For dinner, selected sandwiches are joined by beef Bourguignonne, seafood Parisienne, and poulet de la maison (chicken breast sautéed in spicy marinara sauce, served over fettuccine). There's a small children's menu available. Dessert offerings include fruit tarts, Napoleans, hot apple strudel, and chocolate éclairs. L, D, S.

FRENCH MARKET: Much more than New Orleans Square's largest food facility, this Esplanade Street cafeteria, adjoining the Frontierland depot of the Disneyland Railroad, is a destination in its own right: On sunny days, it's relaxing just to sit on the open-air terrace and lunch on fried chicken, fresh trout filet, spaghetti with a choice of meat or meatless sauce, spinach tortellini, or a French dip sandwich. The dinner menu also includes beef and

SNACKS

MINT JULEP BAR: The aforementioned fritters rank among Disneyland's tastiest tidbits, and when the last grains of sugar are polished off, it's hard to fight the desire to go back for more. Not so with the mint juleps, which taste like lemonade spiked with mint syrup. The real lemonade and the hot chocolate are better choices. Cookies-and-cream ice cream sandwiches, cookies, and chocolate-covered frozen bananas round out the selection here. B, S.

LA PETITE PATISSERIE: A snack spot located behind *Café Orleans*, where six different pastries tempt passersby. Chocolate, fruit, and whipped cream are just a few of the prime ingredients. Hot and cold beverages are also served. B, S.

ROYAL STREET VERANDA: Located opposite the Café Orleans and next door to the entrance to Pirates of the Caribbean, this small snack stand is Disneyland's only other source of those delicious fritters. Hot chocolate, frozen bananas, ice cream bars, chips, a fruit punch that goes by the name of Mardi Gras Julep, and a creamy clam chowder served in a bread bowl complete the menu. Be sure to look at the wrought-iron balustrade above the *Royal Street Veranda*'s small patio. The initials at the center are those of Roy and Walt Disney, and the balcony itself belonged to an apartment that was being constructed for Walt before he died. B, S.

FRONTIERLAND

BUFFETERIAS

BIG THUNDER BARBECUE: Open on weekends and during busy seasons, this cafeteria specializes in beef and pork ribs, and chicken cooked slowly over hickory logs and served chuck-wagon style. Bring your appetite: Each lunch platter comes with ranch-style beans, coleslaw, and cornbread. Dinner plates also include corn-on-the-cob. There's only outdoor seating at picnic tables. Children's portions are available. Presented by Beatrice/Hunt-Wesson. L*, D*.

CASA MEXICANA: This Frontierland landmark offers the kind of Mexican food most often found in the American Midwest, so real aficionados of authentically spiced south-of-the-border specialties will find this restaurant's version lacking bite. But because this is California, a state where residents know their tacos and tostadas, hot jalapeño peppers are served on the side, and there's hot sauce on every table. The tables on the west end of the patio offer terrific views of the runaway mine trains of the Big Thunder Mountain Railroad as they race around those sandstone-colored buttes, and the ramadas overhead and the stucco walls around the patio make for a pleasant dining ambience. The restaurant doesn't feel like Mexico—but it doesn't seem much like downtown Anaheim either. Burritos, enchiladas, tacos, tamales, tostadas, rice, and refried beans are on the menu, so mix and match as you prefer, or select one of the menu's combination platters. Presented by Lawry's Foods. L, D, S.

RIVER BELLE TERRACE: Walt Disney himself used to breakfast here, beside the Rivers of America, most Sunday mornings. The terrace offers one of the best views of the activity on the Rivers of America and of the passing throng, and the food is hearty and wholesome. Breakfast is served all day during slower times; until 11:45 A.M. on weekends and during busy seasons. The menu features regular stacks and short stacks of pancakes or waffles, topped with strawberries or blueberries, or eggs in any style with pancakes, bacon, sausage, or ham. This is the only cafeteria in the park that serves breakfast cooked to order. After 11:45 A.M., a selection of sandwiches, salads, and other such stuff—chicken salad with alfalfa sprouts on granola bread, ham-and-swiss-cheese sandwiches, spaghetti with meat sauce, chicken cutlets, and breaded catfish—is offered for lunch and dinner. Don't miss the "Southern Belle" salad, made with freshly sliced seasonal fruits and topped with raspberry-yogurt sauce. Children's portions of some of these items are available. Among the fare fixed specially for the younger set at breakfast, the prize goes to the Mickey Mouse pancakes—a large flapjack for the face, two silver-dollar-size pancakes for the ears, a curve of pineapple for the mouth, a maraschino cherry for the nose, and two blueberries for eyes. With its many mirrors, ornamental pillars, green terrazzo floor, and pale-pink walls, it's as delightful to eat inside this restaurant as it is to dine outside. A pleasure. B, L, D, S.

DISNEYLAND RESTAURANTS WITH ATMOSPHERE

Most of the food served in Disneyland would hardly send a true gastronome into paroxysms of ecstasy. But the Disney talent for designing a dining spot that oozes atmosphere is another matter entirely, and the best here are the equal of many, en-hanced by food prices as reasonable as one can find anywhere.

Main Street: *Town Square Café* during the daily parades, Coke Corner when the pianist is performing, and Carnation Plaza Gardens during concerts and for dancing in the evenings.

Adventureland: *Tahitian Terrace*, for peace and quiet at lunch and for the lively Polynesian show at dinnertime.

Critter Country: *Hungry Bear* restaurant, for its superb feeling of being right in the heart of it all, yet curiously removed.

New Orleans Square: The *Blue Bayou* restaurant, for its perpetual moonlight, its Spanish moss-draped cypresses, its stars, and its fireflies; the *French Market* when the Royal Street Bachelors and any of the park's Dixieland musicians are playing.

Frontierland: The *Golden Horseshoe*, for its slightly slapstick, but terribly funny, old-fashioned show.

Fantasyland: The *Village Haus* restaurant, for its picture-perfect views.

FAST FOOD

STAGE DOOR CAFE: This small fast-food stand, adjoining the *Golden Horseshoe*, serves good grilled hamburgers and cheeseburgers, plus hot dogs, french fries, and brownies. When you're afflicted by a bad case of the eleventh-hour munchies, one that sweets from Main Street's Candy Palace simply can't satisfy, this is a place that usually stays open until about a half hour before park closing, so it can probably help you survive. L, D, S.

GOLDEN HORSESHOE: While you're watching Sam the bartender and his boys welcome back Lil and her girls, frontier-style, by dancing and singing around the tables, lunch on a sliced roast beef or turkey sandwich, a flour tortilla stuffed with meat, cheese, and jalapeño peppers or chili made with buffalo meat, plus cookies and chips. Reservations are required; you must make them in person at the *Golden Horseshoe* on the day you plan to dine here, and since they go quickly, be sure to present yourself at the saloon as soon after park opening as possible. L, D, S.

SNACKS

FORT WILDERNESS CANTEEN: Tucked away in a corner of Fort Wilderness on Tom Sawyer Island, this stand, which looks a bit like an old-fashioned store that might actually have been found in a 19th-century stockade, sells cookies,

dill pickles, beef jerky, candies, nuts, ice cream novelties, and apple juice, and an assortment of other thirst-quenching essentials such as Coke and lemonade. S.

WHEELHOUSE: One of the few spots in Disneyland where soft-serve ice cream is sold, this stand near the *Golden Horseshoe* and the *Stage Door Café* sells hot dogs, meal-size baked potatoes topped with vegetables and cheese, root beer floats, soft drinks, brownies, and chocolate and vanilla soft-serve cones. S*.

FANTASYLAND

TABLE SERVICE

VILLAGE HAUS: Located near Pinocchio's Daring Journey, this fast-food spot—a rather quaint creation with many gables, steep roofs, and wavy-glass windows—serves hamburgers, hot dogs, turkey burgers, salads, and snacks. A special children's meal features a hot dog or turkey burger, juice, raisins, and a cookie, all packed in a souvenir box with a free character-cup prize. Be sure to note the attractive murals, which are painted with such care that they do look almost like the tapestries they are supposed to represent. The fox that appears in many of them is Foulfellow, while his feline companion is named Gideon. The *Maytenus boaria* trees out in front were moved at a cost of nearly $10,000 each from the berm (which rings the park), where they had been for two decades. L, D, S.

SNACKS

YUMZ: Located within the Videopolis complex, this snack stand is open during Videopolis' operating hours. Cheese or pepperoni pizza bread, ¼-pound hot dogs, nachos with cheese, Coke, Cherry Coke, and iced tea are available. S.

TOMORROWLAND

FAST FOOD

LUNCHING PAD: Hot dogs, fine for a light lunch, round out a menu of ice cream bars, frozen juice bars, chocolate-covered frozen bananas, soft drinks, and popcorn. L, D, S.

SPACE PLACE: The menu at this large eating spot inside the Space Mountain complex features non-kosher and kosher-style hot dogs, along with hamburgers and seasoned cottage fries. Ham and tuna sandwiches, picnic-style chicken, "Healthy Tuna" (cholesterol-free mayonnaise), tuna salad, frozen yogurt, fresh fruit, cookies, and children's meals are also on the menu. Soft-serve chocolate and vanilla ice cream and root-beer floats round out the desserts. L*, D*, S*.

TOMORROWLAND TERRACE: One of the largest of Disneyland's dining facilities, this is one spot that always seems to be crowded with visitors bearing their small cardboard trays stacked with french fries, fried onion rings, hamburgers, cheeseburgers, hot dogs, and even an occasional salad. It can handle approximately 3,000 people an hour when operating at full capacity—as it often does. Couple this bustle with lively rock music and it's easy to understand why this eatery seems as frenetic as it sometimes does. The dance floor near the stage can get really crowded on summer nights. Fried chicken, tuna and ham sandwiches, ice cream bars, frozen juice bars, chocolate-covered frozen bananas, nonfat yogurt shakes, yogurt cups, fresh fruit, and chocolate cake and cookies are among the other offerings. The burgers are charbroiled. Presented by the Coca-Cola Company. B, L, D, S.

Some of the best restaurants in Anaheim are found in the hotels closest to Disneyland. There are, however, a number of other establishments in the area offering a surprisingly diverse range of culinary choices. The food runs the gamut from basic hamburgers and fries to seafood, Mexican specialties, and some respectable French dishes. Our recommendations for dining both in the hotels and elsewhere in and around Anaheim follow.

To provide some sense of what food will cost, we've designated restaurants as expensive (lunches over $20, dinner over $40), moderate (lunches from $10 to $20, dinners from $20 to $40), and inexpensive (lunches under $10, dinners under $20). These prices are for an average meal for two adults, not including drinks, wine, taxes, or tips. Remember, however, that meal prices change frequently. When credit cards are accepted, they are abbreviated as follows: AX=American Express; CB=Carte Blanche; D=Discover; DC=Diners Club; MC=MasterCard; and V=Visa.

IN THE HOTELS

HYATT REGENCY ALICANTE: One of the restaurants here is located in the tallest atrium in the western United States.

Café Alicante: Al fresco dining in a 17-story, glass-enclosed atrium, with flowering plants, palm trees, and fountains. A California-style menu is featured, including salads, sandwiches, seafood, and Mexican specialties. Breakfast and lunch buffets, low-calorie items, and a lavish Sunday brunch are also available. 971-3000, ext. 6047. AX, MC, V, D, DC, CB. Moderate. B, L, D, Sunday brunch.

Papa Geppetto's: The ambience is Mediterranean, with panoramic scenes of coastal Alicante, Spain. It serves family-style country Italian cuisine. The menu features a wide variety of pasta, veal, and nightly non-Italian specialties. The adjacent lounge offers live entertainment every night. Casual attire. Valet parking available. Ext. 609. Major credit cards. Moderate. D (Tuesdays through Sundays).

DISNEYLAND HOTEL: Some of the restaurants have fine views of the hotel's lovely manmade marina.

Monorail Café: A pretty standard breakfast and coffee-shop menu—eggs, salads, soups, and burgers. It's a good place for snacks or early-bird breakfasts. 778-6600, ext. 6401. Major credit cards (AX, CB, DC, MC, V). Moderate. B, L, D.

Chef's Kitchen: This country-style dining room features the immensely popular Disney character breakfasts, which offer personal encounters with Minnie Mouse, Goofy, and other Disney friends. Service here is buffet style, so fill your plates with

Mickey Mouse-shaped waffles, scrambled eggs, bacon, potatoes, juice, cereal, and fruit. Open weekends year-round; daily during the summer and holiday periods. Ext. 1327. Major credit cards. Moderate. B.

Granvilles' Steak House: An intimate, 104-seat restaurant that offers generous portions of steak, prime ribs, fresh Maine lobster, swordfish, and poultry. A highlight is the "Land and Sea Delight," both juicy prime ribs and fresh lobster. This is the hotel's top-of-the-line eatery, decorated with oak paneling, etched glass, and an all-American burgundy, white, and blue color scheme. Servers personally deliver a visual menu presentation, bringing a serving cart tableside that's stocked with examples of menu selections. Ext. 6402 or dial direct 956-6402. Reservations suggested. Jackets are no longer required here. Major credit cards. Expensive. D.

Caffé Villa Verde: An indoor/outdoor restaurant. The open, Mediterranean decor—fountains, hanging plants, and a sidewalk-café area that runs along the hotel's marina—make this a lovely spot. The emphasis is on Italian favorites, and the homemade ice cream is delicious. A children's menu is available. Ext. 6403. Major credit cards. Moderate. B, L, D.

Mazie's: In the Plaza Building, across from the swimming pool. This is, perhaps, the eating place within the hotel that is the most fun. It is light and airy inside. The tables outside provide the feeling of a sidewalk café. Its menu offers garnish-your-own burgers, hot dogs, and salads. Cravings for sweets can be satisfied with freshly baked cookies. Beer and wine are sold by the glass. Ext. 1570. Major credit cards. Moderate. L, D.

Shipyard Inn: On the wharf, overlooking the hotel's marina, with a nautical look befitting what may be Anaheim's only waterside restaurant. It offers a spectacular view of the Dancing Waters show at night. Fresh seafood specialties are the fare here, and there is also an oyster bar. A children's menu is available. The California Wine Cellar—a lounge that serves 100 award-winning California wines as well as desserts, grapes, bread, and cheese—is downstairs. Ext. 6404. Major credit cards. Moderate to expensive. L, D.

DOUBLETREE: The restaurants here have a very contemporary Southern California style.

Napa Brasserie: A casual, café-style eatery, serving soups, salads, sandwiches, omelettes, burgers, and light pasta dishes. Prime ribs, swordfish, smoked breast of chicken, and filet mignon are among the dinner specialties. 634-4500, ext. 53. MC, V. Moderate. B, L, D.

Dover's: This innovative eatery offers such dinner entrées as mesquite-broiled chicken served with red-onion marmalade; blackened tenderloin served with dry Cajun seasonings, and spinach pasta with lobster meat, shrimp, snow peas, almond slivers, and sweet red pepper sauce. The Sunday buffet brunch draws a devoted clientele from among area residents. The wine list offers a nice variety of California and French wines. Reservations recommended. Ext. 52. AX, MC, V. Moderate to expensive. L (weekdays), D (except Sundays), Sunday brunch.

ANAHEIM MARRIOTT: One of Orange County's best restaurants is located here.

JW's: Named for the late J. Willard Marriott, Sr., there is usually a wait here at dinnertime. Appetizers might include glazed fresh baby artichokes with reggiano cheese, potato pancakes with three kinds of caviar, and a seafood consommé with diced lobster and fresh sea scallops. Also on the menu are aged rib eye steak, with a sauce made of Stag's Leap Petit Syrah wine and mushrooms, plus Muscovy duck with a sweet and sour sauce, and bouillabaise. There is a comprehensive wine list. Reservations recommended; 750-0900. Major credit cards. Expensive. D.

La Plaza: Just off the hotel's lobby, this restaurant is decorated in a contemporary Southwestern style. There is a fine breakfast buffet, with everything from fresh-baked pastries to omelettes made to order. Lunch and dinner menus include burgers, sesame chicken, and grilled liver and onions. For a snack, try the nachos or potato skins with cheese. There is a special menu for children 12 and under. Beer and wine are available, as well as piña coladas and strawberry margaritas. 750-8000, ext. 116. Major credit cards. Moderate. B, L, D, Sunday breakfast buffet.

INN AT THE PARK: One of the draws here is the Wild West feeling of the *Overland Stage*.

Coffee Shop: Conveniently located off the hotel lobby, the fare is standard coffee shop. 750-1811, ext. 7166. Major credit cards. Inexpensive to moderate. B, L, D.

Overland Stage: The decor tries to re-create the Old West, circa 1880s, with a salad bar set up in a chuckwagon, high-back chairs, red-velvet-draped booths, and western antiques. The wild game offered nightly has a decidedly frontier flavor, with specialties like buffalo, venison, and quail. For less adventuresome eaters, there are the conventional prime ribs, rack of lamb, chicken, veal, filet of sole, and the fish of the day. Beer and imported and domestic wines are available. 750-1811. Major credit cards. Moderate to expensive. L, D.

The adjoining *Territorial Saloon* may be booked for private parties of up to 50 people. Ext. 7170.

SHERATON-ANAHEIM: Dining here can be an experience in eating in a home of gothic proportions.

Adrienne's: Specializes in American food. Steak, lobster, and rack of lamb are among the specialties. Reservations suggested. 778-1700, ext. 3948. Major credit cards. Moderate. D.

Continental Café: A complete breakfast, lunch, and dinner menu is available here, in a café setting. Open from 6 A.M. to 11 P.M. daily. Ext. 3808. Major credit cards. Inexpensive to moderate. B, L, D.

Deli: Serves continental breakfasts. Featured fare includes a variety of sandwiches, salads, domestic wines by the glass, and domestic and imported beers. Open 18 hours daily. Ext. 3834. No credit cards. Inexpensive. B, L, D.

GRAND: A bit of Broadway (see "Dinner Theaters" in *Anaheim*) right across the street from Disneyland.

Coffee Shop: Located near the swimming pool and patio area, it has a row of extra-large windows that keeps it light and airy. Quick meals, and the price is right. 772-7777, ext. 270. Major credit cards. Inexpensive. B, L, D.

Green's : Serves continental dishes, as well as some traditional American menu items. The extensive dinner menu includes such selections as prime ribs, poached salmon, lobster tails, and rack of lamb. Reservations suggested. Ext. 273. Major credit cards. Moderate. L, D, Sunday brunch.

ANAHEIM PLAZA: Fresh produce is the star on the menu of this establishment's restaurant.

Palm Court Café: A particularly pleasant and

comfortable restaurant with an airy, gardenlike atmosphere. Eggs are available at all meals, with fried potatoes and a choice of sausage, bacon, or ham. The lunch menu offers various burgers and sandwiches, quiche lorraine, fried chicken, fried shrimp, and light pasta specialties. For dieters, the dinner menu has a low calorie section which lists the calorie counts for the various entrées. Other dinner entrées include filet mignon, New York-cut steak, crawfish fettuccine, and fresh fish (selection varies daily). At lunch and dinner, there's a terrific salad bar—full of out-of-the-ordinary toppings. At the dessert bar, brownies, cookies, and soft-serve ice cream top it all off. Several items are priced and sized for kids (see box on children's menus later in this chapter). 772-5900, ext. 140. Major credit cards. Moderate. B, L, D.

ANAHEIM HILTON: A casual, "Casablanca-style" café, a sushi bar, as well as two other specialty restaurants round out the Hilton's dining spots.

Café Oasis: A café designed to create the atmosphere of a safari. A soup and salad buffet is featured at lunchtime. Relax with espresso or cappuccino and enjoy pastries and cakes baked fresh daily in the hotel's kitchens. 750-4321, ext. 412. Major credit cards. Moderate. B, L, D.

Pavia: Fresh seafood—with an emphasis on Italian specialties, such as scampi and a delightful fish soup—and homemade pastas amid a setting of marble floors, Roman arches, and cut-crystal windows. Live entertainment. Reservations suggested. Ext. 419. Major credit cards. Expensive. D.

Hasting's Grill: An elegant yet casual grill featuring California-style cooking. An unusual option is "hot rock" cuisine, where guests may grill their own food on 700° hot rocks. Reservations suggested. Ext. 422. Major credit cards. Expensive. L, D.

Sushi Bar: Seafood (delivered fresh daily) is prepared as you watch, by a master sushi chef. Ext. 422. Major credit cards. Moderate. D.

PAN PACIFIC, ANAHEIM: Both restaurants here are located on the ground floor, and offer casual dining.

Summertree: A California bistro setting, with indoor/outdoor dining. Seafood (delivered fresh daily) and pasta specialties are features, along with a good selection of California wines. Children's menus are available. 999-0990, ext. 44. Major credit cards. Moderate to expensive. B, L, D, Sunday brunch.

Marushin: Features authentic Japanese food, with the choice of private rooms with floor seating or a spot at the sushi bar. Reservations suggested. Ext. 46. Major credit cards. Moderate. L, D.

QUALITY ANAHEIM: Here's where the captain will take your order.

Tivoli Gardens: A small, attractive café, in a gardenlike setting. Soups, salads, sandwiches, and omelettes are among the menu selections. 750-3131, ext. 3300. AX, DC, MC, V. Moderate. B, L, D.

Captain Greenhorn's: Nautical trimmings and a seafood and steak menu. Drinks are available from the adjoining lounge. Reservations are suggested for dinner. Ext. 3945. AX, DC, MC, V. Moderate. D.

CONESTOGA: Early Western is the word here, pardner.

Chaparral Café: A very pleasant establishment among hotel coffee shops. The high-back chairs are oak and look antique. Flowered valances adorn the windows, and linen napkins come with the place settings. After 5 P.M., out come the tablecloths, too. The menu isn't especially imaginative, but it does offer a wide selection: hearty sandwiches, various salads, and Mexican foods. Hot entrées include chicken-fried steak, fried chicken, and beef teriyaki. There are several items for light eaters, and some especially for kids—like a good, old-fashioned peanut butter-and-jelly sandwich. Wine, beer, and cocktails are available. 535-0300, ext. 616. Major credit cards. Moderate. B, L, D.

Original Cattleman's Wharf: In a building adjacent to the *Conestoga* at 1160 West Ball Road. Modern and angular design on the outside, eclectic inside. The five dining rooms each have an individual, elaborate design plan (running the gamut from a simple garden to a formal dining room). The food—steak, chicken, seafood, prime ribs—is surprisingly good given the emphasis placed on decor. A lavish Sunday brunch is served. There is entertainment Thursdays through Sundays in the lounge. And on summer nights, the fireworks at Disneyland are visible from the observation tower. Reservations are suggested; 535-1622. AX, D, DC, MC, V. Moderate. D, Sunday brunch.

AROUND ANAHEIM

MR. STOX: A favorite with people who live in the area, not only for the food—veal scallopini, rack of lamb, beef Wellington, fresh salmon—but for the wine list, which offers more than 500 selections of California, French, Italian, and German vintages. Also a good spot for a business lunch. A real plus: Häagen-Dazs ice cream. They are also known for fine pastries. A nightly musical accompaniment to dinner is provided by either a pianist or harpist. Valet parking. Reservations encouraged. 1105 East Katella Ave.; 634-2994. Major credit cards. Expensive. L (Mondays through Fridays), D, Sunday brunch when the L.A. Rams play at home, and on holidays.

THEE WHITE HOUSE: The exterior of this turn-of-the-century mansion bears a resemblance to the President's residence. Inside, the menu is Northern Italian, and the food would please even a Presidential palate. Several veal dishes are noteworthy, in addition to scampi, quail, rabbit, and chicken specialties. Reservations recommended. 887 South Anaheim Blvd.; 772-1381. Major credit cards. Moderate to expensive. L (except weekends), D (except Sundays).

CHARLEY BROWN'S: Located near Anaheim Stadium, it's part of a chain best known for its beef specialties (particularly prime ribs), but the extensive menu offers much more, including several seafood, pasta, and chicken specialties. Full bar. Reservations recommended. 1751 South State College Blvd.; 634-2211. Major credit cards. Moderate to expensive. L (Mondays through Fridays), D, Sunday brunch.

THE CATCH: Located directly across the street from Anaheim Stadium, this popular eatery is best known for its fresh seafood. Also on the menu are some beef specialties, including prime ribs. Reservations suggested. 1929 South State College Blvd., 634-1829. AX, DC, MC, V. Moderate to expensive. L (Mondays through Fridays), D.

BENIHANA OF TOKYO: The first *Benihana* on the West Coast to have a sushi bar. In the dining room, it's communal-style seating, with tables for eight. One of the restaurant's main attractions is the show put on by the chefs, who prepare the food (hibachi steak, chicken, seafood, and vegetables) at the table/stove with a great flourish of knives and other utensils. Cocktail lounge. Reservations recommended; there can be a wait of 20 minutes

or so from 6:30 P.M. to 9 P.M. 2100 East Ball Rd.; 774-4940. Major credit cards. Moderate. L (except weekends), D.

CASA MARIA: From the moment the hostess greets you with, "Buenos días," you'll think you've crossed the border. The shrimp fajitas are a specialty. Several taco, burrito, tostada, and enchilada combinations are offered, too. Cocktail lounge. Reservations are recommended. 1801 East Katella Ave.; 634-1888. Major credit cards. Moderate. L, D, Sunday brunch.

EL TORITO'S: If there's an occasion to celebrate, the waiters will gather with guitar and tambourines to salute it. The atmosphere is definitely lively. There's an extensive Mexican menu, and you can make your own fajitas. Margaritas are a specialty. Reservations are suggested. 2020 East Ball Rd.; 956-4880. Major credit cards. Moderate. L, D, Sunday brunch.

CHAO'S: This establishment is bright red and resembles a Chinese temple—but only on the outside. The lunch and dinner menus are a mix of Chinese and American dishes, but breakfast here may be the best bargain in town. The breakfast special (a plate with bacon, pancakes, and an egg) costs only 99¢. There is a children's menu, and the lounge serves beer and wine, as well as tropical drinks. 1560 South Harbor Blvd.; 776-1880. Major credit cards. Inexpensive to moderate. B, L, D.

FITZGERALD'S: Located closer to Anaheim Stadium than to Disneyland. The breakfast menu includes top sirloin and eggs; spinach, bacon,

and swiss cheese omelettes; and biscuits and gravy. They also feature homemade chili, and the house specials offered at lunch and dinner help to keep meal prices very reasonable. 1810 East Katella Ave.; 634-9660. AX, MC, V. Inexpensive to moderate. B, L, D.

TIFFY'S: The menu is strong, obviously, in homemade ice cream, but there are also some good sandwiches, all sorts of egg combinations at breakfast, and some more ambitious dinner entrées than at similar restaurants in the area. 1060 West Katella Ave.; 635-1801. MC, V. Moderate. B, L, D.

TONY ROMA'S: This member of the national chain, located across the street from Disneyland, specializes in ribs served with plenty of tangy homemade barbecue sauce. Other typical dinner selections include New York-cut steak, breast of chicken teriyaki, and grilled halibut. Full bar. Reservations not accepted. 1640 South Harbor Blvd.; 520-0200. AX, DC, MC, V. Moderate. L, D.

NEW DRAGON: Chinese food is the fare here. Luncheon specials start at $3.95. For dinner, there are the predictable American-Chinese choices: chow mein, chop suey, lo mein, plus some interesting house specialties like lemon chicken, beef and squid with broccoli, and orange beef. Beer and wine. 1550 South Brookhurst; 491-0447. Major credit cards. Inexpensive to moderate. L, D.

ACAPULCO: Small and pleasant, with hanging plants, the decor conveys the atmosphere of a courtyard in Old Mexico on a summer evening. A large menu, features more than 100 items. Fajitas filled with shrimp, chicken, or beef are a specialty. There's a cocktail lounge that offers 15 flavors of margaritas. Reservations recommended. 1410 South Harbor Blvd.; 956-7380. AX, MC, V. Inexpensive to moderate. L, D.

MARIE CALLENDER'S: Best known locally for its variety of pies (30 in all), but the hamburgers are quite good here, too—the kind that ooze over your fingertips with every bite. There's a salad bar—try the spicy tomato dressing. Besides burgers and pies, there's also a complete menu of breakfast, lunch, and dinner selections. Several locations in

the area: the two closest to Disneyland are at 408 South Brookhurst Ave.; 635-1370; B, L, D; and 540 North Euclid St. (Anaheim Plaza Shopping Center); 774-1832; L, D. MC, V. Inexpensive to moderate.

SPAGHETTI STATION: Eat spaghetti amidst a collection of Winchester rifles and Colts, a Cheyenne war bonnet, and other Old West relics in a building that looks like a frontier hotel. Full bar on the premises and the sounds of a player piano. Reservations accepted for parties of eight or more. 999 West Ball Rd.; 956-3250. AX, MC, V. Inexpensive. L (Mondays through Fridays), D (nightly).

NOTEWORTHY ORANGE COUNTY RESTAURANTS

Some of the restaurants listed below are only a short distance from Anaheim; others are a bit farther afield. Here are our recommendations for dining in the area.

DINING ROOM AT THE RITZ-CARLTON: Formal dining at one of Southern California's poshest resort hotels. The service is outstanding, as is the French and continental food, featuring lamb, beef, rabbit, duck, and seafood specialties. Jackets required. Valet parking. Reservations are a must for weekends, recommended for weekdays. Ritz-Carlton Dr., Laguna Niguel; 33533 Ritz-Carlton Drive, Laguna Niguel; 240-2000. AX, DC, MC, V. Expensive. D.

CELLAR: In the basement of a graceful old Spanish-style building lurks one of the county's best restaurants, serving French and continental cuisine. Ingredients are flown in fresh from around the country and from as far away as New Zealand. There's an extensive and excellent wine list. Elegant dining for sure, and reservations are a must. Jackets required. 305 North Harbor Blvd., Fullerton; 525-5682. Major credit cards. Expensive. D (Tuesdays through Saturdays).

FIVE CROWNS: Fashioned after *Ye Old Bell*, England's oldest pub on the Thames River. With heavy leaded glass windows and cozy fireplaces, this is every inch the proper setting for meals like roast prime ribs of beef accompanied by creamed spinach and Yorkshire pudding, or roast duckling. Watney's beer, an English import, is on tap, and the wine list is impressive. Reservations suggested. 3801 East Coast Highway, Corona Del Mar; 760-0331. Major credit cards. Expensive. D, Sunday brunch.

PAVILION: Located at the luxurious *Four Seasons* hotel in Newport Beach, the menu offers first class continental cooking with a contemporary California touch. Roasted New Zealand loin of lamb is a dinner specialty. There's an extensive wine list. The Sunday champagne brunch is particularly opulent (a good thing, considering the $39 price

SCOOPS, SUNDAES, AND SOFT SERVE

IN DISNEYLAND: The *Main Street Cone Shop* serves ice cream and frozen yogurt in cones only.

IN THE HOTELS: Whether you like it in sugar or wafer cones, by the dish, smothered with gooey chocolate, or accompanied by strawberries, bananas, whipped cream, nuts, and chocolate chips, there is an ice cream place here to suit your fancy: The *Wharf Ice Cream Galley* at the *Disneyland* hotel, the *Coffee Shop* at the

Inn at the Park, *La Plaza* at the *Anaheim Marriott* (Haägen-Dazs served here), and the *Chaparral Café* at the *Conestoga* hotel.

IN THE AREA: *Tiffy's* (1060 West Katella Ave.; 635-1801), *Baskin-Robbins* (1646 West Katella Ave.; 772-8441, and other locations), and *Quinn's*, located in a funky mall (1192 West Katella Ave.; 535-6093).

CONES

Tiffy's; *Baskin-Robbins*; and *Quinn's* (waffle cones are made fresh daily on the premises).

SOFT-SERVE ICE CREAM

Palm Court Café at the *Anaheim Plaza* features soft-serve vanilla ice cream.

ASSORTED SUPER SUNDAES

IN THE HOTELS: The *Coffee Shop* (at the *Inn at the Park*) serves a chocolate-fantasy sundae: brownies surrounded with chocolate ice cream, and covered with lots of hot fudge and chocolate chips. It also serves a "banana boat" topped with three scoops of ice cream, crushed pineapple, strawberries, whipped cream, and nuts.

IN THE AREA: *Tiffy's*, *Baskin-Robbins*, and *Quinn's* all offer a variety of sundaes. *Quinn's* serves a three-scoop sundae in an enormous waffle cone.

---

tag). It features a splendid buffet including meats and fish with sublime sauces, omelettes, caviar, sushi, oysters, jumbo shrimp, hot and cold vegetable and pasta salads, breakfast rolls and pastries, cheese and cold cuts, and a heavenly dessert table. Valet parking. Reservations required for Sunday brunch, recommended for lunch and dinner. 690 Newport Center Dr., Newport Beach; 759-0808, ext. 4338. Major credit cards. Expensive. B (except Saturdays), L (except weekends), D, Sunday brunch.

BISTANGO: Modern art decorates the interior of this fashionable restaurant. The contemporary California/Italian cuisine is outstanding, and there's an excellent wine list. The menu offers many enticing appetizers and salads: duck, chicken, and cilantro sausage, for example, or smoked chicken salad with watercress and walnuts. Pasta is homemade and nontraditional (jalapeño linguini is a specialty). There are also California-style pizzas. Main entrées include a wide range of fish,

veal, beef, chicken, and other specialties. Don't miss dessert. The fresh fruit tarts, in particular, are veritable masterpieces. Live music (usually light contemporary jazz) is featured daily. Valet parking available. Reservations suggested. 19100 Von Karman Ave.; Irvine; 752-5222. AX, DC, MC, V. Expensive. L, (except weekends), D.

ANTONELLO: Located in the South Coast Plaza Village, across the street from the major shopping mall and just a block from the Orange County Performing Arts Center and South Coast Repertory, this fine Northern Italian restaurant has a reputation for attentive service and excellent food. Calamari is one of the seafood specialties. Several veal dishes are noteworthy, and pasta is made fresh daily on the premises. The dessert pastries are quite delectable. Semi-formal dress. Valet parking available. Reservations recommended. 3800 South Plaza Dr. (South Coast Plaza Village); Santa Ana; 751-7153. MC, V. Expensive. L (except weekends), D (except Sundays).

LA BRASSERIE: The charming country-style decor of this French café restaurant is warm and inviting. Traditional French and continental cuisine is served, and there's an excellent selection of wines. Veal forestiere (veal in a Madeira sauce with mushrooms) is a specialty. The dessert pastries are homemade. Reservations suggested. 202 South Main St.; Orange; 978-6161. MC, V. Expensive. L (except weekends), D (except Sundays).

RITZ: The decor is that of a classic, formal European dining room. Continental cuisine is the specialty at this restaurant across the street from Newport Center's Fashion Island mall, and the wine selection is excellent. Service is first-rate, too. Valet parking. Reservations suggested. 880 Newport Center Dr.; Newport Beach; 720-1800. AX, MC, V, DC. Expensive. L (except weekends), D (except Sundays).

KID STUFF

Almost every restaurant in the Magic Kingdom offers a children's menu. A bit rarer in the Anaheim area, there are still establishments that cater to children.

CASA MARIA: Children under 12 can order a hamburger or chicken strips with french fries; or enchiladas, quesadillas, tacos, or burritos with rice and beans (about $2.75). Adult entrées cost $5 to $10. 1801 East Katella Ave.; Anaheim; 634-1888.

DENNY'S: At breakfast, child-size portions of pancakes and French toast are offered. Choices for lunch and dinner include hot dogs, grilled cheese sandwiches, hamburgers, and corn dogs. Children's dinners cost about $2.50. Regular entrées cost $3 to $9.50. 14300 East Firestone Blvd. in La Mirada; 994-1490 or 1610 South Harbor Blvd. in Anaheim; 776-3300.

HANSA HOUSE SMORGASBORD: Children from ages 4 to 12 are charged 40¢ per year of age at breakfast (i.e., $4 for a 10-year-old), 45¢ per year at lunch, 60¢ at dinnertime, and 55¢ per year at Sunday brunch. For the same buffet selections, their parents pay $4.95 at breakfast, $5.95 at lunch, $9.50 at dinner, and $7.50 for Sunday brunch. Prices include dessert, but not a drink. 1840 South Harbor Blvd.; Anaheim; 750-2411.

HOF'S HUT: Near the Crystal Cathedral and the City Shopping Center, this full-service, American-style restaurant has a fairly extensive children's menu at breakfast, lunch, and dinner. Cost of a child's dinner, including dessert, is about $2.65. Adults can order steaks, seafood, ribs, a half dozen kinds of burgers, and quiche for $4.50 to $11.25. 4050 West Chapman Ave.; Orange; 634-8606.

MRS. KNOTT'S CHICKEN DINNER: Children's portions of the chicken dinner that made Mrs. Knott famous in the first place are smaller and less expensive than those their parents order. Cost is $9.45 for adults, $4.95 for youngsters under ten. 8039 Beach Blvd., Buena Park; 220-5080.

MARIE CALLENDER'S: Spaghetti, pizza, hamburgers, cheesburgers, chicken tenders, and turkey or ham sandwiches cost $1.99 including a bakery treat and a drink. Regular entrées go for $6.95 to $8.95. Visit either Anaheim location: 540 North Euclid St.; 774-1832 or 408 South Brookhurst Ave.; 635-1370.

AND THEN SOME: The following restaurants also have menus that cater to child-size appetites.
- **Chao's**
- **L Plaza** (*Anaheim Marriott*)
- **Palm Court Café** (*Anaheim Plaza*)
- **Chaparral Café** (*Conestoga Hotel*)
- **Caffé Villa Verde** (*Disneyland* hotel)
- **Coffee Shop** (*Inn at the Park*)
- **Coco's**
- **Summertree** (*Pan Pacific*)
- **Café Alicante** (*Hyatt Regency Alicante*)

NIEUPORT 17: Dine in the midst of a wonderful collection of aeronautical memorabilia. The food is continental, a good mix of fish and meats. Cocktails, imported and domestic wines, and entertainment. Reservations recommended. 13051 Newport Ave.; Tustin; 731-5130. AX, MC, V, DC. Expensive. L (Mondays to Fridays), D.

CHANTECLAIR: A French and continental menu is offered at this lovely restaurant in Irvine, about 12 miles southeast of Anaheim. Filet mignon is a specialty and all desserts and pastries are made on the premises. The strawberries Chanteclair, served with Grand Marnier and chocolate, are particularly noteworthy. Men are asked to wear jackets at dinner. Reservations necessary. 18912 MacArthur Blvd., Irvine; 752-8001. Major credit cards. Expensive. L (Mondays through Fridays), D, Sunday brunch.

ROYAL KHYBER: A bit of India comes to the beach. The menu includes about 20 different curries, "Chicken Tikka" (diced chicken marinated in spices and herbs and cooked tandoori-style in a clay oven over charcoal), leavened bread stuffed with roast lamb, and rice mixed with lamb or chicken and nuts. Diners are served under a canopy. Full bar. Reservations requested. 1000 Bristol St. North, Newport Beach; 752-5200. All major credit cards. Expensive. L (except Saturdays), D, Sunday brunch.

BELISLE'S: You can't miss this bright-pink building. The food is first rate, fresh, and of Brobdingnagian proportions. Open 24 hours a day, nearly everything on the menu—including the mile-high pies (wondrous extravaganzas of whipped cream)—is available at all times. 12001 Harbor Blvd., Garden Grove; 750-6560. MC, V. Expensive. B, L, D.

REX: Now in a new location in Newport's lovely Fashion Island shopping center, this restaurant has been highly acclaimed for its outstanding seafood. The fish is always fresh and well prepared. Abalone almondine and poached salmon with an orange butter sauce are among the specialties. Reservations recommended. Valet parking available. 1141 Fashion Island, in Newport Center; Newport Beach; 644-4400. Major credit cards. Expensive. L (Mondays through Fridays), D.

WATERCOLORS: Located at the Dana Point Resort. Dine in a restaurant where every table has a dramatic view of the Pacific Ocean. The contemporary American menu is innovative, and the food is first-rate. Spiced Maine lobster with tarragon fettuccine, garlic, and basil with a cognac cream sauce, is a specialty. Semi-casual dress. Complimentary valet parking. Reservations recommended for dinner. 25135 Park Lantern; Dana Point; 661-5000. Major credit cards. Moderate to expensive. B, L, D, Sunday brunch.

FISH COMPANY: One of the best values in Orange County, serving first-rate, fresh fish at surprisingly moderate prices. It is a very popular eating place,

---

EATING ETHNIC

Mexican food is certainly the ethnic favorite in Southern California, but you need not go far afield to satisfy other international preferences as well.

MEXICAN
- **Acapulco**—1410 South Harbor Blvd.; Anaheim
- **Casa Maria**—1801 East Katella Ave.; Anaheim
- **Café El Cholo**—840 East Whittier Blvd.; La Habra
- **El Torito's**—2020 East Ball Rd.; Anaheim
- **Casa Mexicana**—Frontierland, Disneyland

CHINESE & JAPANESE
- **A Thousand Cranes**—120 South Los Angeles St.; Los Angeles
- **Benihana of Tokyo**—2100 East Ball Rd.; Anaheim
- **Chao's**—1560 South Harbor Blvd.; Anaheim
- **Marushin**—Pan Pacific Hotel, Anaheim

INDIAN
- **Royal Khyber**—1000 Bristol St. North; Newport Beach

PIZZA AND PASTA
Here's where to mangia, mangia.
- **Angelo's & Vinci's Café**—516 North Harbor Blvd.; Fullerton
- **Chicago Pizza Works**—11641 Pico Blvd.; Los Angeles
- **Spaghetti Station**—999 West Ball Rd.; Anaheim

---

and since reservations are not accepted, there's usually a wait at peak dining hours. Desserts are quite good (try the cheesecake). 11061 Los Alamitos Blvd. (at Katella), Los Alamitos; 213-594-4553; AX, MC, V. Moderate. L, D.

CAFE EL CHOLO: Orange County is full of places promising authentic south-of-the-border cooking, but this is probably the best. Its enchiladas, combination plates, and margaritas are real knockouts. 840 East Whittier Blvd.; La Habra; 525-1320. Major credit cards. Moderate. L, D, Sunday brunch.

ANGELO'S & VINCI'S CAFE: The menu offers pizza, pasta, seafood, plus other Italian specialties. Part of an old theater complex, the ceiling goes up, up, and up, and the Italian opera recordings in the background sound as full-throated as the originals in this cavernous room. Summer dining on the patio. Reservations required for groups

of 10 or more. 516 North Harbor Blvd., Fullerton; 879-4022. MC, V. Inexpensive to moderate. L, D, Sunday brunch.

BACK BAY ROWING & RUNNING CLUB: The soups, salads, quiche, burgers, and sandwiches served here are all tasty. But the real draw is the salad bar—regarded by many locals as the best in Orange County. It features myriad fresh fruits and vegetables, many varieties of lettuce, imaginative pasta and taco salads, unusually delectable potato salads, and much more. The house dressings are fresh and delicious (the honey and mustard dressing is particularly good). 3333 Bristol St. (South Coast Plaza), Costa Mesa; 641-0118. AX, MC, V. Inexpensive. L, D.

MRS. KNOTT'S CHICKEN DINNER: Started as a way to augment income from the family's berry farm during the Depression, a full-fledged amusement park (see *Anaheim*) has grown up around this restaurant. The same good chicken dinner that Cordelia Knott once served is still available. The menu includes homemade biscuits, chicken, mashed potatoes with gravy, salad, choice of desserts (try the boysenberry pie), and a beverage. 8039 Beach Blvd., Buena Park; 827-1776. Major credit cards. Inexpensive. D (daily); B, L (Mondays through Saturdays).

LOS ANGELES RESTAURANTS

In spite of the overwhelming number of fine restaurants in Los Angeles, finding one is not all that easy. Many of the more famous places reward the unsuspecting first-timer with lost reservations and tables beside the kitchen door. Be sure to confirm reservations on the day of your meal. Our choices follow.

L'ERMITAGE: Housed in a Parisian-style home, a typical meal here begins with a velvety-smooth mousse of duck livers laced with Armagnac, followed by a sautéed filet of beef in

vinegar sauce, concluding with an individual chocolate soufflé. Celebrate a special occasion here because the tab (without liquor or wine) will probably run more than $100 for two. Closed Sundays and holidays. Reservations necessary. 730 North La Cienega Blvd., 213-652-5840. Major credit cards. Expensive. D.

SPAGO: The unusual menu here is described by owner Wolfgang Puck as "California cuisine." The establishment is best known for its pizza with toppings like duck sausage, mozzarella, oregano, and tomato, or smoked lamb, eggplant, and roasted peppers. Entrées include chicken dishes, roasted baby lamb, and grilled fish. Reservations required (weeks ahead for weekends). 8795 Sunset Blvd., 213-652-4025. Major credit cards. Expensive. D.

BISTRO GARDEN: The very same Beverly Hills celebrities who for years parked their Rolls-Royces up the street at the *Bistro* have made its sister restaurant the hottest spot in town. Lunch is especially chic, with popular fare like bratwurst and hot potato salad. Reservations required. 176 North Canon Dr., Beverly Hills; 213-550-3900. Major credit cards. Expensive. L (Mondays through Saturdays), D (daily).

PEPPONE: Possibly the best Italian restaurant in L.A., tucked away in a tiny West Los Angeles shopping center. Splendid pasta and veal dishes are the cornerstones. Reservations essential. 11628 Barrington Court; 213-476-7379. Major credit cards. Expensive. L (Mondays through Fridays), D.

MUSSO & FRANK GRILL: It really is a grill, in Hollywood since 1919, and apparently not redecorated since. Orthodox American food. Breakfast is served starting at 11 A.M. An L.A. classic. Closed Sundays. Reservations recommended. 6667 Hollywood Blvd., 213-467-7788. Major credit cards. Moderate to expensive. B, L, D.

A THOUSAND CRANES: This Japanese restaurant is well versed in the traditional art of serving beautiful food. Several tatami rooms and a western dining room. Reservations recommended. In the *New Otani* hotel, 120 South Los Angeles St., 213-629-1200. Major credit cards. Moderate to Expensive. B, L, D.

LAWRY'S CALIFORNIA CENTER—THE GARDEN: The gardens surrounding Lawry's (the sauce people) headquarters are open for lunch and dinner year-round. Meals are served in a Mexican fiesta atmosphere (to the sound of Mariachi music). Only four set meals are available: charbroiled New York steak, fresh fish of the day, hickory-smoked chicken, or rack of lamb. All include a salad, fresh vegetables, corn on the cob, a delicious sourcream tortilla casserole, and herb bread. Reservations recommended. 570 West Avenue 26; 213-224-6850. Major credit cards. Moderate. L, D.

RIB JOINT: Known locally as *RJ's*, this is the place for sumptuous spare ribs, seafood, and salads. Portions are very generous and best accompanied by the steam beer on draft. The chocolate cake is colossal. Reservations recommended. 252 North Beverly Dr., Beverly Hills; 213-274-7427. Major credit cards. Moderate. L (Mondays through Saturdays), D (daily), Sunday brunch.

CHICAGO PIZZA WORKS: The pizzas are deep-dish style, and a wide range of toppings is available. The lasagna, spaghetti, salads, and desserts are good too. Open daily. Reservations not necessary. 11641 West Pico Blvd., 213-477-7740. MC, V. Moderate. L, D.

ORIGINAL PANTRY CAFE: Once a truck stop, now a diner. Dinner is thick sirloin or platter-filling T-bones. Lunch tends to be short ribs and beef stews. But the ham omelette at breakfast is truly outstanding—filled with half a pound of chunked pieces of ham steak. The hash browns are heavenly. Ninth and Figueroa, 213-972-9279. No credit cards. Inexpensive. Open 24 hours.

NIGHTLIFE

Anaheim/Orange County boasts plenty of after-dark entertainment. For information on dinner theaters in the area and the Orange County Performing Arts Center, see our *Anaheim* chapter.

NIGHTSPOTS: All the larger hotels have lounges offering soft jazz or piano or guitar music. Some of the hotel lounges and other area nightspots offer even more. **Sgt. Preston's**, at the *Disneyland* hotel, has a rowdy, Yukon Territory atmosphere. The sergeant himself, mustachioed and dressed like a Canadian Mountie, is a singing host. He's helped out by dancehall girl Klondike Kate and by the saloon's mascot, Yukon Klem, a dancing bear. It's vaudeville in the Yukon. Contemporary music with a country-western twang is offered at another of the *Disneyland* hotel lounges, **The Wharf**. The *Anaheim Hilton* has an upbeat nightclub called **Pulse**, which offers dancing nightly to Top 40 music. **The Bandstand** (1721 South Manchester Ave., Anaheim; 956-1412) has country-western nights on Tuesdays, Thursdays, and Sundays, Top 40 music Fridays and Saturdays, and live rock music on Wednesdays (closed Mondays). **Crackers** (710 East Katella Ave., Anaheim; 978-1828) features singing waiters and waitresses, musicians, jugglers, and audience participation. **The Original Cattleman's Wharf** (adjacent to the *Conestoga* hotel at 1160 West Ball Rd., Anaheim; 535-1622) features a pianist and live band in the **Baron's Lounge** upstairs. **Mr. Stox** (1105 East Katella Ave., Anaheim; 634-2994) caters to young professionals. **The Righteous Brothers' Hop** (18774 Brookhurst St., Fountain Valley; 963-2366) bears its owners' name; music and special events take guests on a nostalgic trip through the 1950s and 1960s. **Medieval Times** (7662 Beach Blvd.; 521-4740) features knights on horseback and a four-course dinner. **Crazy Horse Steakhouse and Saloon** (1580 Brookhollow Dr., Santa Ana; 549-1512) has music with a swinging western beat and often features name country performers. **The Cannery** (3010 Lafayette Ave., Newport Beach; 675-5777), besides its light rock music, is notable for the building itself—an old cannery, with some of the original equipment still in place. It's a good spot for dinner and drinks and attracts a large singles crowd (see *Getting Ready to Go*). A dinner/dancing spot of note is **Peppers** (12361 Chapman Ave., Garden Grove; 740-1333). It features dancing nightly to Top 40 hits, and offers a free shuttle to and from Disneyland-area hotels. **The Coach House** (33157 Camino Capistrano Suite, San Juan Capistrano; 496-8930) has showcased the music of top stars such as Rod Stewart, Roberta Flack, and Ray Charles.

COMEDY: The **Laff Stop** (2122 Southeast Bristol St., Newport Beach; 852-8762) has comedians nightly. There's comedy Thursdays, Fridays, and Saturdays at the **Pan Pacific** hotel (999-0990).

BREAKFAST

DISNEYLAND

Main Street: Belgian waffles and omelettes at the *Town Square Café*, biscuits and honey at the *Plaza Pavilion**.

Adventureland: Buttermilk doughnuts at *Sunkist, I Presume*.

New Orleans Square: Fritters at *Mint Julep Bar* and *Royal Street Veranda*.

Frontierland: Waffles, pancakes, and Mickey Mouse pancakes at *River Belle Terrace*.

ANAHEIM: Bacon, pancakes, and eggs at *Chao's* (request the 99¢ breakfast special).

ORANGE COUNTY: Texas-style breakfast (12 eggs, a 26-ounce top sirloin, a stack of hotcakes, potatoes, cornbread) at *Belisle's*.

LOS ANGELES: Ham omelettes, hash browns, grilled sourdough bread, and strawberry preserves at the *Original Pantry Café*.

LUNCH

DISNEYLAND

Main Street: Omelettes at the *Town Square Café*, sandwiches and salads at *Carnation Ice Cream Parlor*.

Adventureland: Burgers and salads at *Tahitian Terrace**.

New Orleans Square: The *fletan à l'acadienne* at *Blue Bayou*, interesting sandwiches and salads at *Café Orleans*.

ANAHEIM: Cobb salad or New York-cut steak at *Mr. Stox*.

ORANGE COUNTY: Hot and cold salads from the salad bar at *Back Bay Rowing & Running Club*.

LOS ANGELES: Deep-dish pizza at *Chicago Pizza Works*.

DINNER

DISNEYLAND

Main Street: Omelettes at the *Town Square Café*, sandwiches, salads, and steamed vegetables at *Carnation Ice Cream Parlor*.

Adventureland: Shrimp in Tahitian sauce, as well as steak, ribs, and pineapple upsidedown cake at *Tahitian Terrace**.

New Orleans Square: Most offerings at *Blue Bayou*.

ANAHEIM: Wild game—buffalo or venison—at the *Overland Stage*, enchiladas and margaritas at *El Torito's*, wild boar at *JW's*.

ORANGE COUNTY: Chicken dinner at *Mrs. Knott's*, pizza at *Angelo's & Vinci's*.

LOS ANGELES: Steak at *Lawry's California Center*, spare ribs and chocolate cake at *The Rib Joint*.

SNACKS

DISNEYLAND

Main Street: Sodas and sundaes at *Carnation Ice Cream Parlor*, ice cream cones at *Carnation Plaza Gardens*.

Adventureland: Pineapple spears and pineapple juice at *Tiki Juice Bar*, Jungle Juleps at *Sunkist, I Presume*.

New Orleans Square: Fritters at the Mint Julep Bar and the *Royal Street Veranda*, ice cream sodas and sundaes at *Café Orleans*.

Frontierland: Soft-serve sundaes at the *Wheelhouse**.

Tomorrowland: Soft-serve sundaes at *Space Place**.

ORANGE COUNTY: Mile-high pie at *Belisle's*.

* Only open during Disneyland's busy seasons.

SPORTS

No matter what you've heard about Southern California's urban sprawl—one town feeding into another and not an inch of land without a freeway or a house on it—there's still plenty of wide-open space for recreation. That's particularly true in Orange County. There are, for instance, more than 10,000 acres of parkland here—large community greenswards that provide a variety of sports facilities. Some have baseball fields and basketball and racquetball courts. Others offer golf, fitness courses, bike trails, and even nature areas.

In addition, there are close to 70,000 acres of mountain terrain in the Cleveland National Forest in Orange County. They are ribboned with more than 40 miles of hiking trails and 60 miles of fishing streams. There's also fine fishing to be found in several trout-stocked lakes.

Anaheim itself has two municipal golf courses and any number of convenient tennis courts. And though the hotels in the immediate vicinity of Disneyland generally don't qualify as "resorts" (they don't normally offer a multitude of sports facilities right on the premises), most do have swimming pools. The *Disneyland* hotel, for example, has three swimming pools, one of which is shaded by palm trees and is surrounded by a sand beach.

Just 15 miles south of Anaheim are some prime Pacific Ocean beaches. That's the direction to head to pursue a total tan and find the ultimate wave. (Even if you don't want to get out on a board and try it yourself, surfing is a great spectator sport, too.) In all, there are some 42 miles of beaches within an hour's drive of Anaheim, and the Pacific Coast offers plenty of fishing, too.

In winter, there are ski slopes just two hours' drive northeast of Anaheim—with the requisite snow and cold temperatures.

So even with its urban, warm-winter reputation, this part of Southern California offers such a variety of recreational opportunities that no matter what your sports preference, there's someplace here to play or practice it. (Unless otherwise noted, all phone numbers are in the 714 area code.)

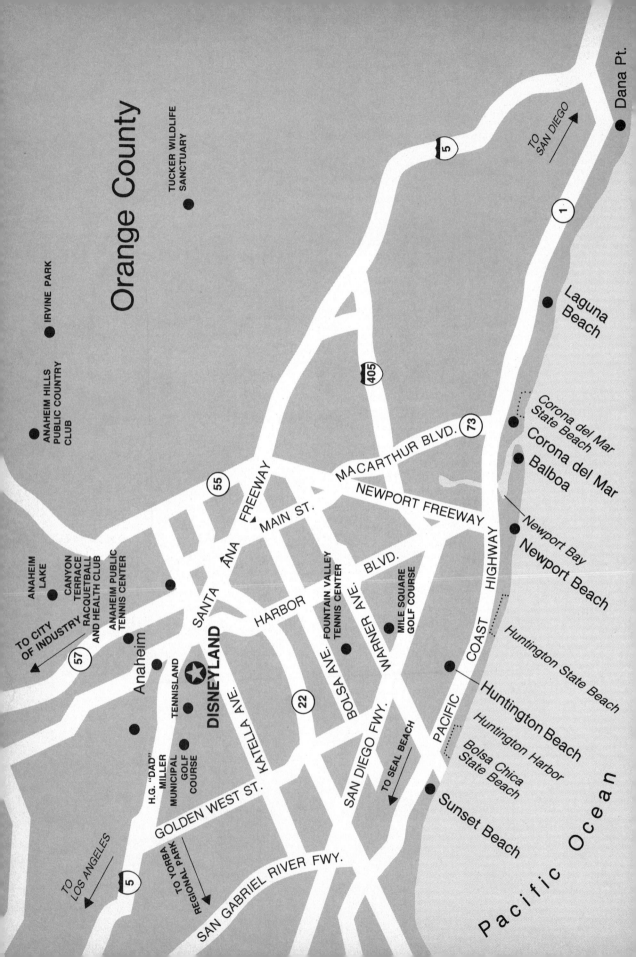

TENNIS AND RACQUETBALL

Almost any day can be a day on the courts in this sunny clime.

TENNISLAND RACQUET CLUB: Just one block west of Disneyland, this private club has facilities available to area hotel guests. There are ten hard-surface courts; nine are lit for night play. Equipment rental: good quality metal-, wood-, or graphite-frame racquets $5; shoes 75¢. Court rental: 7 A.M. to 3 P.M. Mondays through Fridays, $10 per hour; 3 P.M. to 10 P.M., $14 per hour; 7 A.M. to 6 P.M. weekends, $14 per hour. Ball machine use is available with court rental. Between noon and 3 P.M. some courts are generally unoccupied; otherwise, reservations are necessary. Tennisland offers a partner-matching service, group tournament scheduling, and shuttle bus service (advance notice is necessary) to and from the *Disneyland* hotel. The fee for a private lesson is $40 per hour, $25 per half-hour. A semi-private lesson (two people) is $20 per hour per person, $12.50 per person per half-hour. Group lessons for up to four people cost $40 per hour per group; $20 per half-hour per group. Guests at the *Disneyland* hotel, the *Pan Pacific*, the *Residence Inn*, and the *Conestoga* receive a 20 percent discount. There are locker rooms, showers, and a lounge. 1330 South Walnut St.; Anaheim; 535-4851.

FOUNTAIN VALLEY TENNIS CENTER: Located in Mile Square Regional Park, facilities are more spartan than the preceding duo, offering 12 hard-surface courts, all lit at night. Courts are open 8 A.M. to noon and 4 P.M. to 10 P.M. Mondays through Fridays; 8 A.M. to 4 P.M. weekends. A reservation card ($5) is necessary to reserve court time. Reservations may be made up to a week in advance. Cost is $4 per hour during the day; $6 per hour after dark. The busiest hours for play are 9 A.M. to 11 A.M. and 7 P.M. to 9 P.M. You must have your own equipment. Showers and lockers are not available. Near the Fountain Valley Recreation and Cultural Center. 16400 Brookhurst St., Fountain Valley; 839-5950.

ANAHEIM TENNIS CENTER: Another good playing place, about two miles from Disneyland. It has the facilities of a private club—pro shop, Spanish-style clubhouse, computerized practice machines, lockers/showers—but is open to the public. Here, too, they'll try to match you up with a suitable partner, but you must request this in advance. There are 12 fast, hard-surface courts, all lit for night play. The rate is $4 per person per hour; after 5 P.M. and weekends, $5 per hour. Ball machine use is $3.50; it's separated from the courts, but still a good place to practice forehand and backhand strokes. At press time, hours were 8 A.M. to 10 P.M. Mondays through Thursdays, 8 A.M. to 9 P.M. Fridays, 8 A.M. to 6 P.M. Saturdays and Sundays. Racquets rent for $3. Locker and shower facilities are free; towels are not supplied. Professional instruction (by appointment only) is $30 per hour. (The fee is per person for a private lesson; $15 each for a semi-private; $10 each for a group of four.) Advance reservations (bookable up to three days ahead) are a good idea, especially after 5 P.M. 975 South State College Blvd.; Anaheim; 991-9090.

FOUNTAIN VALLEY RECREATION AND CULTURAL CENTER: Located on the west side of Mile Square Regional Park, the center offers indoor and outdoor racquetball. The indoor court fee is $4 per hour. Outdoor courts are free during the day. From dusk to 8:45 P.M. they are $3 per hour. You must bring your own racquet since there are no rentals. Hours are 9 A.M. to 8:45 P.M. Mondays through Thursdays (the three outdoor courts are lit until 8:45 P.M.), 9 A.M. to 5 P.M. Fridays and Saturdays, and noon to 5 P.M. Sundays. For evening play, book reservations a day in advance. 16400 Brookhurst St.; Fountain Valley; 839-8611.

CANYON TERRACE RACQUETBALL AND HEALTH CLUB: This facility has seven air conditioned racquetball courts. Court time is $6 per hour for non-members. Racquets may be rented for $1. The club also has a weight room and aerobics classes that are open to nonmembers for $4. Hours are 6 A.M. to 10 P.M. Mondays through Fridays, 7 A.M. to 9 P.M. weekends. 100 North Tustin Ave.; Anaheim; 974-0280.

INDUSTRY HILLS & SHERATON RESORT: About 25 miles north of Disneyland, the elaborate sports complex here includes 16 hard-surface tennis courts and one grass court, all lit for night play, along with two practice courts with ball machines. The rate is $6 per hour. Ball machines are $6 for 30 minutes' practice. Hours are Mondays through Thursdays, 8 A.M. to 10 P.M.; Fridays, 8 A.M. to 8 P.M.; Saturdays and Sundays, 7 A.M. to 8 P.M. Racquets rent for $2; lockers cost $2. Professional instruction is available by appointment for $34 per hour for pro instruction, $18 per half hour. Reservations are suggested after 5 P.M., and may be booked up to three days in advance. One Industry Hills Parkway; City of Industry; 818-854-2366.

For information on tennis tournaments in the area, contact the Orange County Tennis Association; Box 4801; Newport Beach, CA 92716; 640-7743.

GOLF

Hackers and experienced golfers alike can match their skills to the following courses.

H. G. "DAD" MILLER MUNICIPAL GOLF COURSE: "Dad" Miller made a hole-in-one on this course (on the 112-yard 11th hole) when he was 101 years old, and it's still a favorite course with senior citizens since the terrain is rather flat and easy to walk. But don't let that keep you away even if you're a tad younger. This is the third-busiest golf course in California, partly because of its convenient mid-city location, but also because it's just right for the strictly recreational golfer. It's a 5,920-yard, par 71, 18-hole course. The cost for 18 holes on weekdays is $15; $18 on weekends. Carts are $18 and clubs are available for rent for $8.50 with a driver's license (you leave the license; you get it back when you return the clubs). Reservations are a must, and may be made a week in advance for weekdays and five days ahead for weekends. 430 North Gilbert St.; Anaheim; for reservations call 748-8900.

ANAHEIM HILLS PUBLIC COUNTRY CLUB: This is a far more challenging course than old Dad Miller's. It's a hilly, par 71, 6,330-yard championship layout whose 18 holes are nestled in the valleys and slopes of Santa Ana Canyon. Greens fees are $15 weekdays and $18 weekends. Carts cost $18 and rental clubs are $10 per set. Busiest on weekends; the least crowded days are Mondays and Tuesdays, but even then reservations (you can call seven days ahead for weekday play, five days ahead for weekends) are required. 6501 Nohl Ranch Rd.; Anaheim; 637-7311.

MILE SQUARE GOLF COURSE: The course runs along the southern side of the same Mile Square Regional Park area that offers such other sports as tennis, baseball, basketball, and jogging. It's a very flat 18-hole course, par 72. Greens fees are $14 during the week, $18 on weekends. Carts are available for $18. There are rental clubs (matched sets) for $12. Reservations are required; call seven days ahead for weekdays, five days ahead for weekends. 10401 Warner Ave.; Fountain Valley; 545-7106.

INDUSTRY HILLS GOLF CLUB: The lure of this location is its two 18-hole golf courses—the "Babe Zaharias" and the "Eisenhower." The former is a par 71, 5,994-yard layout; the latter is a par 72, 6,287-yard course. The cost to play the courses is $40 (including cart rental) Mondays through Thursdays; $55 Fridays through Sundays. Rental clubs are $25. Reservations for morning tee-off times can be made three days in advance. One Industry Hills Parkway; City of Industry; 818-810-GOLF.

HIKING AND BIKING

Most of the Santa Ana mountain range lies within the boundaries of the Cleveland National Forest, and the Forest Service maintains campgrounds and hiking trails. There are several areas here for hiking, horseback riding, picnicking, and biking, but two of the more popular are Santiago Canyon and Modjeska Canyon.

IRVINE PARK: Located in Santiago Canyon, near Irvine Lake. Picnic facilities are plentiful, and hiking and equestrian trails wind through the park's 477 hilly and tranquil acres. There are a petting zoo, playground, and 800-year-old sycamores and oaks. The park—the oldest county park in California—also includes several miles of bike trails, a waterfall, and a lake. The park is open from November through March from 7 A.M. to 6 P.M.; the rest of the year 7 A.M. to 9 P.M. On weekends, bicycles-for-two and paddleboats may be rented. The entry fee is $2 per vehicle, which covers parking. 21501 East Chapman Ave.; Orange; 633-8072.

YORBA REGIONAL PARK: Located in Anaheim Hills, the park offers picnic areas with barbecues, playgrounds, hiking, biking, and equestrian trails. Again, you must provide your own bikes and/or horses, but if you have a bike with you the 3½ miles of trails provide a pleasant (but not too demanding) workout. There are also four lakes within this 135-acre park (see "Fishing"). The park is open October through March from 7 A.M. to 6 P.M.; during the summer months it's open from 7 A.M. until 9 P.M. You can walk or bike into the park without charge. To drive in costs $2, which covers parking. 7600 East La Palma Ave.; Anaheim; 970-1460.

MILE SQUARE REGIONAL PARK: Offers four miles of trails for biking, hiking, or jogging. There are a fitness course and two fishing lakes, as well as a public golf course (see "Golf") and tennis courts (see "Tennis and Racquetball"). On the west side of the park, the Fountain Valley Recreation and Cultural Center (located at 16400 Brookhurst St.) has indoor and outdoor racquetball courts (see "Tennis and Racquetball"). The recreation center is open from 9 A.M. to 9 P.M. Mondays through Thursdays; 9 A.M. to 5 P.M. Fridays and Saturdays; and noon to 5 P.M. Sundays. The park is open 7 A.M. to 6 P.M. October through March; during the summer months from 7 A.M. to 9 P.M. 16801 Euclid Ave.; Fountain Valley; 839-8611 (center), 962-5549 (park).

BY THE SEA, BY THE SEA

Fishing, whalewatching, boating, surfing, and swimming are all popular in the area and available at their best where Orange County meets the Pacific. It's hard to find a hotel or motel of any size in the area that doesn't boast a swimming pool, but they are for the most part the cool-off-at-the-end-of-the-day variety, not really suited to exercise or laps. You'll find more serious swimming spots by the sea.

BEACHES: For relaxation or, for surfers, a real workout, head for one of the many free public beaches. There is a fee, however, if you park your car in any of the beach parking lots.

Seal Beach: The Orange County coast begins here and this is its northernmost beach. It's a 1½ - mile expanse of sand stretching south from Long Beach to Anaheim Bay. This is a high-density residential area, and not the prettiest spot along the coast, but there are some good boutiques at Old Town Seal Beach. There is also a variety of eating establishments on Main Street in the Old Town area. The city also has a fishing pier. For further information on the beach area call 213-431-2527 (213-379-8471 for surf information).

Bolsa Chica State Beach: A wide and sandy expanse with its own nature reserve. There are convenient restroom and changing facilities. There is a $6 entrance fee for autos; $14 for recreational vehicles. The beach is located between Goldenwest Street and Warner Avenue. For further information call 846-3460.

Huntington Beach: Driving from Disneyland, beachgoers will reach Huntington before Bolsa. This is probably the best place to surf, since equipment can be rented along Main Street. Unfortunately, the Huntington Beach pier was damaged by high tides in 1988. It has been rebuilt

and it provides an ideal spot for fishing and a good vantage point from which to watch the surfers. Huntington Beach calls itself the "Surfing Capital of the USA," and annual surfing competitions are held here. It's also been the site of world surfing championships. On any given summer Saturday or Sunday, surfers swarm into the water. Diehards in wet suits are out in winter, too. Huntington Beach boasts a long stretch of sand, and it's a rare day when there isn't a beach volleyball game to join. It's also a good beach for jogging. For further information call 536-5281 (536-9303 for surf information).

Newport City Beach/Balboa Beach: This, too, is a popular area with surfers, as well as sightseers, especially since Newport Harbor shelters nearly 10,000 boats, including those of the dorymen who go out in their small, wooden craft each morning at dawn. These hardy souls leave from the pier at Newport Beach and return at about 10 A.M. to clean and sell their catch. The scene quickly becomes a large, open-air fish market, and is quite picturesque. This is also the place to sample the much revered Balboa Bar in its native habitat.

The Balboa Peninsula juts into the Pacific here, and the beaches—Newport on the mainland, Balboa on the peninsula—are long and horseshoe-shaped. They are pleasant and sandy, albeit a bit far from Anaheim if you just want to catch some rays for only an hour or so. It's sightseeing that makes these beaches worth the drive. From your place in the sun you can see the boats at sail (some of them are particularly interesting to see, since Newport is host each year to the Wooden Boat Festival, the Newport Seafest Celebrations, and the Christmas Boat Parade. The total value of the boats anchored here is estimated between $50 and $60 million.

For a good view of the harbor, drive along Newport Boulevard to Balboa Boulevard on the Balboa Peninsula. Turn right on Palm Street to find parking for the Balboa Pier. Or stop at Main Street, near the landmark Balboa Pavilion. Adjacent to the Balboa Pavilion is Davey's Locker, where it's possible to rent 14-foot skiffs with outboard motors if you'd like to do some fishing, go parasailing, or just take a tour of Newport Bay. There also are regularly scheduled sightseeing boats that provide a view of local residences, and since Newport/Balboa is Orange County's answer to Beverly Hills, the shorefront houses are quite opulent and fun to look at. For more information contact the Newport Harbor Area Chamber of Commerce (644-8211).

> **WHALEWATCHING:** Each winter, hundreds of California gray whales migrate along the coast to the warm waters of Baja California and western Mexico, then early in spring swim back to feeding areas off the Alaska coast. From December through March, the 50-foot-long leviathans are usually easy to spot from cliffs along the ocean. Boats will take the adventurous out for even closer looks from Dana Point Harbor (named after Richard Henry Dana, who wrote *Two Years Before the Mast*) and from Newport Harbor.

Corona Del Mar State Beach, Laguna Beach, Doheny State Beach, and San Clemente: These beaches farther south are not quite as dramatic as the more northerly strands, yet they are scenic in somewhat the same way. High cliffs and sheltered coves are common, and there are plenty of tidal pools to explore. If you wend your way south along the Pacific Coast Highway from Huntington Beach to San Clemente, the county's southernmost beach outpost, you'll find these beaches all in a 20-mile stretch, as well as many smaller ones. Signs lead to parking nearby and on the bluffs overlooking them, where it's possible to get the full effect of the Southern California ocean vistas. In general, beaches are open from 6 A.M. to midnight, with lifeguards present in summer.

FISHING: Anglers will find no shortage of action—both saltwater and freshwater—around Anaheim. You can go out for mackerel, whitefish, or halibut in the Pacific; try catching grunion on the beach from March through September; or take youngsters to one of a handful of stocked lakes to cast for trout, crappie, catfish, or bass.

Sportfishing: The Dana Wharf (in Dana Point) sportfishing fleet generally makes four trips a day in season. Prices run about $20 to $30. For details and to confirm schedules, call 831-1850. Boats from Davey's Locker (Balboa) also go out several times a day; prices are comparable. Details: Balboa Pavilion; 400 Main St.; Balboa; 673-1434.

Boats from Dana Wharf and Davey's Locker go out for bonita, barracuda, bass, and yellowtail. Reservations are required at Davey's Locker and can be made a day in advance. The price of a full-day boat rental (which is equipped with some bunks and a galley; food is extra) is $32 for adults and $22 for children 12 and under; for half a day, $22 for adults and $12 for children 12 and under. Pole rental is $7. Fourteen-foot skiffs (which accommodate six people) with outboard motors are also available for rent—$45 for a full day, which includes bait, motor, and gas. Fishing licenses, which are necessary for deep-sea sportfishing, can be obtained at Davey's Locker; $17.75 per year, $6 for 1 day. Dana Wharf boats go out at 7 A.M. for ¾-day fishing (returning between 3 P.M. and 3:30 P.M.). The cost is $30 for adults, $20 for children under 12. For a half day of fishing, the price is $20 for adults, $15 for children. Poles rent for $6. Licenses may be obtained on the premises. Reservations are advisable, and they can be made a day in advance, two days in advance for weekends.

Irvine Lake: Another stocked local fresh waterway. The gate fee is $10 for adults, $8 for children 4–12, under 4 free. There's no charge for fish caught, and a fishing license is not required. Fishing poles rent for $4 a day. Boats with motors can be rented for $30 a day, including gas. The rate is $18 for half a day, beginning at noon. Rowboats rent for $18 a day; $12 for half a day. You can launch your own boat ($5 launch fee), but it must be at least ten feet long. Caution: the five-mph speed limit is strictly enforced. There is a tackle shop and a snack shop on the lake. Hours are 6 A.M. to 4 P.M. daily. 4621 Santiago Canyon Rd.; Orange; 649-2560.

Yorba Regional Park: Three of the four lakes within the boundaries of this 135-developed-acre park are stocked with catfish. To fish you'll need a valid California fishing license. You can buy one at most of the local sporting goods stores, but they are *not* available at the park. 7600 East La Palma Ave.; Anaheim; 970-1460.

Bolsa Chica: It's also possible to catch grunion in the vicinity, and Bolsa Chica is one of the better beaches on which to try your hand—literally. From March through September, the tiny fish are swept onto beaches here to lay their eggs in the sand; they head to sea again on outgoing waves. Best times to get them are on the second through fifth nights after a full moon, about an hour after high tide. You must catch grunion with your bare hands—they're slippery, but easy to see, for they shimmer in the moonlight. A fishing license is required if you're over 16 years of age. For information call the State Department of Fish and Game at 213-590-5132. Fishing catch reports, trout plant reports, and best beaches and times for grunion can generally be found in the sports sections of area papers.

NATURE: Bird- and wildlife-watchers will be pleasantly surprised to learn that they can easily spend anywhere from an hour to a full day close to nature in this land of freeways and parking lots.

Bolsa Chica Ecological Reserve: Offers 250 acres of Pacific Ocean marshland in which to observe fish and wetland birds. From the parking lot, cross the bridge and follow the trail that loops through the marsh. Binoculars are useful, but not absolutely necessary. The parking lot is on Pacific Coast Highway 1½ miles south of Warner; Huntington Beach; 897-7003.

Upper Newport Bay Ecological Reserve: During the fall and winter months, this 750-acre reserve at Newport Beach is teeming with birds—great blue herons and ospreys among them. Six times during the migratory season (October through March), Friends of Newport Bay guide groups on walking tours through the reserve and point out the birds, as well as fossils, marsh plants, and fish. But it's easy enough to enjoy the area all on your own. To reach the reserve, begin at the intersection of Back Bay Drive and Jamboree Road. Drive or walk along Back Bay Drive for the length of the reserve. Information: 646-8009.

Tucker Wildlife Sanctuary: Located in Modjeska Canyon in the Santa Ana Mountains, this sanctuary is a beautiful oasis of trees, flowers, plants, and wildlife. Walk along the lovely stream and listen to the birds sing—over 140 species have been identified here. Naturalists are on duty to answer questions. The sanctuary is open daily from 9 A.M. to 4 P.M. For information call 649-2760.

CATALINA ISLAND: This special island is a sportsperson's wonderland. Golf, horseback riding, snorkeling, scuba diving, and sportfishing are all available. Tours of inland Catalina provide a glimpse of buffalo, wild goats, deer, and boar, and glass-bottomed boat tours offer crystal-clear views of underwater life. From Orange County, Catalina Passenger Service (673-5245) has a high-speed catamaran, the *Catalina Flyer*, which makes a one-way trip in 75 minutes. Call ahead for schedules and to make required advance reservations. Tours leave from the Balboa Pavilion, 400 Main St., on the Balboa Peninsula. From Los Angeles County, Catalina Cruises (800-888-5939) has daily service year-round from Long Beach, plus weekend service year-round and daily service in season from San Pedro. Advance reservations are required for hotels, condo rentals, and campsites (it's best to make these at least a month ahead). Details: Catalina Chamber of Commerce; Box 217; Avalon, CA 90704; 213-510-1520.

SKIING: Although it's unlikely that you'd come to Southern California solely for the skiing, it is not at all out of the question. In fact, you'll find fine areas like Big Bear (in the San Bernardino Mountains) just 90 miles from Disneyland. You even can do a little skiing right in Anaheim—indoors. California Ski Center (Port-A-Slope) carries full equipment for skiers, as well as offering indoor ski lessons on their two slopes (one covered with a plastic material called Pro-Snow, the other, which rotates, covered with something similar to low-pile carpeting). Private and group lessons for beginning through advanced skiers are given here, and boots, skis, and poles are included in the cost of the lesson. Open from 10 A.M. to 9 P.M. Mondays through Fridays, and 9 A.M. to 6 P.M. Saturdays. 1011 North Harbor Blvd.; Anaheim; 776-7669.

SPORTS PACKAGES: Ask at your hotel about sports packages available in the area. One example is the two-night/three-day tennis package at the *Newport Beach Marriott*, which costs $275 per couple, including one dinner and one breakfast (if you are there on Sunday, you can substitute the champagne brunch). The hotel's tennis club is open from 8 A.M. to 9 P.M., and they guarantee 1½ hours per day of court time on one of their eight asphalt courts. All are lit for night play. Court fees are $15 per hour for hotel guests, $20 for the public. For hotel guests and club members, there's a ball machine available for practicing strokes at the rate of $8 per half hour. They do rent racquets for $3, but you must buy balls. There are four pros on staff who give private lessons for about $40 per hour ($20 for a half hour). There's also a fully equipped pro shop. Reservations are requested. The Newport Beach Marriott Tennis Club is open to the public. 900 Newport Center Dr.; Newport Beach; 640-4000.

AERIAL SPORTS: Parasailing and hot-air ballooning have become popular year-round sports in this sunny clime. A parasailing excursion from Dana Point runs $45 per person. Each individual ride lasts ten minutes. Details: 496-5794. Hot-air balloon tours, which take off at sunrise or sunset, offer a bird's-eye view of some of the area's most scenic spots. Most tours leave from locations about an hour or two from Disneyland. The following companies offer balloon tours of the area: Above All Balloon Charters (546-7433) features flights over the Perris and Temecula areas of Riverside County, and the Del Mar area of San Diego County. Prices range from $80 to $175 per person, depending on the options chosen. Cloud 9 Champagne Balloon Flights (800-677-3600) offers flights over the Temecula area; champagne picnics and winery tours are available. Prices range from $90 to $110 per person. Rainbow Flights (800-634-7174) takes guests on one-hour flights over the Temecula area. Rates are $120 per person. Brunch at a nearby winery is an option.

MEETINGS AND CONVENTIONS

Compared with the majority of cities vying for convention business, Anaheim is small. Still, in the minds of meeting planners—and meeting goers—it consistently ranks among the country's top five meeting destinations.

It no doubt helps that Anaheim is not only the home of Disneyland, but also offers—within a half-hour's drive—beaches, desert, and just about every other recreational and entertainment possibility for which any attendee could wish. It is also not insignificant that in midwinter, when much of the rest of the country is buried in snow and ice, Anaheim's daytime temperature usually hovers around 70°. (Summers are warmer—in the 85° to 95° range—but there's usually very little humidity.)

Another strong drawing card is Anaheim's accessibility: It's less than an hour's drive from Los Angeles International Airport and a half-hour drive from John Wayne/Orange County Airport (which recently opened a new terminal and parking structure as part of an extensive expansion). Transportation from either airport to Anaheim is quite convenient; both are served on a regular schedule by the Airport Coach and Airport Cruiser motorcoach fleet (see *Transportation and Accommodations*). Scheduled transportation to the Los Angeles Airport is also provided by Airport Cruiser buses. Limousine and van fleets also are available for airport pickup and delivery. And for those who plan to rent cars, Anaheim is surrounded by five freeways and is only 27 miles south of the Los Angeles Civic Center.

But the city's meeting and convention facilities themselves are by far the biggest draw, for Anaheim has the largest convention center on the West Coast, and it was recently expanded so there's even more exhibition space and parking than ever. It also happens to be the sixth-largest convention center in the entire United States.

Furthermore, the exhibit space and meeting rooms at the 70,500-seat Anaheim Stadium can be used to supplement those in the Convention Center (for groups that require additional space), and there are still more facilities available at the *Disneyland* hotel, the *Grand*, the *Sheraton*, the *Marriott*, the *Inn at the Park*, the *Hyatt Regency*, the *Quality*, the *Hilton*, the *Pan Pacific*, the *Doubletree*, and the *Anaheim Plaza*. So space and facilities exist to meet any group's needs.

(Unless otherwise noted, all phone numbers are in the 714 area code.)

ANAHEIM CONVENTION CENTER

The Convention Center facilities are versatile and multifaceted. A major expansion was completed in 1990, so there is now a total of 835,000 square feet of air conditioned space—a 27,000-square-foot arena with 9,000 seats and three 100,000-square-foot exhibition halls, each accommodating up to 550 ten-foot-by-ten-foot booths; and a new 150,000 square foot exhibition hall. In addition, the South Exhibition Hall adjoins the California Room, which has 21,000 square feet available for exhibit and meeting space. The Southwest Exhibition Hall and its adjoining Pacific Room offer identical configurations. The center's 46 meeting rooms have individual temperature controls, telephones, sound systems, and seating for anywhere from 10 to 2,800 people.

Each of the Convention Center areas is really multipurpose in itself. The meeting rooms can be used for exhibition purposes, and the larger ones can even accommodate trucks and motor homes. The arena is similarly flexible. It can accommodate exhibits, theatrical events, and a variety of other activities—including banquets.

Food is provided by ARA Leisure Service, a national organization that counts executive dining rooms, hospitals, and universities among its clients. They serve more than 250,000 dinners a year here, and can handle as many as 18,000 guests for a sit-down meal, with everything prepared within the Convention Center itself.

In fact, practically anything required can be created on the premises: The Anaheim Convention Center has its own carpentry shop, plus welding, electrical, and sound facilities. There are portable stages and booths. Television hookups are no problem.

Located directly across the street from Disneyland and within walking distance of many hotels and motels, the center is designed to accommodate virtually any type of public performance—concerts, sporting events, circuses, closed-circuit telecasts with approximately 9,000 people in attendance—and that's in the arena alone. Each year the nation's largest home and garden show, a recreational vehicle show, and a boat show are held here. "Disney on Ice," Ringling Bros. and Barnum & Bailey Circus, and various other entertainments are also presented. Billy Graham has even staged a crusade here, using the Convention Center as well as the Anaheim Stadium (two miles away) for his outdoor rally. And recent conventions have included the Merchants Music Association, the American Heart Association, and the International Reading Association.

Center personnel have moved 800 tons of dirt into the arena for a rodeo and have frozen the floor for ice shows. Rocket engines and a computer display (that took five days to set up) have come across the loading docks—or through one of the 40-foot truck-doors built into the side of each of the ground-level exhibition halls. Cleanup time never takes more than eight hours; so the ice show can move out one day, and the computers set up the next.

Total attendance for the Center has grown from about 45,000 conventiongoers in 1967, its opening year, to a current attendance of about one million attendees per year. Nearly 70 percent of Anaheim's conventions are national meetings; the majority in the education, scientific, technical, or medical fields.

The Anaheim Area Visitor & Convention Bureau and the Convention center sales and booking staff will help meeting planners arrange everything, and their housing bureau can help organize and reserve hotel accommodations. The center has paid parking for more than 4,500 cars. Anaheim Visitor and Convention Bureau; 800 West Katella Ave.; Box 4270; Anaheim, CA 92803; 999-8999.

AT DISNEYLAND

In an effort to keep pace with Anaheim's growing convention business, Disneyland now offers several group programs ranging from Private Parties for 20 to Enchanted Evenings for 1,000. Groups of up to 18,000 can be accommodated for special events. Though Disneyland does not serve alcohol during its regular operating hours, drinks are available for these scheduled functions. The unique Disney touch can make any event extraordinary. For details on group events call 999-4123.

ACCOMMODATIONS AND FACILITIES

There are some 17,000 hotel rooms in the immediate Anaheim area, and 40,000 in all of Orange County. Many of the city's hotels and motels have special convention rates, which vary according to the number of rooms required. All of these hotels have parking (generally free) for guests.

More than one million delegates convene in Anaheim annually. The average meeting consists of about 5,000 participants. The major meeting facilities in the Anaheim area, apart from the Convention Center, are described below.

DISNEYLAND HOTEL: 1,132 guestrooms, including 65 suites, and 150,000 square feet of space provided for convention facilities. The Entertainment and Convention Center on the Marina houses two ballrooms, exhibit halls, meeting rooms, an audiovisual center, restaurants, and cocktail lounges. There are 52 meeting rooms in all, including those located in three separate meeting centers. They can be set up theater style to accommodate groups ranging from 20 to 3,200 people, or from 20 to 1,900, banquet style. There's also 97,000 square feet of exhibit space. Several rooms have adjacent convention-registration or guest reception areas. Exhibit booths, food service, staging, and audiovisual equipment are also available. In the Grand Ballroom, lit by an Italian-crystal chandelier 30 feet in diameter, the stage can be raised or lowered hydraulically. This ballroom has electronically controlled drop and side curtains, a movie screen, and three dressing rooms in the back. A particularly nice aspect of convening here is that the hotel's convention-service staff can help set up special theme parties on any one of several out-of-the-ordinary outdoor sites on the hotel grounds, including a marina, a white sand beach, horseshoe waterfalls, and flowering gardens. Details: Disneyland Hotel; 1150 West Cerritos Ave.; Anaheim, CA 92802; 778-6600.

PAN PACIFIC: 502 guestrooms, 15 meeting rooms. There are almost 25,000 square feet of meeting and banquet space here. The 7,250-square-foot Grand Ballroom (which seats 725 theater style, 600 for banquets) breaks down into four rooms. Adjacent to it is a 2,000-square-foot foyer for registration and preconvention activities. Up a staircase are nine separate "breakout" meeting rooms, ideal for gatherings of 15 to 125 people. Outdoors on the third-floor pool deck is the 8,000-square-foot, flower-lined Garden Pavilion and Reception Plaza; it is used for events such as cocktail receptions and weddings. The new 3,800-square-foot Pacific Room accommodates 200 for a banquet or 250 for a reception. The hotel offers state-of-the-art public address systems and audiovisual capabilities. Details: Pan Pacific; 1717 South West St.; Anaheim, CA 92802; 999-0990 or 800-321-8976.

GRAND: 240 guestrooms, 22 banquet rooms, and several meeting rooms that will accommodate from 5 to 700 people. The main-floor Crystal Ballroom holds 550 for dinner and 700 for meetings. It can also be separated into 13 smaller rooms, each of which can be set up in classroom, "U" shape, conference, theater, banquet, round-table, or reception style. The Sky Room, on the top floor, overlooks Disneyland and holds 300 people. Any equipment—stages, decorative elements, floral arrangements, audiovisual equipment—as well as food service from the hotel's kitchens, can be provided. The hotel also has a nightly dinner theater with a buffet and a show. It holds 400 people and can be reserved for an evening's entertainment. Details: Grand; One Hotel Way; Anaheim, CA 92802; 772-7777.

ANAHEIM MARRIOTT: 1,039 guestrooms, 27 meeting rooms, and 72 suites at present. The Grand Ballroom has 16,000 square feet of exhibit space. It will hold from 1,160 to 3,000 people, depending upon how the seats are arranged. It can also be divided into ten rooms, the largest of which is 5,187 square feet, the smallest 644 square feet. Several rooms can be combined, so configurations can be created to satisfy most needs. The Orange County Ballroom (5,000 square feet) also divides into five smaller rooms. All can be set up in various configurations. Marriott Hall (25,000 square feet, which can be broken down into four rooms) adds still more meeting and exhibit space. There is parking for about 2,000 cars. Food service, portable stages, audiovisual, or other equipment can be provided. Details: Anaheim Marriott; 700 West Convention Way; Anaheim, CA 92802; 750-8000.

INN AT THE PARK: 500 guestrooms and 16 meeting rooms; more than 20,000 square feet of meeting space, capable of accommodating groups from 10 to 1,700 people. All meeting rooms are soundproof. The Park Plaza Ballroom (11,988 square feet) has the largest exhibit space. It is on the ground floor of the lobby building. The Garden Rooms, also in the lobby building, will hold 200 people, theater style. The hotel's special-function room, Tiffany Terrace, has a beautiful, antique stained-glass ceiling and an indoor/outdoor meeting area, which can be used for special theme parties and events. All rooms can be set up in varying styles. Required audiovisual equipment and food service can be provided. Details: Inn at the Park; 1855 South Harbor Blvd.; Anaheim, CA 92802; 750-1811.

ANAHEIM PLAZA: 300 guestrooms right across the street from the main entrance to Disneyland. Meeting rooms include the Lanai Ballroom, which holds 250 participants, theater style, and can be divided into four separate rooms holding about 50 people each, depending on how they are set up. Two of the rooms can be combined to hold 120 or so. The Valencia Ballroom, on the second floor, has a capacity of 350 people, theater style, or 500 people standing at a cocktail party. When divided into two or three rooms, each can accommodate from 100 to 225. The Rainbow Room on the second floor seats 75, theater style. The bright, airy Celebrity Room, right off the patio, holds 400, theater style. All rooms can be set up in any desired configuration, and the hotel has full convention facilities: audiovisual equipment, podiums, screens, risers, and the like. Large displays are easily accommodated. Food is prepared in the hotel's kitchens. The hotel has an Olympic-size pool. Details: Anaheim Plaza Resort; 1700 South Harbor Blvd.; Anaheim, CA 92802; 772-5900 or 800-228-1357.

QUALITY: 284 guestrooms; 9 meeting rooms. The largest display space is 4,272 square feet. The Orangewood Ballroom can hold as many as 500; classroom style, it holds 350. It can be broken up into three rooms holding 150 people each. The California Room can be divided into four rooms. There is also a Conference Theater, with raised floor and graduated seating, that holds 56 people. Poolside parties can be arranged, and all banquet facilities are on the first floor. Audiovisual equipment, portable floors, stages, and a message center with direct phone lines are available. Because the hotel's kitchen was designed to handle conventions as well as its own restaurants, menus can be flexible. Details: Quality; 616 Convention Way; Anaheim, CA 92802; 750-3131.

ANAHEIM HILTON: 1,600 guestrooms and approximately 60 meeting rooms. This hotel is just steps away from Anaheim's Convention Center, but the hotel's facilities are fine in their own right. There are two 29,000-square-foot ballrooms, the largest ballrooms in Southern California. They are served by a registration and prefunction foyer of 15,216 square feet. There are another 52 meeting rooms of varying sizes and configurations, too; and there's a spacious boardroom with a special anteroom. The rooms can be set up in any style and any necessary audiovisual or other equipment

and food service are available. One other nice touch: The hotel's suites have been designed with double- and triple-wide parlors, which can easily accommodate receptions. Details: Anaheim Hilton and Towers; 777 Convention Way; Anaheim, CA 92802; 750-4321.

HYATT REGENCY ALICANTE: 400 guestrooms, including 17 suites, with almost 16,000 square feet of meeting space. The 6,940-square-foot Royal Ballroom accommodates up to 770 for a banquet, up to 1,200 for a reception, and up to 1,000 theater-style. The Ballroom can be divided into six smaller sections. There are also seven conference rooms. The atrium and garden areas can be booked for special functions. Audiovisual equipment and props are available at the hotel. Special menus can be arranged through affiliated catering services. Details: Hyatt Regency Alicante; 100 Plaza Alicante; Harbor Blvd. and Chapman Ave.; Garden Grove, CA 92640; 971-3000.

DOUBLETREE: 461 guestrooms, including 19 suites, plus 20,000 square feet of meeting space. The 8,085-square-foot Grand Ballroom seats 550 for a banquet or 1,000 for a reception, and divides into as many as five separate sound-resistant rooms (various room configurations are possible). The 2,960-square-foot California Ballroom, divisible into three rooms, accommodates about 200 for a banquet, 380 for a reception. There are seven conference rooms, ranging in size from 312 to 1,036 square feet. The largest of these accommodates 130 for a reception, 50 classroom-style. There are also 11 conference suites with seating for 10 to 20 people. Catering services offer extensive menu options for a variety of functions, ranging from small receptions to buffets to sit-down meals. Audiovisual equipment and props for staging can be provided. Details: Doubletree; 100 The City Dr.; Orange, CA 92668; 634-4500.

SHERATON-ANAHEIM: 493 guestrooms and 14 meeting rooms, varying in size from banquet/ballroom to suite, accommodate from 12 to 1,200 for cocktails or about 600 for a sit-down dinner. Most rooms include a public-address system and individual temperature control; audiovisual equipment, podiums, floral arrangements, entertainment, and photography can all be arranged. There is a separate, free parking area for convention-goers, and equipment can be brought directly into the exhibition and display areas. The largest display room, the Kensington Ballroom, is 8,280 square feet. Details: Sheraton-Anaheim; 1015 West Ball Rd.; Anaheim, CA 92802; 778-1700.

ANAHEIM

145 Sights and Attractions
150 Shopping

With a population of about 243,000, Anaheim is Orange County's largest city and the eighth largest in the state of California. It is an amalgam of apartment complexes, mobile-home parks, graceful adobe residences, and housing tracts full of those "little boxes on the hillside." The general landscape is softened and shaded and further colored by dignified royal palms, feathery jacaranda, and cascading bougainvillea. And the dry weather claims of the local chamber of commerce notwithstanding, Anaheim is washed clean every once in a while (generally in winter and early spring) by rain. When this happens, the clarity of vista and line makes even smog-jaded residents take a new look at the surroundings.

Anaheim really doesn't look much different from the cities that surround it: Buena Park, Fullerton, Garden Grove, Placentia, Orange, Santa Ana, Stanton, Westminster. One community seems to flow into another, from the mountains to the beach. What sets Anaheim apart is Disneyland, whose creation totally changed the concept of amusement theme parks all over the world. It is the number one tourist attraction in the state of California.

According to local legend, everyone thought Walt Disney was more than a little crazy when he broached the idea of putting his pioneer amusement attraction in Anaheim. After all, who'd go all the way out *there* just to shake hands with a mouse?

It turns out that lots of people would—and did. Disney chose Anaheim as the site for Disneyland on the advice of the Stanford Research Institute, and opened his dream park to the public in 1955. Between 1955 and today, Anaheim has become just what the Stanford Research people must have predicted it would—a compact, well-developed city that's a pleasant place to visit.

(Unless otherwise noted, all phone numbers are in the 714 area code.)

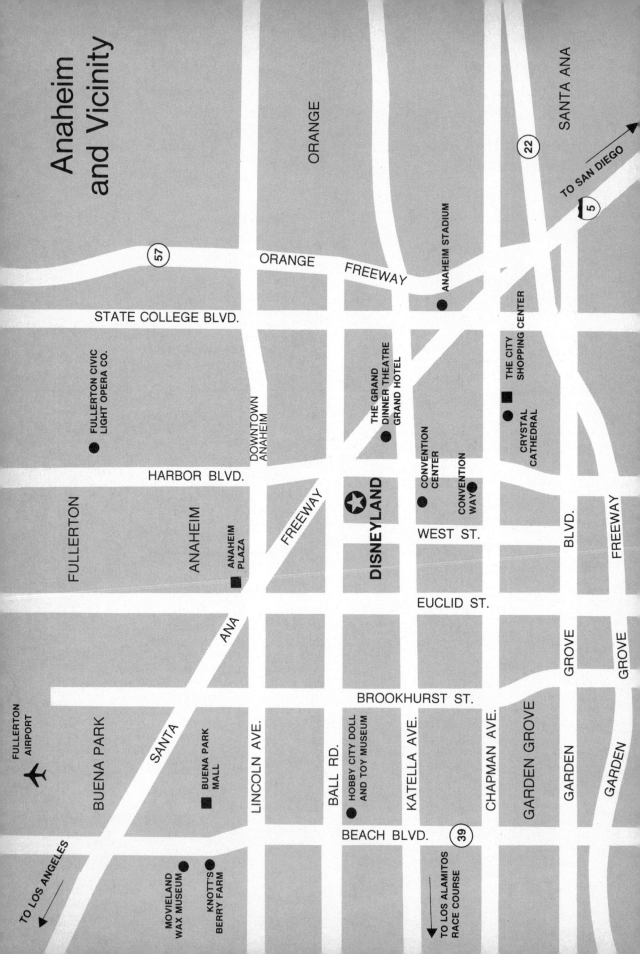

Anaheim and Vicinity

ORANGE

TO SAN DIEGO

SANTA ANA

(22)

(5)

(57)

ORANGE FREEWAY

STATE COLLEGE BLVD.

ANAHEIM STADIUM ●

FULLERTON CIVIC ● LIGHT OPERA CO.

THE GRAND DINNER THEATRE GRAND HOTEL ●

THE CITY SHOPPING CENTER ■

DOWNTOWN ANAHEIM

HARBOR BLVD.

CONVENTION CENTER ●

CRYSTAL ● CATHEDRAL

FULLERTON

ANAHEIM

FREEWAY

CONVENTION WAY ●

★ DISNEYLAND

WEST ST.

ANAHEIM PLAZA ■

BLVD.

FREEWAY

EUCLID ST.

ANA

BROOKHURST ST.

FULLERTON AIRPORT ✈

BUENA PARK

SANTA

LINCOLN AVE.

BALL RD.

HOBBY CITY DOLL ● AND TOY MUSEUM

KATELLA AVE.

CHAPMAN AVE.

GARDEN GROVE

GARDEN GROVE

GARDEN GROVE

BUENA PARK MALL ■

BEACH BLVD.

(39)

TO LOS ANGELES

MOVIELAND ● WAX MUSEUM

KNOTT'S ● BERRY FARM

TO LOS ALAMITOS RACE COURSE

SIGHTS AND ATTRACTIONS

ANAHEIM PIONEER MOTHER COLONY HOUSE: This redwood-frame house, the first residence built in Anaheim, dates from 1857, when George Hansen and 50 German colonists established the town. Artifacts that survive from the families that called it home until the 1920s are on display. The house is open from 1 P.M. to 3 P.M. on Sundays. About three miles from Disneyland. 414 North West St., Anaheim; 774-3840. Tours are available by special arrangement. For information, call the Anaheim Public Library at 999-1850.

ANAHEIM STADIUM TOURS: This is an attraction that's sure to please sports buffs. Guided tours of Anaheim Stadium (home of the California Angels and the Los Angeles Rams) take visitors behind the scenes. You can stand at home plate and imagine you're an all-star, and even visit the locker rooms. The tour also takes in the press areas, where radio, TV, and news reporters watch the games. Tours are conducted daily on the hour on weekdays from 10 A.M. to 2 P.M., except during games and other scheduled events. Before heading to the ballpark, call 937-7333 to make sure that there are no scheduled events at the time you plan to tour.

Rates are $3 for adults, $2 for seniors, $2 for children 15 and under; children under 5 are admitted free. Parking for tour guests is free. Anaheim Stadium is located at the corner of Katella Avenue and State College Boulevard, 2 miles east of Disneyland. Details: Anaheim Stadium tour information; 937-7333.

NEWPORT HARBOR ART MUSEUM: Orange County's premier art museum has expanded its permanent collection in recent years. Post World War II California art is strongly represented, but major works by New York and European artists also are featured. The museum also houses a bookstore and a restaurant (open for lunch Mondays through Fridays). Museum hours are 10 A.M. to 5 P.M. Tuesdays through Sundays. Admission is $3 for adults; $2 for students, senior citizens, and military; $1 for children ages 6 to 17; free to museum members and children under six. 850 San Clemente Dr.; Newport Beach; 759-1122.

ANAHEIM MUSEUM: Exhibits depict the history of Anaheim from its beginnings as a rural society to the opening of Disneyland in 1955 to its present-day role as an important Southern California city. Open Wednesdays through Fridays from 10 A.M. to 4 P.M., Saturdays from noon to 4 P.M. No admission is charged, but donations are accepted. The museum is about a mile from Disneyland. 241 South Anaheim Blvd.; Anaheim; 778-3301.

CRYSTAL CATHEDRAL: Just two miles southeast of Disneyland, in the city of Garden Grove, is what *Newsweek* magazine called "the most spectacular religious edifice in the world." More than 10,000 panes of glass cover a weblike steel skeleton, so that it seems a cross between a greenhouse and a glass obelisk. The glass lets the outdoors come in, and anyone entering the auditorium is surrounded by nature's beauty.

The Crystal Cathedral's pastor, Reverend Robert Schuller, is often seen on television. He began his ministry in a drive-in theater, and his church has been engineered in such a way that a section of it can be opened up for those who prefer to worship in their cars. Open from 9 A.M. to 4 P.M. Mondays through Saturdays and noon to 4 P.M. Sundays. Tours are generally available; group tours must be scheduled in advance. 12141 Lewis St.; Garden Grove; 971-4000.

HOBBY CITY DOLL AND TOY MUSEUM: Bea De Armond has been collecting dolls and toys for more than 60 years. Her collection is displayed here in a half-scale replica of the White House. There are teddy bears, some dating as far back as 1907, and a wooden model of the Kyoto Imperial Palace that was first seen at the Japan Expo, held in Tokyo in 1870 (two of the figures in it resemble the emperor and empress who were reigning at that time). There are cloth dolls; composition, beeswax, papier-mâché, and bisque dolls; Kewpie dolls; and American Indian, Chinese, Haitian voodoo, and Barbie dolls. The oldest doll comes from an Egyptian pyramid. The popular favorite is a "smiling lady" who resembles Mary Poppins, but serious collectors especially want to see "Lady Long Fingers," a carved, wooden pre-Georgian doll made in England, circa 1700. There are 3,000 dolls and other toys in all, easily seen by people of all sizes since some of the display cases run along the walls at floor level. The Doll and Toy Museum is a part of Hobby City, a group of 24 hobby, crafts, and collector shops. Open from 10 A.M. to 6 P.M. daily (tickets are sold until 5:30 P.M.). Admission is $1 for adults and 50¢ for senior citizens and children under 12. Located four miles from Disneyland. 1238 South Beach Blvd.; Anaheim; 527-2323.

KNOTT'S BERRY FARM: This isn't a farm at all but a themed amusement park depicting much of the history and culture of California. Knott's was once a berry patch (hence the name) where Walter Knott propagated a new fruit that had been started and then abandoned by Rudolph Boysen. Knott christened the large, succulent berries *boysenberries* and planted 20 acres of them. At the time, his family was selling berries, pies, and preserves at a roadside stand.

During the Depression, Knott's wife, Cordelia, started a tearoom to help make ends meet. The Knott children helped in the kitchen and waited on tables.

Mrs. Knott's chicken dinners were soon so well regarded locally that visitors had to wait for a seat. Then Walter Knott decided to build a wander-through ghost town. His mother had come to California on a wagon train, and the ghost town was his way of saluting her courage and keeping waiting restaurant patrons from getting impatient. The park just grew from there. Today it ranks as one of the most visited amusement parks in the country, after Walt Disney World and Disneyland.

There is a Topsy-like

"just-growed" feeling about Knott's, and it's worth the better part of a day. It would be wise, however, to put a day or two of other, varied sightseeing between your Knott's and Disneyland visits.

The chicken dinners are still available at *Mrs. Knott's Chicken Dinner* restaurant (they are first class, so there's always a line; it's wise to skip breakfast and opt for a very early lunch, or skip lunch and get there early enough to beat the dinner crowd). Be sure to top off your chicken, gravy, and biscuits with a slice of boysenberry pie.

Headline entertainers often appear at the Chevrolet-Geo Good Time Theatre. All entertainment is included in the price of admission to the park.

The themed areas include Wild Water Wilderness, a turn-of-the-century California river wilderness park (with trees and plants native to California) featuring Bigfoot Rapids, a wet, wild ride down a "raging" white-water river (with a glimpse of Bigfoot). Ghost Town, a reproduction of an 1880s California Old West boom town, includes the Old Trails Hotel (built in 1868 and brought from Arizona to Knott's in 1940), a train that dates from 1881, a stagecoach ride, and a log ride with a final, almost vertical drop guaranteed to inspire some screaming. Fiesta Village is a re-creation of colonial Spanish America. The major thrill ride here is Montezooma's Revenge, a roller coaster that literally rockets through 600 feet of track, a 76-foot loop, and two spires, backward and forward. It's not for the fainthearted. There's also a merry-go-round built in 1890. There are three computer-operated thrill rides. In the Roaring '20s amusement area, Kingdom of the Dinosaurs provides a face-to-face encounter with 21 fully animated figures, including a 32-foot-long Apatosaurus and a menacing Tyrannosaurus Rex. The Pacific Pavilion features an entertaining dolphin and sea lion show.

Boomerang, an exciting roller coaster than turns thrill-seekers upside down six times in less than a minute, premiered in 1990. Other rides include the Wheeler Dealer Bumper Cars and the red-and-white-checked Sky Cabin that is located on the same tower as the Sky Jump. This para-chute ride provides a bird's-eye view of Buena Park before dropping 20 stories in a simulated free-fall. Your feet will reach the ground long before your stomach does. Appealing, especially to the young and the young-at-heart, is Camp Snoopy; it covers some six acres. Built to resemble California's High Sierra terrain, the "camp" includes such attractions as a petting zoo, pontoon bridges, a treehouse, the Red Baron biplane ride, and a video learning center where kids learn the basics of computer programming. In this area, too, they can meet and

have their pictures taken with Snoopy, the world's most beloved beagle, and his friends from the comic strip *Peanuts*. Every year, Knott's presents Camp Snoopy Days with kid-size games, shows, and other activities.

All in all, Knott's Berry Farm sprawls over 150 acres. There are 165 rides, shows, attractions, restaurants, and shops. The main shopping area and the *Chicken Dinner* and *Steak House* restaurants can be entered without paying the park admission.

Across Beach Boulevard from the main gates is another section of Knott's. The entrance is through a tunnel from the main parking area, near the shops. Here visitors can experience Independence Hall West, Knott's exact-size replica of Philadelphia's Independence Hall. More than 140,000 hand-finished clay bricks duplicate the original. Chandeliers, furniture, and the shape and size of

the rooms were exactly reproduced by craftsmen. There is even a replica Liberty Bell, correct right down to the famous crack. Open every day of the year but Christmas. For more information, including operating hours, call the 24-hour "Knott's Line" at 220-5200. Dining spots and shops in the California Market Place, outside the paid admission section of the park, are open daily except Christmas Day. Admission is $21.95 for adults; $9.95 for children 3 to 11; $14.95 for seniors and non-ambulatory persons; free for children under three. Prices include unlimited use of the park's rides and attractions, except for Pan for Gold and the arcade games. Parking costs $4 and is on tree-shaded lots adjacent to several gates and across Beach Boulevard and La Palma and Western avenues. If you don't have your own wheels, Pacific Coast Sightseeing (978-8855) offers tours to Knott's from most Disneyland-area hotels for about $26 for adults and $14 for children ages 3 to 11. Prices include admission to Knott's Berry Farm. About seven miles from Disneyland. 8039 Beach Blvd.; Buena Park; 220-5200.

SHERMAN LIBRARY AND GARDENS: Off the Pacific Coast Highway, in the southeastern Newport Beach area of Corona del Mar, this is a small corner of paradise. The botanical collections surrounding

the library building range from desert plant life to exotic tropical vegetation. The gardens are a veritable museum of plants and flowers, displayed amid a setting of fountains and sculptures, brick walkways and manicured grass. They are open daily from 10:30 A.M. to 4 P.M. Admission is $2. The library also should not be missed. It is a major research center devoted to the history of the Pacific Southwest (particularly the amazing changes that the area has undergone over the past 100 years). Its collection includes maps and photographs, more than 2,000 reels of microfilm, about 15,000 books and pamphlets, and about 200,000 papers and documents. While primarily designed for use by students and researchers, the library is open to visitors. Library hours are from 9 A.M. to 5 P.M. Mondays through Fridays. The Sherman Library and Gardens are about a 35-minute drive southeast of Disneyland. 2647 East Pacific Coast Highway; Corona del Mar 92625; 673-2261.

MOVIELAND WAX MUSEUM AND RIPLEY'S BELIEVE IT OR NOT: The wax museum describes itself as the "greatest gathering of stars," and even if you're not a fancier of sculptures in wax, you'll probably enjoy the glimpses of western-movie heroes, musical-comedy greats, and leading men and women. More than 250 movie and TV performers are portrayed in scenes from their best-known roles: Judy Garland in *The Wizard of Oz*, Robert Redford and Paul Newman (blue eyes looking right at you) in *Butch Cassidy and the Sundance Kid*, John Wayne in *Rio Hondo*, Marilyn Monroe in *Some Like It Hot*, Barbra Streisand as Dolly, and Redd Foxx as Fred Sanford. Performers recently added to the cast of characters include Michael Jackson and Dudley Moore. There is also a Chamber of Horrors.

The costumes and props in many displays are original, donated by the studios or the stars themselves. And some of the "wax" figures occasionally turn out to be real: Be sure to take a very close look at the Keystone Cop!

At Ripley's there are 10,000 square feet of oddities including the tale of the tallest man in history. Combination tickets are available. Both museums are open daily from 10 A.M. to 8 P.M. Seven miles from Disneyland. 7711 Beach Blvd.; Buena Park; 522-1154.

SPECTATOR SPORTS

CALIFORNIA ANGELS: Anaheim is home to the American League California Angels baseball team (ticket office 634-2000). During early April, immediately preceding the regular season, the Angels and the National League Los Angeles Dodgers hold a "freeway series," so called because the teams' home parks are just a short freeway ride apart. The Angels' home games can be seen at Anaheim Stadium between April and October.

LOS ANGELES RAMS: Despite their name, the Los Angeles Rams (ticket office 937-6767) of the National Football League call Anaheim home, too.

They play their home games from August through December. Both the Angels and the Rams play at Anaheim Stadium, two miles east of Disneyland. 2000 State College Blvd. at Katella; Anaheim; 254-3000.

LOS ALAMITOS RACE COURSE: Spotlights night racing. Depending on the season, the course features either quarter horses or harness racing. Seven miles west of Disneyland. 4961 Katella Ave.; Los Alamitos; 995-1234.

MUSIC AND THEATER

FULLERTON CIVIC LIGHT OPERA CO.: Specializes in musical comedy and operetta. The season runs from October to early June. About seven miles from Disneyland. Plummer Auditorium, Lemon Street and Chapman Avenue; Fullerton; 879-1732 for ticket information.

SOUTH COAST REPERTORY: Two stages—the main-stage features large-scale productions of classics. The second, smaller stage is more experimental, showcasing modern plays and new playwrights. The season normally runs from September through July. The theater is across from South Coast Plaza, about ten miles from Disneyland. 655 Town Center Drive; Costa Mesa; 957-4033 for ticket information.

CELEBRITY THEATRE: This 2,500-seat theater-in-the-round has presented such well-known entertainers as Smokey Robinson, Barbara Mandrell, and Kenny Rogers. 201 East Broadway; Anaheim; 999-9536 for ticket information.

ORANGE COUNTY PERFORMING ARTS CENTER: This 3,000-seat multipurpose theater hosts regional, national, and international symphony orchestras; opera; dance; and musical theater in an acoustically advanced performance facility. The center is located about ten miles south of Disneyland, across from the South Coast Plaza. 600 Town Center Drive; Costa Mesa; 556-2787 for ticket information.

DINNER THEATERS: *The Grand Dinner Theatre* in the *Grand* hotel, across from Disneyland, features professional Broadway-style productions accompanied by sit-down or buffet meals. Tickets for Saturday nights go for about $39; Tuesday night is Broadway on a Budget, and tickets cost only $30 (7 Freedman Way; Anaheim; 772-7710). The *Elizabeth Howard's Curtain Call Dinner Theatre* offers a sit-down dinner (there's a choice of three entrées), followed by a performance—usually a Broadway musical. Shows are presented Tuesdays through Sundays, with both a matinee and an evening performance on Sundays. Prices range from $19.95 on Tuesday nights to $30.95 on Saturday evenings. Drinks and dessert are not included. (690 El Camino Real; Tustin; 838-1540). *Medieval Times* (7662 Beach Blvd.; Buena Park; 521-4740), though not a traditional dinner theater, offers a show that kids, in particular, enjoy. There's swordplay and a jousting tournament. Dinner, beverages, and dessert are all included in the admission price of $27.95 for adults, $18.95 for children, Sundays through Thursdays; $31.95 for adults, $19.95 for children on Fridays and Saturdays. Call ahead for special discount programs.

ANAHEIM CONVENTION CENTER: Most concerts here are booked by conventions, but there are some that are open to the public. Check the marquee on Katella Avenue or the concert listings in the local papers. 800 West Katella Ave.; Anaheim; 999-8900 for ticket information.

IRVINE MEADOWS AMPHITHEATRE: Open from March through October; normally presents concerts that range from symphonies to heavy metal. There's reserved seating for 10,500 people and seating on the lawn for 4,500. 8800 Irvine Center Drive; Irvine; 855-6111 for recorded information; 855-2863 for the box office.

SHOPPING

If you're used to shopping in that staid strip of stores known as *downtown* in most cities, an outing to one of Southern California's shopping malls will be an attraction in itself. They are the Western world's version of Middle Eastern bazaars, an everything-in-one-place shopping experience.

Malls may not have been invented here, but Southern California's largely suburban population has refined the phenomenon to a new level. There are 3- and 4-store malls on just about every street corner, and others, built on a far more grandiose scale, are very conveniently located.

The big ones often don't look like much from the outside. They are usually enclosed and air conditioned, with blind concrete exterior walls facing acres of surrounding parking lots. On the inside, however, elevated walkways and ramps lead to two or even three levels of stores. Often there are fountains and lush landscaping and waterfalls, bringing the outside dramatically in. There are domed ceilings with stained-glass skylights at some, merry-go-rounds and a carnival atmosphere at others.

There are also movie theaters, auto-repair centers, and hairdressers. Restaurants range from the quick hamburger-and-fries variety to sidewalk cafés that offer cozy tables, espresso, and a view of fellow shoppers; and menus vary from the carob-and-carrot-cake health-food types to those serving fancy French foods of the highest caliber. There also are stores of every sort and style.

The shopping malls within easy driving distance of Disneyland are generally open from 10 A.M. to 9 P.M. weekdays, from 10 A.M. to 6 P.M. Saturdays, and from noon to 5 P.M. Sundays.

ANAHEIM PLAZA: On Euclid at Crescent, the Anaheim Plaza is only three miles from the park. It's a straightforward shopping center, with The Broadway, Mervyn's, and 75 other shops and restaurants.

WESTMINSTER MALL: One of the bigger, better shopping centers in Orange County, with a Buffums, May Company, and Robinson's, among others. It's got an upper level, a lower level, a mezzanine level, and enough stores and restaurants to keep you busy and nourished for an entire day. When you're tired of shopping, go see a movie. There are two United Artists theater complexes, one in the parking lot area, one in the mall itself. Westminster Mall is about nine miles southwest of Disneyland. Be sure to take special note of where you enter, so you can exit through the same door and find your car most easily.

CITY SHOPPING CENTER: Where the Santa Ana (I-5) and Garden Grove (22) freeways meet at the City Drive exit and Chapman, just three miles from Disneyland. There are more than 100 stores, restaurants, and services, including J. C. Penney and May Company, and a United Artists movie theater complex. The City Shopper bus provides a shuttle service during shopping hours from 13 major hotels in the area.

BUENA PARK MALL: In Buena Park, on La Palma between Stanton and Dale, six miles from Disneyland, and one very long block from Knott's Berry Farm. This older mall has been completely renovated, and includes Penney's, Sears, May Company, and a United Artists movie theater complex.

SOUTH COAST PLAZA: At the intersection of the San Diego Freeway and Bristol Street in Costa Mesa, about 10 miles from Disneyland. It is huge and airy and festive, and houses about 300 shops and restaurants. Along with Bullock's and the May Company are such well-known names as Chanel, Barney's New York, Nordstrom, Mark Cross, Saks Fifth Avenue, and Williams-Sonoma. Located nearby on Town Center Drive are the Orange County Performing Arts Center and the South Coast Repertory. South Coast Plaza Shuttles transport shoppers during shopping hours from Anaheim hotels to the plaza.

MAIN PLACE MALL: The area's newest mall is located at 2800 North Main Street in Santa Ana, near the intersection of the Santa Ana and Garden Grove freeways, about four miles from Disneyland. Along with Bullock's, Nordstrom, May Company, and Robinson's, this attractive enclosed mall houses about 190 stores and restaurants, and a cinema complex. A shuttle transports shoppers from Anaheim hotels to the mall.

NEWPORT CENTER FASHION ISLAND: Located in Newport Beach on Newport Center Drive, about a half-hour drive south of Disneyland. This park-like mall was recently expanded and offers about 150 stores, restaurants, and services amidst a setting of potted flowers and towering palms, plazas with umbrella-covered tables, fountains, and fish ponds. Department stores include The Broadway, Neiman-Marcus, I. Magnin, Buffums, and Robinson's. The enclosed Atrium Court houses many small shops, plus the Farmer's Market. The mall also has an Edwards six-cinema complex.

IN ALL DIRECTIONS

All right, so now you've been to Disneyland. Is there anything else to do in Southern California? You bet!

It's the sheer variety of things to see—both natural and manmade—that makes Southern California such a great vacation destination. Just look at a road map: Anaheim is only about an hour from the center of metropolitan Los Angeles—the home of movie stars, shopping malls, Rodeo Drive, and more automobiles than you've ever seen. It's a place that, as they say in the movies, you won't soon forget.

To the east are rugged deserts. And that doesn't have to mean just cactus and bleached wastelands either: Rich carpets of wildflowers in spring and lush oases of palms are among the many surprises awaiting inland.

Now run your fingers across the map to the north and find the mountains—the towering Sierra Nevadas. Between the Sierras and the sea lies the San Joaquin Valley, a rich and highly developed agricultural region that boasts endless fields of cotton, grapes, and roses.

California's historic Spanish missions also are worth a second thought, especially if you hunger for something with a past. And what about the fabulous Pacific? That road along the coastline to Big Sur (two-thirds of the way to San Francisco) is

Highway 1, and it runs along some of the wildest and most beautiful coastline on earth.

But don't forget that just Southern California itself is *big*, and a day trip can mean a very long day indeed. It's almost certainly best to explore just one region at a time—Los Angeles, the desert, the mission trail, etc. So gather up your road maps, your sunscreen, and your family—Southern California is waiting!

LOS ANGELES

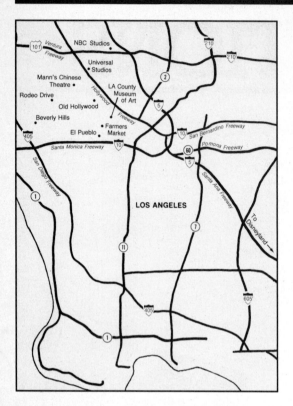

The American dream was invented in Los Angeles—glamour, fame, palm trees, endless sunshine, and incredibly good-looking people posing around their swimming pools. The myth may conflict with reality just a bit, which tends to include a certain amount of yellowish smog, 500 miles of freeways in Los Angeles County, and 4,000 square miles—count 'em—of urban sprawl.

From the rugged ridges of the Santa Monica Mountains to the vast San Fernando Valley and downtown, the city is enormous. It's well known that Angelenos live in their cars, and with good reason. To get a radically different perspective, take a walking tour through downtown L.A. or Old Hollywood.

DOWNTOWN LOS ANGELES: If you ever wondered what the place looked like before shopping centers were invented, work your way into the heart of the downtown area—and abandon your wheels.

El Pueblo: Here's where the great city began, as the tiny Spanish village of El Pueblo de Los Angeles. Built around a wide central plaza, El Pueblo offers an open-air bandstand, the restored fire station of Engine Company No. 1, the tiny Plaza Church, established in 1822, and Olvera Street, a pedestrian walkway paved in cool brick and filled with colorful Mexican shops and restaurants. Sample the spicy tacos, burritos, and enchi-

ladas at food stalls along your way. The oldest house in Los Angeles is here—the 1818 Avila House, made of adobe. Free walking tours are offered hourly from 10 A.M. to 1 P.M. Tuesdays through Saturdays. Details: El Pueblo de Los Angeles State Historic Park; 845 North Alameda St.; Los Angeles, CA 90012; 213-628-1274. To get to El Pueblo and Olvera Street, take the Santa Ana Freeway (Rte. 5) north to the Hollywood Freeway (Rte. 101), then exit at Alameda Street and head north two blocks. During noncommuter hours, it's a 45-minute drive from Anaheim.

Farmers Market: 150 stalls of American, Mexican, Italian, Chinese, and vegetarian foods, and any number of exquisite bakeries and candy shops. If you don't like to eat standing up, there are tables set up in several locations throughout this indoor market. Open in summer from 9 A.M. to 7 P.M. Mondays through Saturdays and in winter 9 A.M. to 6:30 P.M.; 10 A.M. to 5 P.M. Sundays year-round. Free parking. Details: 6333 West Third St. and Fairfax Ave.; 213-933-9211.

Los Angeles County Museum of Art: The Robert O. Anderson Building houses the museum's distinguished collection of 20th-century art, and there's the Pavilion for Japanese Art. Special exhibits come and go in the Armand Hammer Building while a dazzling permanent collection stays put: See pre-Columbian and African art, tapestries, and paintings from the 18th century to the present. Closed Mondays. Admission charge. Details: 5905 Wilshire Blvd.; 213-857-6111.

HOLLYWOOD—OLD AND NEW: A walk through Old Hollywood will delight lovers of the great era of Hollywood movies, though the area is no longer the physical center of film production and its glamour is, sadly, long gone. While the streets are crowded, bustling, and safe by day, it's not wise to walk down Hollywood Boulevard after dark. But there is a lot to enjoy here, much of it at little or no cost.

Mann's Chinese Theatre: Better known to movie fans around the world as the old Grauman's Chinese Theater, this is probably the most visited site in Old Hollywood. But if you wander down Hollywood Boulevard toward Highland Avenue looking for the Grauman's sign, you'll never find it. A new proprietor named Ted Mann took the theater over in July 1973 and replaced the famous old sign with his own—causing considerable local controversy. The Chinese Theatre's forecourt is world-renowned for its celebrity footprints and handprints immortalized in cement. If you buy a ticket to get into the original theater (rather than one of Mann's adjacent new twin cinemas), you'll see one of the world's most impressive and elaborate movie palaces. The ornate carvings, high decorative ceiling, plush seats, and the enormous screen itself are all part of a Hollywood that no longer exists. Details: 6925 Hollywood Blvd.; 213-464-8111.

El Capitan Theatre: This Hollywood Boulevard landmark (formerly the Paramount) has been completely restored to its original elegance. Built in 1926 as a legitimate stage house, it was remodeled in 1942 and became the Paramount movie theater. Thanks to a joint effort by Pacific Theatres and Buena Vista Pictures Distribution, moviegoers can enjoy first-run motion pictures in an elegant atmosphere with a state-of-the-art projection and sound system. El Capitan, the Chinese Theater and several other renovated moviehouses along an eight-block stretch of Hollywood Boulevard offer viewers an alternative to the modern-day mulitplex.

Universal Studios Hollywood: Some of the lingering evidence that the local movie business is still alive and functioning. Tours are conducted on SuperTrams by tour guides, with about 175 people per tour. Highlights include a look at some of the production facilities and 34 soundstages, especially the "World of Cinemagic," where some of Alfred Hitchcock's best-kept secrets are revealed. You'll also see the parting of the Red Sea, a burning house, and a collapsing bridge, an attack on the tour tram by a 30-foot-tall King Kong, and the Doomed Glacier Expedition, in which you plunge down an Alpine avalanche. A popular attraction allows visitors to "experience" an earthquake measuring 8.3 on the Richter scale. This moving experience—ominously called "The Big One"—may not be suitable for younger children. New attractions include "Lucy: A Tribute" and "E.T.'s Adventure." After the tour, you can visit an area of shops and special shows: There you'll see a Miami Vice live-action show and a swords-and-sorcery show called Adventures of Conan. Admission charge; children under three get in free when they are accompanied by an adult. Off the Hollywood Freeway (Rte. 101) at Lankershim Boulevard. Details: 100 Universal City Plaza, Universal City; 818-508-9600.

NBC Television Studios: This behind-the-scenes tour passes through television studios and set constructions, and special effects, makeup, and wardrobe departments. Tours are guided by NBC pages, who make no promises but very often include a view of a few stars. Each tour lasts about an hour. Tours start every half hour on weekdays from 8:30 A.M. to 4 P.M.; on Saturdays tours begin every hour on the hour from 10 A.M. to 4 P.M., and on Sundays every hour on the hour from 10 A.M. to 2 P.M. Admission charge. Details: 3000 West Alameda Ave., Burbank; 818-840-3537.

Beverly Hills: Mansion-studded and compact—one of the most affluent and elegant suburbs in Southern California. Starline-Gray Line offers tours that point out movie stars' homes; for more information, call 213-856-5900.

Rodeo Drive: While you're in Beverly Hills, don't miss Rodeo Drive—perhaps the most expensive shopping street in the world. And that's "ro-DAY-oh," friend. Prestigious European shops and boutiques have opened branches here, and the prices can be astronomical. If you want to make sure you don't get tempted to buy, go in the evening when the stores are closed. This epicenter of conspicuous consumption is located in just three blocks between Little Santa Monica and Wilshire, so the ideal route is down one side of the street and up the other. It's easy to spot:

Fred Hayman—Yellow and white awnings crown this shop which used to be called *Giorgio's*. Clothing for men and women, with a stand up-bar and complimentary drinks are offered. This establishment was the prototype for Judith Krantz's *Scruples*, and is as elegant as its reputation suggests.

Polo—Ralph Lauren—featuring the complete line of Ralph Lauren's "Polo" label.

Hermès—Fine leather goods from France.

Theodore Man—American styles of a distinctly continental cast; a splendid bastion of Southern California fashion.

David Orgell—Such silver, and such china!

Ferragamo—Men's and women's fine Italian leather goods, shoes, and clothing.

Harry Winston—Big-ticket baubles are featured at this jeweler to the rich and famous.

2 RODEO—A $200 million European-style shopping and dining complex fashioned after a small European street where Tiffany, Cartier, and Valentino shops can be found. *Peter Stringfellows* restaurant offers pleasant patio dining.

NOTE: There are many other compelling sites and attractions in Greater Los Angeles. In fact, you could probably spend a full year vacationing here and still not get to see it all. For a more complete sampling, as well as maps and bus information, write the Greater Los Angeles Visitors Information Center; 695 South Figueroa; Los Angeles, CA 90017; 213-624-7300.

Taking I-5 north and Rtes. 101 and 10 west from Anaheim, depending on where you're headed, you can reach all of the sites discussed above. Figure on roughly a 100- to 150-mile round trip.

DESERT LANDSCAPE

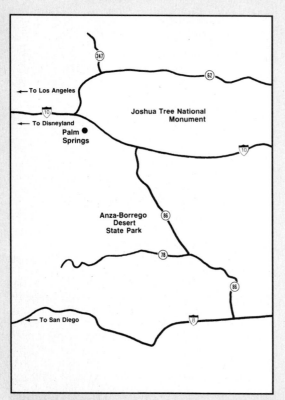

To Los Angeles
To Disneyland
Palm Springs
To San Diego

247
62
10
10
Joshua Tree National Monument
Anza-Borrego Desert State Park
86
78
86
8

The deserts of Southern California have two things to offer—one is a certain quantity of sand, and the other is Palm Springs. Either is worth a look, but don't try to do them both in one day.

DESERTS: The best times to visit are in winter, spring, and fall, when temperatures are a bit less mind-baking and the occasional sudden downpour gives the landscape a striking fresh-washed look.

Joshua Tree National Monument: Created in 1936 over howls of protest from mining companies, it is a haven for the Joshua tree and other desert wildlife and plants. The tree was given its name by early pioneers who felt it resembled the prophet Joshua raising his arms in supplication to God, or at least pointing the way for them to go. Nature trails and good major roads provide access to 870 square miles of park. Split Rock, near Pinto Wye, one of the monument's best-known landmarks, is a giant split boulder more than three stories high, with a natural cave underneath. See rocks carved into weird shapes by the wind, an impressive view of the San Bernardino Mountains, and the distant waters of the Salton Sea. Work your way out of Anaheim via Rte. 91 east to 60 east to I-10 east; about 240 miles round trip. Details: The Superintendent; Joshua Tree National Monument; 74485 National Monument Dr.; Twenty-nine Palms, CA 92277; 619-367-7511.

Anza-Borrego Desert State Park: Loveliest in the spring, when the willow and tamarisk trees, wildflowers, and pine groves are at their best. (Call 619-767-4684 for recorded camping and weather information.) The desert ranges from 100 feet below sea level (near the Salton Sea) to 6,000 feet above (in the Santa Rosa Mountains), and sprawls across half a million acres. See the remnants of long-gone Indian civilizations and more animals than you'd expect: bighorn sheep (*borregos*), jackrabbits, coyotes, gray foxes, mule deer, and round-tail squirrels.

There are hundreds of miles of vehicle trails (for street-legal vehicles only), some accessible to regular autos, some for four-wheel drives only. Self-guided auto and hiking tours describe the region's geology, while ranger-guided tours are available on weekends and holidays from November to May. Check at the visitor's center for schedules.

Camping sites offer tables, wood stoves, shade ramadas, toilets, and running water. Reservations are recommended for any day of the week from November through May, and for weekends and holidays the rest of the year. Reservations can be made using MasterCard or Visa, and information can be obtained about the locations of walk-in reservation outlets throughout the state by calling 800-444-7275. The Visitors Center at 200 Palm Canyon Drive (619-767-4205) is open daily from 9 A.M. to 5 P.M. Take I-5 south from Anaheim to Rte. 78, which rambles east into the park; about 260 miles round trip. Details: Anza-Borrego Desert State Park; Box 299; Borrego Springs, CA 92004; 619-767-5311.

Palm Springs: The dress code is cool and casual as you glide down the boulevard in Palm Springs. The sun shines here only about 350 days a year, the days average 88´ (delightful because the humidity is so low), and the nights average a perfect 55°. In summer, though, daytime highs often reach 105°.

The spot was discovered centuries ago by the Agua Caliente Indians, who considered the hot water (*agua caliente* in Spanish) springs to have miraculous healing powers. While Palm Springs was a spa for many years, people today are more interested in it for its warm, dry climate, its desert scenery, and its superb resort facilities.

Not everyone in Palm Springs is rich, though it sometimes seems that way. The world's densest swimming pool population is said to be found here—some 10,000, or one for every five people. In winter, the wealthy, the famous, and the powerful come to play, and prices soar as high as Mount San Jacinto, the peak overlooking the city. In spring, however, hordes of high school and college students descend on the town—usually at the time of spring break. Summer rates lure many families as hotel prices drop as much as 50 percent. Savvy visitors head farther down Route 111 to Palm Desert and Indian Wells. Golf is very big here, too—on more than 40 courses, with tournaments just about every week from September through May, including the Bob Hope Desert Classic. Don't miss the Palm Springs Desert Museum, a multifaceted cultural center featuring art exhibits, a history museum with unusual Indian artifacts, and outstanding facilities for the performing arts (101 Museum Drive). The San Jacinto Wilderness State Park, which can be reached only by aerial tram, is nearby, as is the larger San Bernardino National Forest. Take Rte. 91 east; about 200 miles round trip. Details: Palm Springs Desert Resorts Convention and Visitors' Bureau; Airport Park Plaza; North El Cielo Rd., Suite 315; Palm Springs, CA 92262; 619-327-8411.

HISTORIC MISSIONS

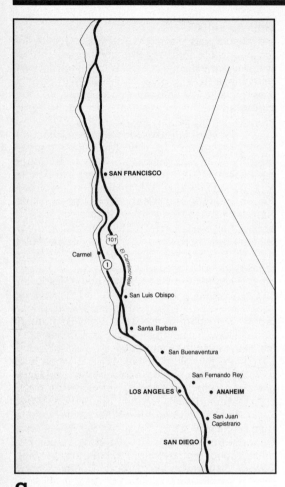

Scattered along the old Camino Real (sometimes called Highway 101) are 21 historic Spanish missions, nine of which were founded by Father Junipero Serra beginning in 1769. These structures originally could be seen for miles from the sea and from inland valleys. They employed thousands of native Indians—or so-called "heathens"—in agriculture and livestock raising. When California became a part of the United States in 1850, the influence of the Spanish missions waned and several of the abandoned structures have quietly crumbled. Others have had their Mexican/Moorish architecture and lush, semitropical gardens meticulously restored. Many of these are open to visitors. The missions are spaced about 40 miles apart, so a good strategy is to concentrate on those in a narrow region, keeping away from the ones in major urban centers.

San Juan Capistrano: Today, the mission is no more than a collection of crumbling structures with a wistful air of decayed grandeur. Its church, once the most remarkable of the entire mission chain, was shattered by a powerful earthquake in 1812, though the 4 bells of the tower and a small sanctuary called Father Serra's Church were miraculously

spared. The other miracle is the swallows, which return to Capistrano every year on March 19 (Saint Joseph's Day) with clockwork regularity. Many Christians take this as a sign of the holiness of the church, while ornithologists explain it as no more than a predictable natural phenomenon.

See the 300-year-old gilt altar, gardens, ancient pepper trees, the remains of tallow vats and an iron smelter where mission Indians did the Lord's—or somebody's—work, an Indian cemetery, a *calabozo* (jail), the quarters of the early padres, and Spanish soldiers' barracks. The mission tour is self-guided, or, for an extra charge, groups of 15 or more can get a docent-guided tour.

The church and grounds are open from 8:30 A.M. to 5 P.M. daily. Admission is $3 for adults, $1.50 for children 3 to 11. Take I-5 south to the mission; about 80 miles round trip. Details: San Juan Capistrano Mission; 31815 Camino Capistrano, Suite C; San Juan Capistrano, CA 92675; 714-493-1424.

San Fernando Rey: Working your way north along the coast, you may want to skip San Gabriel Archangel, which is almost totally lost in the hornet's nest of suburbs around L.A. The next mission along the trail is San Fernando Rey—seven acres of grounds, featuring the Convento, the largest adobe building in California. The museum

here is perhaps the best of all the mission museums. It displays hand-carved, 17th-century gold-leaf altars; a library of priceless volumes; and art treasures of Mexican, Spanish, and Indian origin. The famous Bells of San Fernando faithfully ring "Cantico del Alba," an ancient Indian melody, every hour from 10 A.M. to 6 P.M. Admission is $3, $1.50 for children. The mission is open 9 A.M. to 4:15 P.M. daily. Take I-405 north; about 110 miles round trip. Details: San Fernando Rey; 15151 San Fernando Mission Blvd.; Mission Hills, CA 91345; 818-361-0186.

San Buenaventura: Its church is beautifully preserved, though less striking than San Fernando. The surrounding beaches of coastal Oxnard are superb, and the inland Ojai valley is a favorite haunt of artists and writers. Admission is 50 per adult, 25 per child. The mission, which has a museum and a gift shop, is open 7 A.M. to 6 P.M. daily, while the museum and gift shop are open Mondays to Saturdays 10 A.M. to 5 P.M., Sundays until 4 P.M. Take I-405 north to Rte. 101; about 200 miles round trip. Details: San Buenaventura Mission; 211 East Main St.; Ventura, CA 93001; 805-643-4318.

Santa Barbara: The town of Santa Barbara prides itself on preserving its Spanish heritage—wide sidewalks lined with flowering trees, hybrid Mexican/Moorish architecture, and not a neon sign, billboard, or mailbox in sight.

By contrast, the mission (completed in 1820) offers a Roman temple facade, gleaming white walls, and graceful towers; it is still used by the parish of Santa Barbara. The mission has a good museum and beautiful grounds. Lush expanses of lawn are adorned with flowering trees and shrubs and a lovely Moorish fountain (If you're in the mood for more of the same, the town's superb Botanical Gardens are about 1½ miles north.)

A $2 donation is requested; children under 16 free. Open 9 A.M. to 5 P.M. daily. Take I-405 to Rte. 101; about 210 miles round trip. Details: The Old Mission of Santa Barbara; Santa Barbara, CA 93105; 805-682-4713 or 805-682-4151.

San Luis Obispo: The Los Padres Mountains of central California harbor one of California's best-kept secrets—San Luis Obispo. This picturesque town, midway between Los Angeles and San Francisco, is close to some of the state's best beaches. Restaurants, shops, and boutiques encircle Mission Plaza, dominated by the Mission

San Luis Obispo de Tolosa. The mission boasts a colorful chapel and a superb museum, as well as a garden of brick paths and benches along a sleepy winding creek.

Again, the nearby beaches are splendid—Avila offers deep-sea fishing and perhaps the best swimming in the area; Pismo is dotted with caves, cliff-sheltered tidal pools, and old pirate coves, as well as year-round clam digging; and Morro Bay is a winter and early-spring sanctuary for thousands of wild birds, including the peregrine falcon.

San Luis Obispo also is the home of the *Madonna Inn*, one of California's most famous and unusual hostelries. It is a gingerbread castle with winding outdoor staircases, a shingled roof, turrets, and 109 rooms, each decorated around some idiosyncratic theme—such as the Love Nest, Yosemite Falls, Victorian Gardens, and the Safari Room. Details: The Madonna Inn; 100 Madonna Rd.; San Luis Obispo, CA 93401; 805-543-3000.

The museum asks a donation of $1 per adult. Open from Palm Sunday to Labor Day from 9 A.M. to 5 P.M. daily; the rest of the year from 9 A.M. to 4 P.M. daily. Take Rte. 101 north; the ride is about 400 miles round trip. Details: The Old Mission of San Luis Obispo; 782 Monterey St.; San Luis Obispo, CA 93401; 805-543-6850.

Carmel: The coastal town of Carmel lies about 15 miles west of Rte. 101 and El Camino Real, but getting there via Route 1 is half the fun. The coastal drive is one of the most famous scenic roads in America. See dramatic cliffs skirting vertiginous ocean vistas, shoals of wild birds, seals and sea lions sunning themselves on rocks, and migrating California gray and humpback whales. The forest village is serene and isolated and has long been a haven for artists and writers.

The Carmel mission was one of the largest and most important in the group founded by Father Serra (who is buried here). Today it is one of the best preserved, presenting a complete quadrangle of authentic mission architecture. The splendid exterior tower, adorned with a star window, is Moorish in design. An elegant fountain, olive trees, and a drooping flower garden further enhance the site.

The mission asks a $1 donation per adult. Open Mondays through Saturdays from 9:30 A.M. to 4:30 P.M., Sundays from 10:30 A.M. to 4:30 P.M. Take Rte. 101 north to the junction with Rte. 1, which doubles back to Carmel; about 640 miles round trip. Details: Carmel Mission Basilica; 3080 Rio Rd.; Carmel, CA 93923; 408-624-3600.

THE COASTAL PACIFIC

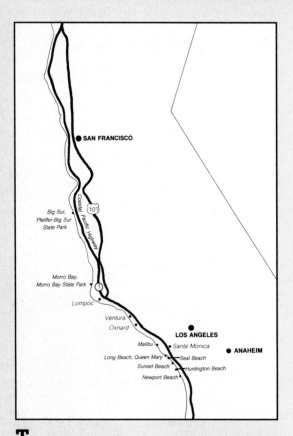

The Pacific Coast Highway (Rte. 1) winds along the California coast for over 400 miles from Los Angeles to San Francisco. For much of this distance, it clings to the water's edge, twisting and dipping through towering, spray-battered cliffs, silent groves of pine, and those legendary electric-blue glimpses of the wide Pacific. The coastline is truly one of the world's most dramatic, and the Pacific Coast Highway is the best way to see it. But drive carefully—"twisting and dipping" is not an exaggeration, particularly along the 115-mile stretch from Morro Bay up to Carmel, which convict chain gangs spent 20 years carving out of solid rock. If you have the time and strength, this is the stretch of road that's likely to be the most dramatically satisfying. Portions of Route 1 are prone to damage during the winter. For highway conditions call 714-972-9980.

Starting from Anaheim, your route begins well south of Los Angeles (generally in Newport Beach). You'll pass fine swimming and surfing beaches, and any number of scenic—though rather densely developed—coastal towns.

The beaches: As you head up Rte. 1, you'll pass Huntington Beach, Sunset Beach, Seal Beach, and so forth. The beach towns blend into one another; the houses—generally weatherworn wood or condos built to look like weatherworn wood—are interspersed with surfing shops, fishing piers, fast-food stands, and broad stretches of classic sand.

Long Beach is next. Don't miss the *Queen Mary*, the famous retired oceanliner permanently docked in the harbor and serving as a hotel and convention center. Adjacent to the ship is a dome that houses the *Spruce Goose*, Howard Hughes's legendary flying boat—the largest airplane ever built of wood. The Walt Disney Company operates both of these attractions and tours are conducted daily (box office open from 10 A.M. to 5:30 P.M., with extended hours during spring and summer holidays). Special exhibits include the ship's sound and light show in the engine room re-enacting a near-collision, a World War II display on the *Queen Mary*'s role as a troop ship, and other changing shows. A platform adjacent to the *Spruce Goose* allows guests to view the cockpit, cargo area, and flight deck up close. There are also displays and films describing the plane's construction, its one-and-only flight, and Howard Hughes's aviation career. For ticket information call: 213-435-3511.

Farther north: Drive up through Santa Monica, Malibu, Oxnard, and Ventura to charming, Spanish-flavored Santa Barbara (see ``Historic Missions'' in this chapter). By now it's almost certainly lunchtime, so pause for a picnic by the sea.

For the next 100 miles, the highway tends to drift away from the coastline. Unless you are urgently moved to see Lompoc, stay on Route 101 and cover the distance swiftly, picking up Route 1 again in San Luis Obispo and making your way another 10 or 12 miles to the coast.

Morro Bay: At the harbor entrance to this seaport town is Morro Rock, a 576-foot volcanic dome discovered by Juan Rodriguez Cabrillo in 1542. A large commercial fishing fleet sails from here, and many boats are docked along the Embarcadero. Morro Bay State Park, a 2,500-acre tract with hiking trails, picnic areas, and campsites, also has an interesting natural history museum that primarily focuses on local marine biology.

San Simeon: About 25 miles north of Morro Bay, William Randolph Hearst's fabled castle contains decorative elements (and even whole sections) of castles shipped to this site from all over the world. Stunningly elegant, this $150 million treasure house is now a state historical monument set on 123 acres overlooking the ocean. There are four tours available, including an evening tour that runs during the spring and summer. For reservations call 800-444-7275. Tickets are available on arrival but reservations are suggested. Open year round.

Big Sur: The most dramatic piece of shoreline on the continent. About 65 miles to the north of San Simeon, Big Sur's rolling, grassy hills end abruptly in cliffs towering high above the sea. There are many places to stop and watch sea otters, seals, sea lions, and occasionally even whales spouting in the waves far below. You won't need to be told which specific spots on the road are especially scenic—when you round a hairpin curve and find yourself gasping at the view and simultaneously reaching for your camera, you'll know you've found one.

Pfeiffer—Big Sur State Park, a deep forest of redwood and other trees, provides a change of scenery from the bare grassy hills of Big Sur. It has hiking trails, fishing spots, picnic areas, campgrounds, food service, and a lodge. At Jade Cove, about 20 miles south of the park, you can hunt for pieces of jade at low tide. Details: Pfeiffer—Big Sur State Park; Big Sur, CA 93920; 408-667-2315.

Thirty-Mile Drive: The 30 miles from Big Sur to the Monterey-Carmel area include some of the most dramatic scenery in the country. Though you've driven about 300 miles by now, push on for the extra hour to cover this coast-hugging, twisting road. Here's where the Santa Lucia Mountains meet the sea. Bixby Creek Bridge, just south of Carmel, is a 260-foot-wide observation point where you can park, watch the ocean pound the beach, and gaze hypnotically at the Point Sur Lighthouse, which flashes every 15 seconds.

Ever northward: It's quite possible to let this route get out of hand—you're not too far from San Francisco, and before you know it, a fired-up imagination may lead you on to Seattle and into the shouldery blue pines of British Columbia. But that's really terrain to tackle on another trip.

Instead, turn your eyes and your heart to the mild, dreamlike paradise of Southern California, the ocean, the highways, the sports, the oil wells, the sun. This may be your first visit here, but it needn't be your last. Take in as much as you can reasonably enjoy, but no more. For there's always more to see and, after all, Southern California never goes away. Come back and catch it next time.

FERTILE FARMLANDS

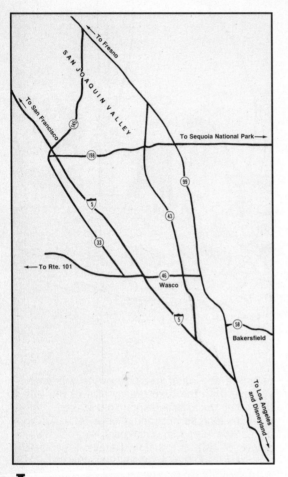

While you're in town, think about seeing the Kern County Museum—14 acres of 56 historic structures, both originals and reproductions, laid out as a model turn-of-the-century town. The main museum building houses fossils, Indian relics, and wildlife dioramas. Open from 8 A.M. to 5 P.M. weekdays and from 10 A.M. to 5 P.M. weekends and holidays. Ticket offices close daily at 3:30 P.M. 3801 Chester Ave.; 805-861-2132. Take I-5 north to Rte. 99 north to Bakersfield.

As you head toward the Sierra range, you'll be passing through some of Southern California's richest farmlands—the San Joaquin Valley at the southern end of California's Central Valley. The setting for Steinbeck's *The Grapes of Wrath*, the area is rich in pasturelands, orchards, and vineyards (with some oil fields thrown in).

Flowers, flowers, flowers: Over 75 percent of the rose plants sold in the United States begin life in the little town of Wasco. Peak bloom times are May and September, when the blossoms are arrayed in technicolor splashes of reds, pinks, salmons, corals, oranges, yellows, creams, and whites. Bear Creek, the well-known rose growers, are located on Kimberlina Road, just off Route 43. To arrange to tour their fields, call 805-758-5186 about a week before you want to visit. Plan to arrive no later than 1 P.M. To reach the flower fields around Wasco, take I-5 north from Anaheim to Rte. 46 north; about 320 miles round-trip.

Bakersfield: Just short of Wasco lies Bakersfield, the largest city in the region. It is known locally as "Nashville West" because it is home to country music stars Buck Owens and Merle Haggard.